U.S.A. AND THE NEW MIDDLE EAST

U.S.A. AND THE NEW MIDDLE EAST

Eddie J. Girdner

GYAN

GYAN PUBLISHING HOUSE

NEW DELHI-110002

U.S.A. and the New Middle East

Rs.

ISBN: 978-81-212-1001-0

Published in 2008 in India by
Gyan Publishing House,
5, Ansari Road Darya Ganj
New Delhi-110002
Phones : 23282060, 23261060
Fax : (011) 23285914
E-mail: gyanbooks@vsnl.com
Website : http : // www.gyanbooks.com

Laser Typesetting by : Quick Media, Delhi
Printed at : Singhal Print Media, Delhi

Contents

Preface

Five years have passed since the United States launched a colonialist war and illegaly occupied the sovereign state of Iraq. On the drawing board, "Operation Iraqi Freedom" was conceived as a "revolution" which would transform Iraq into a modern democratic state in the pluralist image. It would then serve as a catalyst for democratic change which would spread throughout the region. The attraction of the liberal future wave, in the glorified image laid out by Francis Fukuyama as the "end of history," would be irresistible. The feudal autocracies which the US had underwritten in the past would be tossed upon the trash heap of history.

The neo-conservatives acknowledged that "regime change" through military force could produce regional turbulence, to be sure, but when the dust settled, the local peoples would be forever grateful to the visionary insight of Georve W. Bush in ridding them of rulers like Saddam Hussein. The global situation following the attack on the US on September 11, 2001, was seen as a historical window of opportunity which must be grasped or lost forever.

Five years later, the ranks of the neo-conservatives who launched the Project for a New Americal Century have thinned considerably. Many have simply jumped ship. Their vision of a neoliberal, peaceful, and democratic Middle East has been shattered. The occupation of Iraq has turned out to be a failure far surpassing the earlier warnings of those most knowledgeable about the region.

Iraq has been destroyed, perhaps more devastatingly that even Kora and Vietnam in previous US imperialist ventures. "Operation Iraqi Freedom", alone, has resulted in the deaths of more than half a million people withat least two million in exile. Five years after the invasion, the US command in Iraq has resorted to paying Sunni insurgents, who formerly worked for al-Qaeda, not to attack American soldiers and US installations. The leading Republican candidate for President of the United States, Senator John McCain, spoke repeatedly of an extended US occupation of Iraq of up to 100 years, based upon the more than 60 year presence of US troops in Japan which continues today.

Not only had the neo-conservatives made no inroads whatsoever in addressing the root problem of political instability in the Middle East, the Israeli occupation of Palestine, Iraqi society was shattered and its future uncertain. The US presence in Iraq was destabilizing the entire wider region from the Eastern Mediterranean to Pakistan.

US imperialism had also taken its toll at home as the US relied more heavily upon borrowing hundreds of billions of dollars from China to finance its one trillion dollar war, devalued the US dollar, and pushed the US national debt to 9.25 trillion US dollars by early 2008. While Iraqi neighborhoods were being obliterated by bombs and ethnically cleansed, while thousands of Iraqi civilians died, Americans were losing their freedoms at homes as the American state assumed more authoritarian powers. Some 4000 US soldiers had died in Iraq and no single American had any idea how long the war would go on. On the other hand, the only certainty was that it would go on as the profits of US corporations operating in Iraq continued to soar. Wall Street continued to enthusiastically support the US occupation and looked forward to new opportunities. The largest US embassy in the world, a billion dollar enterprise, was nearing completion in Baghdad and the construction of US military bases across the country proceeded apace. The US was and would continue to be a major power on the Tigris and Euphrates for decades.

Taking the longer view, the US was rapidly following in the path of former great powers whose empires became overstretched and eventually collapsed. Under the rubric of a "war on terror" the United States of America was extending an empire but destroying the American Republic.

February 24, 2008 **Ankara, Turkey**

1

Introduction

"The war we fight today is more than a military conflict. It is the decisive ideological struggle of the 21st century."

George W. Bush (August 31, 2006)

"..[W]e are the most revolutionary force on earth."

Michael Ledeen, neoconservative

George W. Bush took office as President of the United States with an agenda of "regime change" for the Middle East. The neo-conservative ideologues in the Administration had been planning for the US overthrow of Saddam Hussein in Iraq since the mid-1990s. The neo-conservatives founded the Project for a New American Century (PNAC) to ensure the US control of the strategic resource of oil in the Middle East and pursued strategies to ensure that no country could challenge the global hegemony of the one superpower, the United States of America. The US control of oil would also give the United States leverage over the European Union, Japan, and emerging economies in China, South Asia and Russia.

After the attack on the Twin Towers at the World Trade Center in New York and the Pentagon in Washington, on September 11, 2001, US officials at the White House saw that the way was clear for the unleashing of US military power in the Middle East. Demonstrating military might in the region would serve as an example to other countries of the world, such as Latin America, that might attempt to assert their independence.

A debate took place at the White House about whether the US should first attack Afghanistan, the center for the Taliban and al-Qaeda, or Iraq. The US quickly overthrew the Taliban regime in Afghanistan in the Fall of 2001 and the invasion of Iraq was soon to follow in March 2003.

In September 2002, a new strategic security strategy was announced, that of pre-emptive war. What the US meant by "pre-emptive war," however, was actually a policy of preventive war, the policy that the United States claimed the right to go to war against any country simply on the pretext that the target country might present a security threat to the United States at some time in the future. There is no provision for such a policy under international law. It is simply outside of international law and placed the United States squarely within the category of a rogue state.

The George W. Bush Administration then moved on to make a case for the overthrow of Saddam Hussein in Iraq under the false pretexts that Saddam Hussein was linked to al-Qaeda and that Iraq possessed weapons of mass destruction. The attempt succeeded in the United States due primarily to the well oiled propaganda machine of the US media, which has been highly developed since the 1930s to control and "manufacture" public opinion favorable to the US Government. It did not, however, fool the people of any other nation on earth. The United States ignored massive public protests from around the globe and the United States as well, over any and all democratic resistance from the people.

The US Government strategy was to shock the world in a "shock and awe policy," believing that when people saw how powerful the US war machine was they would cower in fear and surrender to the one mighty superpower. A politics of fear was also launched against the people of the United States to stampede them into supporting George W. Bush and the reelection of Republicans and neo-conservatives under the pretext that they would be safer and avoid being attacked by terrorists. This politics of fear, as a powerful weapon, intimidated the political opposition in the US from challenging the neo-conservatives.

The neo-conservative design for the Middle East was based upon the argument that the US policy of supporting pro-US dictatorships and traditional regimes to control the oil had outlived its usefulness. Now the US would demand that the Middle East be globalized, that is, the area would be integrated into the global political economy through the control of US and Israeli capital. Neither traditional feudal nor nationalist secular regimes would be tolerated. Either the regime would buckle under to the demands of US corporate capitalist accumulation and US hegemony or the regime would by crushed, under the principle of "regime change." This also went for any regime that was willing to challenge Zionism, the claim that the Jewish population had a God-given right to the land of Palestine. The Bush neoconservatives and the Israeli right-wing pursued a policy of rolling back the Palestinian Intifada, under the policy of "hot pursuit" of those who resisted. Saddam Hussein would be removed from power and Yassir Arafat would be crushed. Hamas was to be marginalized and starved for funds, even after it won the elections of 2005. Hezbollah in Lebanon and Syria were also targets of the US and Israel. The Israeli attack on Lebanon in the summer of 2006 badly backfired and strengthened Hezbollah. Threats were also stepped up against Iran by the United States, first over Iran's nuclear program, which was legal under international law, and later over the pretext that Iran was interfering in Iraq.

The "new Middle East" would be one that was willing to take orders from the United States and Israel. No dissent would be tolerated. The economic model to be imposed was neoliberalism. If regime change through massive force resulted in chaos, mass destruction and death, it was of little concern to the neo-conservatives, as they claimed that even chaos was better than the status quo. The natives would have learned a lesson and improve themselves in the future.

This program to harvest the oil, labor, and markets of the Middle East for the purpose of US corporate capitalist accumulation was forwarded under a deceptive rubric, that of the Greater Middle East Initiative (GMEI). It was claimed that the US would bring democracy to the Middle East. In practice, however, the US has always defined democracy as that which produces profits for US multinational corporations.

The result, as the seventh year of the neo-conservative reign of fire came to a close in 2007, was a dismal failure and a catastrophe of world historical proportions for the people of the Middle East and indeed for the entire world. The United States was held hostage in Iraq and the larger Middle East caught in its own trap from which it could not easily survive nor easily escape. One outstanding characteristic of the neo-conservatives is their absolute refusal to listen to sound advice from any quarter whatsoever. In their view they are always right. And they have been brought down by their hubris taking the nation with them. Every missile that the neo-conservatives have fired in the name of regime change has back fired to bring greater resistance against the brutal force unleashed by Washington, sometimes taking the form of genuinely democratic resistance, sometimes religious radicalism, and more often terrorism. Indeed, the invasion of Iraq by the United States has resulted in the mushrooming of Islamist terrorism around the world as confirmed by the entire United States intelligence community in a major report released in September 2006.

In the end, it has been the rulers in Washington who have suffered "shock and awe" at the people's resistance to US force and occupation. Unable to respond to the historical reality, the Bush Administration neo-conservatives move on, apparently preparing to unleash military action against Iran. By January, 2008, it was not clear whether the US would launch strikes against Iran, but the pretext that Iranian arms were being smuggled into Iraq was being built up by the White House. It was known that Vice-President Richard Cheney, as well as the Israelis, was pushing for a strike against Iran.

The desperate wars being unleashed by the US and Israel against the peoples of the Middle East are not noble actions on behalf of human ideals. They are not launched to make people more free. They do not make Americans or any one else more "safe." Rather, they reflect the paranoid frenzy of an empire in decline, an empire grown fat from historical European colonialism, American imperialism, and the global repression of freedom under the false rubric of spreading democracy that has outlived its historical time. Europe too, unable to sustain itself under its own weight, limps on, relying upon the cheaper labor of its poorer neighbors in Eastern Europe and Turkey. Today, the rise of East Asia has threatened the superpower and as the Chinese and Russian economies emerge to challenge the US, American intellectuals accuse them of being "selfish."

In truth, the foreign policy of the Bush Administration has not departed radically from post-World War II American foreign policy. Millions have died in the wars and proxy wars fought in Korea, Vietnam, Iraq and elsewhere to maintain the American system of global capitalist accumulation. Today the continued global plunder of the empire is not only threatened by "terrorism" but is quickly being run into bankruptcy. Resistance grows to the institutions, such as the International Monetary Fund, the World Bank and the World Trade Organization, designed to ensure that the entire globe is made to pay for continued imperial wars.

Today, in spite of the massive propaganda from Washington, there is widespread awareness that the drive by neo-conservative "revolutionaries" to consolidate unchallenged US global hegemony has failed. The war against the Taliban in Afghanistan has not secured the country for moderate forces. The war in Iraq has been an unmitigated disaster by any conceivable standard and has been lost. The above was predicted by many sober analysts before the US invasion.

The top US commander in Iraq from June 2003 to mid-2004, Lieutenant General Ricardo S. Sanchez, has stated that the result of the war in Iraq is "a nightmare with no end in sight." In his view, the war was due to a "lust for power" by civilian officials. "The administration, Congress and the entire inter-agency, especially the State Department, must shoulder responsibility for the catastrophic failure, and the American people must hold them responsible."[1] He is correct, within his narrow colonialist perspective that the US "mismanaged the war," in the words of former Secretary of State Madeleine Albright. This book takes a longer historical view, arguing that the attempt by the neoconservatives in the White House to shore up the US as a declining superpower was doomed from the start. It now appears that the Bush Administration has greatly accelerated the decline of American hegemony, even as it desperately clings to its beach head in Iraq. The American people are increasingly dependent upon the rest of the world and community life has degenerated under the lack of well-paying and secure jobs.

In the 1990s, the group of Washington neoconservatives launched their mein kampf. This was not to be a people's revolution but a global putsch, particularly in the Middle East, with US military force, regardless of the chaos and catastrophes which it might bring about. It was also a putsch against the policy of "realism, maintaining the global status quo built upon the international institutions and international law put into place at the end of World War II." "In just about everything we do, from business and technology to cinema and waging war, we are the most revolutionary force on earth. We are not going to fight foreign wars or send money overseas merely to defend the status quo; we must have a suitably glorious objective."[2] They were out to restore "national greatness" not just political stability. It was all about the American Empire.[3]

The neoconservative neo-Storm Troopers were on the march. Today, as the disaster of the Bush Presidential Coup, launched in Florida in November 2000, limps to its sordid end, the "glorious objectives" of the neoconservatives lie, fallen in the dust, after leaving a swath of vast devastation across the world in their wake. The vast majority of humankind fear the United States as the greatest threat to global peace, prosperity and stability. Indeed, they have done great damage to both national and international order and civil liberties. They have carried out inordinate crimes and owe vast reparations to the people of Iraq. Many people have suffered and died as a direct result of their unbridled folly. They have enriched themselves by saddling the American people with unprecedented levels of public debt to be passed on to new generations. The revolutionary hubris of the neoconservatives has hoisted them on their own petard.

This book explores some dimensions of the Bush Administration's disastrous approach to the Middle East. Chapters two, three and four explore "Operation Iraqi Freedom" and how the United States, as predicted by many, progressed from being perceived as a liberator to a hated occupier of the country. Chapter Five explores the thrust behind the US Greater Middle East Initiative and its real purpose within the context of the drive for unchallenged US global hegemony and a global neoliberal economic agenda. Chapter Six explores some critical dimensions of the Palestinian-Israel conflict and the latest chapter in the Palestinian struggle, with the US-sponsored Israeli attack on Lebanon and its destruction in summer 2006. Chapter seven calls attention to the largely ignored problem of flooding areas of the world that have dared to challenge the west with uranium weapons which is killing untold thousands of people and bringing long-lasting ecological disaster to their countries. It is one of the worst forms of toxic imperialism and almost universally ignored by the western press.

Chapter Eight traces the ongoing debacle in Iraq as the US occupation continued to founder and sink into the quagmire unable to overcome local opposition to the colonial enterprise being carried out by the Americans. The long term future was unclear as to whether the Americans would be able to prevail and keep Iraq in its orbit as an American satellite as South Korea and Japan were after World War II. What was certain was that the cost was going to be inordinate as estimates of future costs soared beyond two trillion dollars. Chapter Nine considers some broader principles of US foreign policy underlying the US colonial occupation of Iraq and US global empire.

The people of the world are today waking up to an awareness of these imperial follies which perpetrate tragedies, suffering and death. The crucial ideological struggle of the age is not in the pursuit of capitalist imperialism, under the deceptive rhetoric of a "war on terrorism." as George W. Bush would have it, but precisely the opposite: the struggle for the freedom of the people in the swift demise of an imperialistic system which is preventing people from working for a better future and a better world. It is a struggle against a system which unnecessarily keeps the majority of the world in grinding poverty and deprivation under the pretext that it is the best of all possible systems. It is hoped that the foolhardy policies of the Bush neo-conservatives in Washington have helped to make people aware that a better world is not only possible but necessary if humanity is to survive.

References

1. David S. Cloud, "Ex-Commander Says Iraq Effort is 'a nightmare,'" *New York Times,* October 13, 2007.
2. Michael Ledeen, "Contribution to American Power- For What," Commentary 19 (1), 2000, p. 36.
3. Michael C. Williams, "What is the National Interest: The *Neoconservative Challenge in IR Theory," European Journal of International Relations* 11 (3), 2005, pp. 307-337.

2

Operation Iraqi Freedom: Invasion, Occupation and Consolidation of US Hegemony in Iraq

"The goal would be to keep the Americans in, the Iranians out and the Iraqis down."

Kenneth M. Pollack

The US invasion and occupation of Iraq in March 2003 marked a test case for the Bush Doctrine of preemptive war, to be examined more fully in the following chapter. On the drawing board, the war was to quickly end a dictatorial regime, rid Iraq of weapons of mass destruction (WMD), and return the country to the fold of respectable nations, while giving the Iraqi people freedom and prospects for a better future. The country was to serve as a test case for "free market capitalism" and democracy in the Middle East, designed by the US, at a relatively small cost.[1]

By the summer of 2004, while the US had set up an interim government in Iraq, "transferred sovereignty," and promised elections, the country was put under military rule by the new Iraqi government. The number of US troops killed in the war had reached nearly 1000 by late summer, explosions were now seen almost daily in the streets of Baghdad, and sabotage of major oil pipelines continued. The future of the country remained highly uncertain. Despite claims that Iraq was "sovereign," it was clear that the US would continue the actual occupation of the country with a large number of US troops for several years, while the rest of the world demonstrated little interest in assisting the US in its attempt to secure the country from the ongoing disruption of civil order. Indeed, most countries felt pressure to pull out their troops as quickly as possible. The mainstream view in Washington was that "no great apologies ought to be made for America's 'unilateralism...' For Pax Americana, Iraq may be worth the effort and the risks." [2] This early optimistic view would begin to fade quickly, however, as the Sunni insurgency began to pick up steam.

While Iraq continued to dominate daily international headlines, the rhetoric emanating from Washington and London seemed completely out of step with the positions of most governments around the world. Global opinion almost universally condemned the US for the invasion and occupation, while the reputation and trust of the US in the international arena had fallen to its lowest level ever.[3] As James P. Rubin, former US Assistant Secretary of State for Public Affairs in the Clinton Administration noted, the US continued to "pay the price" for its "false claims" about alleged Iraqi weapons of mass destruction.[4]

In early March 2003, the Bush Administration had run into rough waters. Neither the UN Security Council nor global public opinion could be convinced that it was necessary for the United States to go to war in Iraq to "disarm Saddam Hussein of weapons of mass destruction." Secretary of State Colin Powell was not convincing in the UN Security Council, attempting to make the case for going to war to remove WMD. Dark notes were sounded from the Bush White House about the demise of the United Nations if it did not wise up and buckle down to American demands. Antiwar demonstrations, the most massive in history, emerged across the globe. The Turkish Parliament surprised the US

Government by voting to deny the US the right to invade Iraq with land forces from Turkey[5] and the Turkish Government was subjected to bitter criticism in the American press. The Bush Administration seemed to be losing momentum, as events threatened to spin out of control and scuttle the best laid plans of US President George W. Bush and British Prime Minister Tony Blair for "regime change" in Iraq.

The Bush administration initially relied upon the rationale that regime change was necessary to "disarm Saddam," removing WMD, and claimed that Saddam was linked with al-Qaeda. These arguments failed to convince world opinion, however, succeeding only in the United States, where the media successfully persuaded more than half the population of the erroneous information that a terrorist link with al-Qaeda did exist. Immediately before the war, the Bush Administration announced that the US would go to war with Iraq, even if Saddam left the country. When no weapons of mass destruction could be found in Iraq, first by the UN Monitoring, Verification, and Inspection Commission (UNMOVIC), and later by the invading American forces in Iraq, the rationale for the war was quickly shifted to the "liberation of the Iraqi people," and finally to bringing democracy to the country and the wider region. The whole project, rhetorically, became subsumed under the rubric of a "war on terrorism," which served to further falsely confound the war with the terrorist attacks in the US on September 11, 2001. Officials attempted to deal with the glaring absence of WMD by shifting to the claim that Iraq needed to be invaded because Saddam Hussein had "possessed the capability to produce WMD." For those paying attention, however, the shifting rationale for the war was transparently revealing and, one would have thought, embarrassing for the Bush Administration. But those in the

White House, seemingly made of sterner stuff, brushed aside such quibbling. When all logic collapsed, as was most frequently the case, it was merely asserted that in any event, whatever the facts, invading Iraq was "the right thing to do." Both US President George W. Bush and British Prime Minister Tony Blair stated repeatedly that they would do nothing differently if they had the chance. Being a fiat accompli, there was no need to look back, to examine the facts, legality, procedure or diplomacy, but just move on. But after being rejected out of hand in the beginning, the rest of the world was now being asked by Washington to lend a hand in the occupation.

Almost universally, global public opinion held that the US went to war in Iraq for the oil. While overly simplistic, this was essentially correct. More accurately, the US recognized the "stupendous prize" to be won by the control of Middle Eastern oil. Iraq and Saudi Arabia together account for at least 65 percent of total global oil reserves in the world. In the words of one prominent analyst, "the goal would be to keep the Americans in, the Iranians out, and the Iraqis down."[6] Five years later and after nearly four years of US occupation this statement was equally valid. As of August 2004, no "weapons of mass destruction" had been found in Iraq and hardly anyone could be found who still believed that WMD would ever turn up in Iraq. Inquiries into the question of WMD, which some bothersome individuals persisted in refusing to forget, held in both Britain and the US, attempted to shift the blame for finding no WMD to the "failure" of intelligence services of both countries. In the US George Tenet, former head of the Central Intelligence Agency, was made a scapegoat and was forced to resign. A similar scripted act was played out in London, with more obscuring subtlety and added farce, keeping to British tradition. Blair, fearing the wrath of voters at the polls, lowered his profile considerably. But the reality of events was appallingly transparent. It is pretty clear that whatever Saddam did was quite irrelevant because the US had already made the decision to go to war.

Regime change in Iraq having been carried out in March and April 2003, it was in the hands of the United States and Great Britain, to justify the use of outright force to overthrow a sovereign regime. In reality, Operation Iraqi Freedom was an American operation and patently illegal under international law. We examine this more fully in Chapter Three. US Defense Secretary Donald Rumsfeld stressed, before the war, that Britain's help was not needed, making it clear that the US would go to war alone if the British did not join. A few other nations did join, mostly small nations with small populations, but with little effective commitment.[7] In fact, opposition to Operation Iraqi Freedom was almost universal, with public opinion running as high as 85 to 95 percent against the war in many countries. Only in the US could it be said that there was initially strong support for the war, largely as a result of the US media succeeding in convincing more than half of the population of the erroneous information that there was a significant terrorist link between Saddam Hussein's government and al-Qaeda.

Nevertheless, the United States proceeded rapidly, brushing aside the opinion of the overwhelming majority of the world's people, as well as that of most of the governments represented in the United Nations. Delegations in the Security Council were spied upon by the US and rigorous efforts were made to coerce, or intimidate uncommitted nations into siding with the US, all of which failed to produce a second resolution in the Security Council, which might have been seen to authorize the overthrow of a sovereign government. US action in opposition to popular opinion may say a great deal about the respect for democracy and the expression of free will by the current US administration. Apparently no one was expected to notice the irony that "bringing democracy" to Iraq meant defying the democratic voice of practically the entire world and attempting to punish countries, like Turkey, where the Parliament listened to the democratic voice of the people. The US calculation that the most powerful countries in the G-8, which opposed the war, would soften, once the operation to overthrow Saddam Hussein was launched, however, proved substantially correct.[8] Nevertheless, most countries have continued to distance themselves from the US effort in Iraq and almost all have pulled out of the "coalition." Voters in Spain reacted to Prime Minister Jose Maria Azner's support for the US by voting his government out of office and the Philippines pulled out of the coalition after threats to its workers in Iraq. Other governments began to accelerate their withdrawal after hostage takings picked up by 2004.

Leaving aside the question of democracy, establishing a stable regime in Iraq was going to be one of the most difficult problems which the US faced. Anglo-American aggression in Iraq had substantially alienated public opinion in the Arab world. Most Iraqis, while happy to see Saddam go, did not welcome the US occupation, a US established government dominated by Iraqi exiles, and the wealth of their nation being appropriated by US corporations. It was clear from early on that the people were going to fight for the freedom the US said they should have, but was not about to allow. A common sentiment in Iraq has been "No to Saddam, no to the US." And merely living from day to day became a tremendous challenge. Operation Iraqi Freedom increased terrorism not only in Iraq but against Americans and the British around the world. While US officials claimed in public that "Americans are safer," US intelligence officially predicted more terrorist attacks would occur as a result of the US occupation and continued deployment of US troops in Iraq.

Moreover, small and relatively weak countries around the world quickly learned the dangerous lesson from the launching of a "preemptive war." The message was that in the essentially lawless world of "preemptive war," or more accurately preventive war, as promulgated in the US national strategic security document, it is vital that defenseless countries obtain weapons of mass destruction, particularly nuclear weapons. It was clear that diplomacy was used in dealing with North Korea, precisely because the country possessed nuclear weapons. The Bush Administration has made the world a much more dangerous place and all indications are that the US is committed to forge ahead to achieve "full spectrum dominance," in the global arena. To the extent resources allow, any challenge by any country will be met with a full range of options, political, economic and military, to prevail over any and all challenges. Iraq has been called a "test case" for the Bush doctrine and one can expect more of the same if the cost is acceptable to the American people. There are likely to be sequels to Iraq if troops, money, and public support can be secured. The bill for replenishing the stocks of weapons after the Iraq War was sent to the American taxpayers, with the cost approaching some $200 billion by mid 2004. This was just the beginning. This convenient division of labor, calls for the American taxpayers to pay for "preemptive wars" while politically connected corporations, which have donated heavily to Bush election campaigns, reap the spoils in lucrative contracts and excessive profits. This agenda has marched forward, even as the social welfare provisions and the fabric of American society has become more stressed under the continuing and deepening neoliberal policies of the Bush Administration, primarily by continuing to pound the drums of "the war on terrorism."[9]

Planning and Pretext

The case for "Operation Iraqi Freedom,"[10] was laid out years before by CIA analysts in the Clinton Administration. Kenneth M. Pollack, Director for Gulf Affairs, at the National Security Council from 1999 to 2001,[11] wrote in 2002 that "The United States should invade Iraq, eliminate the present regime, and pave the way for a successor prepared to abide by its international commitments and live in peace with its neighbors."[12] The argument claimed that there were no longer any good policy options toward Iraq, but since Saddam might develop nuclear weapons and use them, the US had no choice but to overthrow Saddam in an "invasion" and occupy the country. It was argued further that neither weapons inspectors nor deterrence were adequate to eliminate Iraq's weapons of mass destruction (WMD); that the sanctions against Iraq had begun to unravel; that US policy had led to "ludicrous Iraqi propaganda" claiming the death of a million Iraqis since 1991 due to the economic sanctions; that the smuggling of oil to Jordan, Syria, Turkey and the Persian Gulf states had doubled since 1998, benefiting these countries; that the US could not stop the smuggling of such items as the fiber-optic communications system installed by the Chinese in the 1990s; and that a policy of deterrence was too risky, since Saddam could threaten Saudi oil fields and Israel. Kenneth Pollack pointed out that an air campaign could not succeed in overthrowing the Iraqi regime. Consequently, the strategic logic for a full scale invasion was "compelling." Sufficient forces would be deployed to make "success almost certain" and would be well within US capabilities. The oil fields would be seized early on and after the war the US troops would be on hand for occupation. The military buildup for the invasion would take three to five months, and the actual war would last about a month. The diplomatic fallout would be more difficult. To be palatable, it would have to be a quick victory, the only country vital to the operation, being Kuwait. While the French, Russians and Chinese would object, they would be unable to stop the invasion and the US would be "left owning a country of 22 million people...[I]nvaders...get to decide the composition and form of a future Iraqi government..." The Saudis, Kuwaitis, Jordanians, and Turks would be "co-opted." Following the operation, the US would quickly repair the diplomatic damage. Funds would be mobilized from the Gulf Cooperation Council, Europe, East Asia, and Iraqi oil for reconstruction. Clinching the argument, Pollack hammered home the idea that the "shock of September 11" was still fresh in the minds of Americans, so the US Government and the public were ready to "make sacrifices." The rest of the world recognizes that the US is angry about September 11, and "may be leery about getting on the wrong side of it." But time, Pollack stressed, was of the essence.[13]

In fact, there are compelling indications that the Bush Administration team had planned the war even before taking office. On September 13, 2001, two days after 9/11, Rumsfeld, Wolfowitz, and others in the Bush Administration discussed a war against Iraq with President George W. Bush. While there seemed to be a general consensus for a war, the substance of the debate was whether Afghanistan or Iraq should come first. It is also known that Dick Cheney, Paul Wolfowitz, and others brought into the Bush Administration wrote to President Clinton in 1998, asking for "regime change" to be carried out in Iraq. [14] Control of the vast Iraqi oil reserves meant potentially large profits and Texas oil men dominated the Bush Government. It was also feared that if the United States did not overthrow Saddam and gain control of Iraqi oil wealth quickly, the opportunity could slip out of their hands.

Since there seemed to be little chance, in the summer of 2002, that the weapons inspectors would ever return to Iraq, the best rationale for "regime change" seemed to be "the disarmament of Saddam," the elimination of weapons of mass destruction (WMD). According to Wolfowitz, to pin the cause on WMD was just a bureaucratic decision that everyone could agree on. In fact, it was argued by many that Iraq had very few, if any, remaining WMD. The bulk of Saddam's military forces had been destroyed in the 1991 Gulf War. The arguments of former weapons inspector Scott Ritter that Saddam really threatened no one seemed convincing at the time.[15] But no one in the American Government with any influence was listening. In early May, 2003, the US Defense Intelligence Agency stated that there was no proof that Saddam had WMD back in October 2002. Bush, Rumsfeld, Powell and others in the Administration continued to insist in public statements, however, that Iraq's possession of WMD was certain.

The new imperial agenda embarked upon by the George W. Bush Administration is deeply rooted in the first Bush Administration. The "war on terrorism" was first declared, not after September 11, but at the beginning of the 1980s.[16] By 1997, the "Project for a New American Century" (PNAC) had been organized. Among the original signers were Dick Cheney, Donald Rumsfeld, Paul Wolfowitz, Jeb Bush, Elliot Abrams, Francis Fukuyama and Norman Podhoretz. The PNAC is basically about using American force "wherever and whenever necessary."[17]

The roots of unilateral US aggression have deep roots and can be traced back to at least the 1960s. Hans Morgenthau wrote in 1964 that "America has a transcendent purpose" or as Andrew Bacevich stated, "History has a discernible direction and destination. Uniquely among all the nations of the world, the United States comprehends and manifests history's purpose."[18] In this ideology, US global hegemony is the "realization of history's purpose." The doctrine of preemptive strike can be traced to the views of senior US statesman Dean Acheson more than 40 years ago. Acheson, responding to the failed effort of the Kennedy Administration to overthrow the government of Fidel Castro in Cuba in the Bay of Pigs fiasco, stated that "legal issues do not arise in the case of a US response to a 'challenge to its power, position, and prestige." Cuba had engaged in a "successful defiance" of the US. For the Kennedy Administration, the principle of preemptive war was not raised to the level of official policy, as under the current Bush Doctrine. Today, under the Bush Doctrine, it is possible for James Baker to suggest that "Washington could appeal to Article 51 [of the UN Charter] to authorize the conquest and occupation of Iraq, because Iraq may someday threaten the US with WMD, or threaten others while the US stands helplessly by."[19] These principles were clearly applied in the invasion and occupation of Iraq with the question of examining the legality of the war rejected out of hand.

The Forgotten US Track Record in Iraq

Since the past relationship of the US with Saddam Hussein's Iraq seems to have disappeared down the "memory-hole"[20] during the War on Iraq, it is well to briefly recall some well known, but widely ignored, facts. To the extent that Iraq was able to develop programs for weapons of mass destruction, chemical, biological, and nuclear, in the past, it was primarily due to the willingness of the US and Western European countries to assist these efforts. The US assisted Iraq in the use of chemical weapons during the Iran-Iraq war to help contain Iran. It was during this time that

Iraq used chemical weapons against the Kurds in Halabja with the full knowledge of the US. Further, as revealed in the Iraqi report to the United Nations in December 2002, there is a long list of both American and European firms which sold materials to Iraq, prior to 1991, relating to weapons of mass destruction.[21] US officials never mentioned this past record while going to war to "disarm Saddam." The US and British media also cooperated, withholding these facts from the public. As noted above, these WMD were largely destroyed or rendered harmless by the end of the 1990s.

Further, the facts about Saddam's invasion and occupation of Kuwait in 1990 was not been put into context in the 2003 war. At the time of the first Gulf War, Iraq was burdened with a $40 billion debt as a result of the Iran-Iraq War. The drop in the price of oil, at times, to $12 dollars per barrel, was costing the Iraqi economy some $7 billion dollars a year. This was due to the hike in production of oil by the Gulf states and Saudi Arabia. Further, Kuwait was engaged in pumping oil from the Rumaila oil field by slant-drilling which seemed to be a "provocation." Saddam had expected that the West would offer some sort of compensation in return for his collaboration with the US in the war against Iran.

When Saddam met the US Ambassador to Baghdad, April Glaspie, a week before the invasion of Kuwait in 1990, Iraq had placed troops at the Kuwaiti border indicating that Iraq was about to invade. The US Ambassador, rather than indicating that the US would intervene militarily if Iraq invaded Kuwait, stated "We have no opinion on the Arab-Arab conflicts, like your border disagreement with Kuwait." Following this, Saddam seems to have "badly misread America's real intentions" encouraging him to invade Kuwait.

Whether or not a trap was set for Saddam, the invasion of Kuwait afforded an opportunity for the US to dismantle Iraq and establish effective hegemony over the country for the next twelve years under the crippling sanctions regime that was near-genocidal.[22] The 1991 Iraq war could be described as massive overkill which "greatly exceeded the UN-endorsed mission of expelling Saddam from Kuwait. This may have been carried out for the purpose of making an example of Saddam to other nations of the perils of getting on the wrong side of the US. Aerial bombing was massive lasting forty-three days, during which the United States and its allies flew 109,876 sorties, dropping 84,200 tons of bombs. The US pitched the campaign to suggest that bombing raids were surgical strikes against military targets while much of the civilian infrastructure, water and electrical facilities, was actually taken apart. This spread disease and killed many children after the war. Actually 93 percent of munitions were unguided bombs dropped mostly by B-52 carpet bombers. About 70 percent of the bombs missed their targets. Private homes were destroyed and many civilians killed. Many antipersonnel weapons were used including fuel-air explosives, 15,000 pound "daisy-cutter" bombs, petroleum-based incendiary napalm (which incinerated Iraqi soldiers in trenches), and 61,000 cluster bombs containing 20 million small bomblets. Civilian air raid shelters were bombed, such as in the Ameriyya district in Baghdad. Estimates are that some 15,000 civilians died while from 100,000 to 200,000 Iraqi soldiers died.[23]

The 1991 war spelled the destruction of Iraq as a modern nation and placed the US in a position to halt any possibility of development as long as Saddam Hussein was in power. The events at the end of the war, in which President George H.W. Bush encouraged the Shias and the Kurds to rise up against Saddam, and then allowed Saddam's forces to carry out brutal repression, slaughtering thousands, further contributed to the loss of civilian life. It was apparently calculated that Saddam would not be able to cling to power, but this, of course, was not the case. The US targeted the civilian infrastructure of Iraq during the 1991 war, in violation of the Geneva Convention, with full awareness that the degradation of the drinking water supply would result in large numbers of civilian deaths. The targeting of civilian infrastructure is said in official U.S. documents to be the official policy of the US Air Force.[24]

It has been argued that the sanctions which devastated civilian society for almost 13 years in Iraq actually helped to strengthen Saddam and forced the population to rely upon him for survival. US policy actually helped to ensure that Saddam would not be overthrown. There is much documentation of how even items like art supplies, pencils, paper and other school supplies were denied under the UN sanctions program. These sanctions served to punish the Iraqi people, while allowing Saddam Hussein to stay in power. The suffering and large-scale death of the civilian population of Iraq, through the degradation of the water supply, was planned and executed by the US government in direct violation of the Geneva Convention on War.[25]

The War This Time

UN Security Council Resolution 1441 was not meant to authorize the invasion and occupation of Iraq by the US and Britain when passed. It was the intention of the US to push through another resolution authorizing the war, but when the UN Security Council held out against repeated attempts by the US to pressure hesitant members, the US was forced to launch the war without the additional resolution. It was clear from early on that the Bush Administration was determined to go to war in Iraq. The only question was just how serious the diplomatic damage would be in such a near-unilateral act. Probably nothing could have stopped the war, given the brazen attitude of the Bush Administration, willing to go against world opinion, and international law. The US, however, calculated correctly, that the members of the UN Security Council would give retroactive sanction for the war, once the deed had been carried out, and France and Russia stood to lose their interests in Iraqi oil. The US made dire predictions about the demise of the UN if the organization did not authorize US and British intervention. After the war, little concern was raised by other members that the US had violated the Charter and principles of the UN.

The US strikes against Baghdad began on the morning of March 20, 2003, said to be preliminary strikes carried out in an attempt to assassinate Saddam Hussein, who could be hiding in a bunker. It turned out later, however, that the bunker did not actually exist. Simultaneously American tanks cruised through the desert, invading from Kuwait and heading for Baghdad. The campaign of "Shock and Awe," a concept from Harlan K. Ullman, was expected to follow. This was designed to destroy the "enemy's' will." While the Anglo-American forces often encountered stiff resistance from elements of the Iraqi Army and the Republican Guard as they made their way to Baghdad, it is probably not quite correct to call the action which followed a "war." Iraq had very little to fight with and no air force or navy. Any units which put up serious resistance were certain to be slaughtered in short order. The country which spends more than the entire rest of the world combined for weapons was now pounding a small country, whose major military capability was destroyed by the US more than 12 years ago, and had been under sanctions for the entire period since. Part of the resistance involved futile guerrilla tactics but it seemed that the bulk of the forces had little stomach for this only to be pounded into the earth by American bombers. The speculation by some that the US would become bogged down in urban guerrilla warfare from Saddam's forces did not materialize during this phase of the war, major opposition taking about a year to emerge. The highly-equipped American and British soldiers were seen rounding up the rag-tag and often barefoot remnants of the Iraqi Army, who began to surrender by the hundreds and thousands. Most Iraqi troops simply abandoned their positions as the war progressed.[26]

As expected, Baghdad was being bombed in massive attacks and much of it left burning. The result could not be in doubt. The only question was how many Iraqi military and civilians would be slaughtered. Similar to Colin Powell in the first Gulf War, the Commander of Centcom, General, Tommy Franks, stated that "We don't do body counts." The estimates of the dead vary widely. Some 7000 civilians killed in the initial phase of the war was given as a reasonable estimate but the figure was likely much higher. It has been estimated that some 5 to 10 percent of the Iraqi troops died, somewhere between 13,500 and 45,000.[27] The number of US and British soldiers killed were, of course, very small, around 166 during the initial phase of the war. By July 2003, the figure had reached 200, and by one year later, nearly 1000. These figures were deceptive as the ongoing occupation took tens of thousands of Iraqi lives over the coming years and the number of US soldiers reached nearly 4000 by the end of 2007, with more than 30,000 wounded. Many suffered severe psychological effects as in all wars. One in ten Iraqis would be displaced from their homes, some two million in exile. The inevitable health effects from depleted uranium weapons were impossible to predict.

Both sides were condemned for committing war crimes. The Iraqis deliberately stationed tanks and missiles inside civilian areas hoping that the Americans would not bomb them, but the Americans proceeded to bomb them anyway.

Children were hit by American cluster bombs which were used in civilian areas. Many civilians were hit, causing much suffering and death. The Iraqis are partly to blame for this situation. In the Mansur area of Baghdad, the Americans decided to bomb a residential area dropping four 2000 pound bombs. The rationale for this was that it was thought that Saddam was in the area. At least 14 civilians were killed in this action. In Hilla too, a civilian area, the Iraqis had probably placed military vehicles. But according to the Geneva Convention, civilians are supposed to be protected even if there are enemy combatants. Many have pointed out that intentionally dropping such bombs in civilian areas is a clear violation of the Geneva Conventions.[28]

There were also incidents involving journalists, and it is hard to escape the conclusion that there was some deliberate targeting of journalists by frustrated elements in the US military. In the case of al-Jazeera, the network was targeted and bombed in Afghanistan. One of its newsmen injured there was killed by a US bomb dropped on the rooftop of the al-Jazeera headquarters in Baghdad. Tariq Ayoub was killed just three hours before an incident at the Palestine Hotel in Baghdad where a US tank on the Jumeirah Bridge on the Tigris swiveled its turret and fired into the hotel. This was filmed by French TV. The Americans initially denied that the shelling had happened, but were forced to change their story when they discovered that the French had filmed the firing, which was shown on Euronews. Then the story was changed to charge that the tank was under sniper fire and an RPG (rocket propelled grenade) attack. This also was not true. Robert Fisk reported that the 3rd Infantry Division Commander, General Buford Blount, lied about the sniper fire and claimed that it ceased after a round of depleted uranium was fired into the Reuters office. A journalist, who survived, Samia Mahul, had a piece of metal in her brain. A Spanish cameraman was also killed along with a Ukranian cameraman from Reuters.[29] There were many other events in which journalists died in the war.

The main phase of the war, which was never in doubt, lasted less than a month, with US forces occupying Baghdad and watching as the Iraqi ministries, museums, and libraries were burned and looted. The Americans, in the view of Secretary of Defense Donald Rumsfeld, had freed the Iraqis to engage in looting. In fact, anarchy prevailed, as drivers were dragged from their cars and private homes, shops, and offices were looted. In the North of the country, the Turkish Army was held back, while the Kurds were allowed into the Turkmen city of Kirkuk to loot for two days before returning home.

The civilian toll was horrendous, with bombs landing in civilian areas, and the Iraqis forced to endure without electricity and a proper supply of drinking water. The lack of functioning infrastructure would continue to take its toll. In fact, the American and British occupiers had not able to restore essential services to some areas of the city by 2006 in the midst of increase violence. Even by the end of 2007, most of Baghdad was without electricity for the major part of every day.

Deconstructing Iraq: Looting, Anarchy and Emerging Resistance

By any standards, the scale of anarchy, looting, and destruction, after the fall of the Iraqi regime, was very great. A state of anarchy continued to prevail in the country with American soldiers afraid to go out at night.[30] Security for almost all Iraqis continued to deteriorate. Some observers questioned why American tanks were not deployed to key institutions, such as at museums and libraries, to prevent looting. US tanks were reportedly idle while American soldiers were doing little at the time. Under the Geneva Convention, the Americans had a legal obligation to maintain order and prevent massive looting, especially of art and literary treasures. On the other hand, Donald Rumsfeld seemed to take a cavalier attitude, saying that free people were free to do bad things.

The Office of Reconstruction and Humanitarian Assistance (ORHA) urged that the National Museum should be the second priority after the National Bank. A website had been set up by American Archaeologists and information available to the Pentagon several weeks before the war. The Americans claimed they wanted to preserve the national heritage of the Iraqi people, but in fact, they allowed the looting to go on. At least 158 government buildings in Baghdad alone were burned as the US forces took control of the city. Some 35 ministries were gutted by fire. Only the Ministry of Oil and the Ministry of Interior were protected. Among these were the National Archaeological Museum, the National Library of Archives (Ottoman and State Archives) and the Koranic Library of the Ministry of Religious Endowment. It was reported that petrol was poured on the documents before burning. Under the Geneva Conventions, the US occupation forces had a legal duty to protect these historical documents and the embassies.[31] According to the US, there were Saddam Regime remnants that wanted to destroy these documents, but Robert Fisk suggested that there were some institutions and organizations which apparently wanted to destroy these documents and artifacts. Why the US military did not act to preserve the national treasures is not clear. According to Fisk, the generals refused to deploy even one tank, even though there were plenty of them available.

Many priceless treasures disappeared, such as earrings, gold ornaments, and bullring gods, which appeared for sale in Europe and America in a few days. Many Grecian statues were destroyed, shattered on the floors. The looters knew what they wanted and got it out of the country quickly. Some, such as Maguire Gibson of the University of Chicago, believe that the museum looting could have been orchestrated from outside the country. The arsonists knew what to burn and what the Americans would not defend. They had maps and knew where to go in the city The Department of Higher Education and Computer Science was also burned down. The ministry of Agricultural Irrigation was burned, right next to the Ministry of Oil. US Marines reportedly watched the buildings burn and did nothing. Also there was much looting in Basra under the British, with British Defense Secretary Geoff Hoon stating that the Iraqis "were liberating their own property." Rumsfeld ridiculed alarmed reporters and claimed that there was no widespread looting in Baghdad.[32] Kirkuk in the north was looted by the Kurds for two days, in a rerun of what happened in 1991. This was allowed to happen, with apparently no effort to stop it, until the Kurdish leaders, Masud Barzani and Jalal Talabani, called their forces back from the city.

The occupiers, however, were faced with the situation on the ground in Iraq and this increasingly proved to be problematic. The Americans and British were now occupiers and no longer "liberators." Some Shi'ite clerics, who clearly envisioned some form of Islamist government similar to that of Iran, had returned from Iran. One Imam, Sheikh Ahmed al-Kubeisy, was quoted as saying: "We will not accept a government that will oppress us. There must be an elected government...You are masters today. But I warn you against thinking of staying. Get out before we force you out." [33] But major resistance also emerged from Sunni areas.

The United States feared that the resistance to US occupation was growing among the Shia community, supported by thousands of Badr Brigade Iraqis trained in Iran. Most Iraqis wanted the Americans to leave but it took several months for systematic opposition to emerge.[34] Shias suffered the worst from the bombing as most victims were Shia, such as around Nasiriyah and Hillah. Several brutal incidents with the Americans happened, in which the Shias were acting in self defense, but the resistance was portrayed as carried out by remnants of Saddam's regime or terrorists. Increasingly, this situation came to resemble the Israeli occupation of the West Bank and Gaza. The Shias greatly admired the Lebanese Hizbollah and knew the art of guerrilla resistance, after years of enduring Saddam's torture chambers. Yet, the US expected the Shias to take orders from ex-General Jay Garner, who they knew had strong connections to Israel. At lease 17 Sunni demonstrators, as well, were killed in the first week of May, 2003.[35] Some 20,000 Shias protested at Nasiriyah at the attempt of the US and Iraqi opposition to form a government. Iraqis were reportedly shot in the back while trying to buy bread. The US Marines, repeatedly attacked in Mosul, opened fire, killing seven. There was also growing unrest over the long period with little or no electricity. Americans were blamed for this, as well as for the looting.[36] The US occupation force quickly issued a "colonial message". "Please avoid leaving your homes during the night hours after evening prayers and before the call to morning prayers...During this time, terrorist forces associated with the former regime of Saddam Hussein, as well as various criminal elements, are known to move through the area... please do not leave your homes during this time. During all hours, please approach coalition military positions with extreme caution..." This came from the command of the 1st US Marine Division. It was essentially a lock-down with no water or electricity.[37]

The situation was compared to what greeted the British in Greece in 1944. The resistance was genuine but Winston Churchill supported the nationalist government of George Papandreau, who was then the Ahmed Chalabi of Greece. The Elas communist guerrillas, who had fought the Nazis, wanted power, and feared exclusion. The British fought battles with the Communists and imposed martial law. Today, the US and Britain are not ready to accept any help from Iran, even though it has been offered. Both Syria and Iran were accused of supporting "terrorist networks and this has increased in recent years."[38]

This was very similar to the historical situation the British found themselves in after the invasion of Iraq in 1917. The British claimed that they came as liberators, not as conquerors. But within three years, the British were losing hundreds of men every year in a guerrilla war as the Iraqis sought liberation from the British.[39] Today those fighting the occupation are simply called "insurgents."

It was predicted at the time that the same thing would happen with the Americans as the resistance increased and the prediction has proved correct. The Iraqis were convinced that the Americans had come only for the oil.[40] By August 2004, the anarchic situation continued, with almost daily attacks on US soldiers around the country and an increasing fear among the occupying Americans. The Americans in Iraq found themselves in a situation very similar to that of the Israelis in the occupied territories. One could only expect the American soldiers to turn more brutal in their tactics for self preservation as resistance increased.

Health dangers to Iraqis also remained great, not only due to the collapsed infrastructure, but also the toll to be taken in years to come from depleted uranium weapons, and the looting of radioactive materials, such as at the Tuwaitha reactor facility near Baghdad, where villagers looted barrels which had been filled with radioactive waste to use for storing drinking water.[41] There is likely to be a long and deadly legacy as a result of the massive use of depleted uranium munitions all across the country as discussed in Chapter Seven.

US-British Occupation of Iraq

Gabriel Kolko has written that "[t]he US has never been able to translate its superior arms into political success, and that decisive failure is inherent in everything it attempts. Iraq has now confirmed this pattern; its regionalism and internecine ethnic strife promises to produce years of political, social, and economic, instability."[42] Gideon Levy predicted early on that

> "As soon as the United States starts to become mired in the occupation, today's enlightened soldiers will become tomorrow's inhuman troops. They will lose the remnants of their moral image and will kill, destroy and abuse. The children huggers will become the children persecutors, the food distributors will turn into agents of starvation, the wound healers will block ambulances at checkpoints, the liberators will become jailers. Humiliating the occupied and stripping them of their rights will become the norm. The liberated Iraqi people will pay in the form of heavy losses, hunger and humiliation, even if these are temporary. And they will not forget. That is the impact of occupation, whether in the narrow alleys of a Gaza Strip refugee camp or in the sprawling city of Baghdad."[43]

This proved to be true all too soon in Iraq and was to be revealed in stark detail in the pictures from Abu Gharib Prison. Nothing has changed this picture and only the Iraqis can reclaim their own country.

US officials continued to claim that the US had fought a war for the "self determination" and "freedom" of a people.[44] The American approach implied that Iraqis could now become "free" only if they submitted to being under the de facto occupation by a foreign power. Those who resisted, as the American Patriots did when the British were fighting for their US colonies, were seen as criminals, terrorists, and rogue elements. In short, "insurgents."

Prior to the war, there was much speculation about how the US occupation would be carried out.[45] It was suggested in some quarters that post-war Japan would be the model for Iraq, with US general, Tommy Franks, playing the role of General Douglas MacArthur in Japan. After a period of military rule, the US would establish "a broad-based representative democracy." There would be a civilian administration to run the economy. The Iraqi opposition would have a limited initial role and there would be a need for some 150,000 troops for "several years." The US would also need a "legal basis" to take control, presumably, under the cover of the UN. Stated goals would include preservation of Iraq as a unitary state and preventing outside interference. An unstated goal would be the control of oil and its sale in such a way that it would cover reconstruction contracts held by the large American firms, Bechtel and Halliburton. There was concern about how to deal with oil sales, without giving the appearance that oil was the principal aim of the war. Various periods of occupation were suggested from 1.5 years up to three years or more. The occupation, many claimed, could be a bigger challenge than the war and there were "enormous uncertainties." It was also uncertain at what point former members of the Ba'ath Party would be allowed to serve in the new administration to be set up, if at all.

Historians subsequently pointed out that only in the most superficial sense could Japan serve as a model for post-war Iraq. Some analysts accurately predicted widespread chaos. John Dower, a scholar of the US occupation of Japan, which lasted six and a half years, pointed out that Iraq was too dissimilar to Japan for the model to be useful. In Japan, the US had total legitimacy and the US role was readily accepted. There were no ethnic, religious or tribal factions. Unlike Iraq, Japan had surrendered. Democratic institutions would be harder to establish in Iraq and the focus would be on what the Americans did with the oil. Another critic, Herman Eilts, a former Ambassador to Egypt and Saudi Arabia, expressed great skepticism about developing a democratic structure in Iraq. Robert Fisk pointed out that this was the first occupation of an Arab capital by a Western army since General Allenby entered Jerusalem and Sir Stanley Maude entered Baghdad in 1917. Now American troops were occupying the wealthiest Arab country in the world. Fisk wrote of "shock waves for decades to come" and predicted that the price of the oil would be very high in the end. His predictions have proved to be on the mark.

In fact, planning had already been made to privatize not only the Iraqi oil industry, but virtually the entire economy, setting up Iraq as a neoliberal show case for the rest of the Middle East.[46] But it was also clear that Iraqi oil, while vast, would not pay for everything, at least not in the beginning, and the operation would need to be funded by American taxpayers. They would get the news and the bill later.

Progress lagged in getting even a hand-picked government up and running in Iraq. While the end of the War was officially announced on May 1, 2003, American soldiers continued to come under attacks and there were continuous uprisings and demonstrations by militant

Iraqis.[47] Ex-General Jay Garner, named Iraq's temporary post-war civilian administrator, came under considerable criticism in May 2003. He was fired and the US quickly rushed a replacement to Baghdad, L. Paul Bremer III, a former foreign service officer.

Another concern was the lack of legal cover for the U.S. to start running Iraq. This was speedily patched up with UN Security Council Resolution 1483, presented by the US, Britain and Spain on May 9, 2003, and passed on May 22 by a vote of 14-0. Syria did not vote. The European Union and France wanted a central role for the UN, but the US would have nothing to do with this. The capitulation to US demands that the occupation be "legitimized" and that the oil be controlled by the "occupying powers," the US and Britain, nevertheless came smoothly. The resolution lifted the oil and trade sanctions against Iraq, which technically was not supposed to happen until the weapons inspectors had declared Iraq free from weapons of mass destruction. The oil for food program was to be phased out. Iraq's oil reserves were transferred from the UN to the "US led coalition." The UN would have an "advisory role," while oil money would finance the country's reconstruction. UN Secretary General, Kofi Annan, would appoint a "special coordinator" to work with the US and British occupiers and Iraqis. Washington and London were to control the oil wealth "until an internationally recognized, representative government was established." The US refused to accept any time limit on the period of US-British occupation. The UN Security Council was given the power to "review" the implementation of the resolution within 12 months. The role of the weapons inspectors was left to be "discussed later." The US would take charge of an "Iraqi development fund" which would be derived from Iraqi oil. An "international advisory monitoring board was to be set up to provide "transparency." Finally, "[t]he resolution granted immunity from law suits involving oil and natural gas until an internationally recognized government was in place and Iraq's $400 billion debt restructured."[48] Kofi Annan proceeded to name UN High Commissioner for Human Rights, Sergio Viera de Mello, as the UN representative to Iraq. The fate of the oil contracts, held by France, Russia, Italy, and China, was left to be decided later. Ultimately they would become a casualty of the war.

In June 2003, things were not going well on the ground, and civil order in the country seemed to be collapsing. Besides the looting and car-jacking, and thieves robbing shopkeepers, radical shi'ite mobs began attacking cinemas and liquor stores. Some clerics called for an end to the US occupation. It was dangerous on the streets and in the countryside. Iraqis had no security, little electricity and water, and many were running out of food. Garbage piled up in the streets. People were forced to sleep inside miserably hot houses due to bullets flying around, rather than on their roofs. Shiite imams began programs of charity to distribute food on their own. It is clear that some in the Bush Administration already feared that the situation could veer badly off track and were being warned of the coming chaos by the Israelis. The Coalition Provisional Authority (CPA) was coming in for the blame and demands that the US get out of the country were increasing, including criticism from elements of the US military itself.

There were increasing midnight raids on villages, such as "Operation Planet X", at Ad-Dawr village near Takrit by American soldiers where 260 prisoners were taken. It was reported that some 500 soldiers searched 200 houses beginning at 2:00 AM and continuing through the night. The hands of the prisoners were tied with plastic, and those with firearms to be arrested.[49] Some of the prisoners were released but many ended up in Abu Gharib prison being given the Guantanimo Bay treatment, being tortured and abused to elicit information from them. Such operations were to become routine as the occupation ground on.

The new civil administrator, L. Paul Bremer III, was dispatched two months early, to replace Garner. Bremer made a number of grievous mistakes, which later backfired. He fired the West Baghdad police chief and declared that 30,000 former high Ba'ath Party officials would be barred from jobs in the new administration. On May 24, the Iraqi Army was officially abolished, along with the former security apparatus, and Defense and Information ministries. This put some 400,000 Iraqis officially out of a job, leading to a riot in front of a Baghdad mosque a few days later. There were also initial efforts to get on more friendly terms with the local people by removing some tanks from central Baghdad and sending US soldiers on friendly foot patrols, where they would interact with the people and even make friends with local clerics in the mosques. But the American headquarters had been set up in one of Saddam's presidential palace compounds, completely isolated from the people. George Bush was becoming the new Saddam. An edict was issued that all weapons larger than 7.62 semi-assault rifles must be turned in, but this would still leave the local population with Kalashnikov rifles. Helicopters with search lights would be flown over Baghdad continuously.

At the end of May 2003, the U.S. scrapped its plan to call a convention of 300 elites to set up an interim government, until elections could be held. Things were moving too slowly and there was too much dissension among the various groups. In fact, the seven leading political groups, including the Iraqi National Congress (INC), had reached the point of presenting a demand for an end to

American political control to the Americans, due to the unsatisfactory situation in the civil order and accused the Americans of a "systematic stripping of sovereignty from the Iraqi people." At the same time, it was reported that more than a hundred Iraqi exiles, experts chosen by the Bush Administration to restore order, were still waiting, some in the US and some in Kuwait, to be brought into the country. It seems that their role was to clue the Americans in on what was actually going on and how to go about putting the country back together.

The new U.S. political plan to appoint 25-30 "representative Iraqis" to a political council that would nominate Iraqis to serve in senior positions in ministries was put into place by mid-July. At the same time, a constitutional convention was planned to write a new constitution that would then be approved in a national referendum. Following this, a national election could be held to put a permanent government into place.

The new plan was seen to militate against the main Iraqi opposition groups, such as the Iraqi National Congress, the Iraqi National Accord, the main Kurdish groups and some Shiite factions. The US claimed that it also wanted to bring in some Iraqis who had not been exiles. The shift of plans seemed driven by a sense of urgency about the yet unsettled situation in the country. Meanwhile, sporadic attacks on US soldiers continued to take place, with soldiers being killed and wounded almost daily, and there were warnings from the more militant Iraqis that things would get worse for the occupiers. They did. On June 2, more than 3000 former Iraqi soldiers, dismissed from Saddam's army by Bremer, marched on the headquarters of the Coalition Provisional Authority (CPA) at the Presidential Palace, demanding that the Americans and British leave and threatening to become suicide bombers. Later, many of them would. Former Army

Secretary Thomas White, who had been fired by Rumsfeld a few days before, stated that US defense officials were not ready to come to grips with the fact that 150,000 US troops would need to be maintained in the country indefinitely to keep order and that the occupation would be long. US officials talked of setting up a Western-style police force in Baghdad, with the help of a former New York City police commissioner.[50] Considerable uncertainty about the future remained as the toll of dead in combat, since the end of the war, continued to mount.

In August 2004, the US continued to try to contain the ongoing disruptions in daily life in Iraq while the 2004 presidential campaign was underway. US Administrator Paul Bremer left the country at the end of June after officially returning sovereignty to the new interim Iraqi government and disbanding the Coalition Provisional Authority. Meanwhile, some 135,000 US troops remained deployed on the ground in Iraq, mostly on the streets, in an effort to maintain civil order. Clearly, the Bush Administration hoped to convince enough of the American electorate that the US had done the right thing in invading the country, to win another term in office, and seemed to have substantially weathered the damage from the Abu Gharib prison abuse scandal and the alleged abuse of prisoners at US prison facilities in Guantanimo Bay Cuba. While workers and drivers of various nationalities continued to be captured and held by terrorist groups in Iraq, and sometimes executed, the US sought to convince the American people that the war had been worth the effort, that the one-thousand American troops had not died in vain, that the American people were safer than before, and that George W. Bush should lead the American people for another four years. Opinion polls, however, showed that somewhat less than half of the American people were actually convinced of these assertions.

With the invasion and occupation of Iraq the United States embarked upon its first test case under its National Strategic Security Doctrine, launched in September 2002. This marked a new phase in the effort of the United States to control and rule the world by force.[51] As Gabriel Kolko has observed, the world has entered a "new era" in international relations, although the roots of this "age of unilateral war" are deep in past US foreign policy. The US, under its current doctrine, is determined to prevent any challenge to its supreme power globally and seems to be ready to severely punish or destroy any country which presents a significant challenge to US power. Powerful countries will be dealt with diplomatically. Weak countries run the risk of being systematically dismantled, with great damage to the infrastructure, and inordinate, immeasurable loss of human life and suffering. This means that weapons of mass destruction, including nuclear weapons, are likely to quickly proliferate. Terrorism against US interests is likely to increase around the globe. Washington's policy of unilateral preemptive war has clearly made the world a more dangerous place.

At the same time the relationship between the United States and the world has been sharply altered. As the unilateralists in the Bush Administration continue to pursue and maintain US global hegemony, largely outside the bounds of international law, resistance around the world against the policies of the United States of using massive military force is growing. NATO has been weakened as the U.S. shifts its alliances from "old Europe," to the less-democratic, but easier to dominate, emerging states in Eastern Europe, Portugal and Italy. Germany and France wish to pursue more sovereignty from Washington. Eastern

Europe, along with the poorer fringes of Europe, with a less democratic tradition, can be whipped into line for the assistance they need, and largely sideline public opinion, as Washington has demanded. Turkey had been warned. The Turkish Parliament, under considerable pressure from the United States and the IMF, went against the wishes of the people and voted to provide a large contingent of Turkish troops to shore up the US occupation in 2003. However, Turkish troops were not deployed due to opposition from Iraqi Kurds. The US, after acting as if it was too powerful to need allies, found itself in a difficult position when US troops were hard pressed to contain the volatile uprising in Iraq.

The invasion of Iraq caused a sharp shift in the perception of the US around the world, with greater numbers of the global population believing that US claims about the values of democracy and human rights are empty shibboleths in its foreign policy, serving its goal of controlling global resources and markets. This shift in public perception was very marked, practically universal, in Turkey. Even mainstream political economists in the US, like Joseph Stiglitz and Jeffrey Sachs, stated frankly that the era of IMF structural adjustment had badly failed. The growing awareness and revolt against the policies of the Bretton Woods institutions became a growing global phenomenon, and the arrogance of the US in its power and oil grab in Iraq was certain to impart greater momentum to the growing movement against corporate globalization. Global inequality continued to increase by leaps and bounds as neoliberalism was forced upon more and more developing countries. When economic recovery did succeed, it was generally on the backs of the working class, after real wages had been forced down sharply.

The attempt to reshape the Middle East to make it more congenial to the interests of the US and a belligerent Israel, under the rubric of bringing democracy to the region, is sure to breed more resentment in the area. The so-called "Road Map," which Israel was determined to resist, was essentially dead and the US now had its own Palestine in Iraq under occupation. Israel and the US have become fellow occupiers of the Arabs and control the oil in the Middle East. Indeed, Israelis have been heavily involved in the US occupation of Iraq.

At the same time, there are increasing domestic doubts in the US as to the direction of US foreign policy. The Bush Administration has continued to use the tried and true formula of former President Harry Truman and Senator Arthur Vandenburg, of "scarring the hell out of the American people" to push their agenda of force. "Terrorism" has replaced "communism" as the pretext for the unleashing of American force around the world. However, the Bush Administration increasingly lacked credibility and its claims about "Operation Iraqi Freedom" were now understood by great numbers of people to have been "false claims." The assault on the poor and working classes of America had been ratcheted up greatly with tax giveaways to the rich, while the American working class was suffering and unemployment growing. Social welfare in the U.S., in relation to the wealth of the country, can truthfully be described as a national and international shame and this agenda is bound to be pushed harder by the radical right fringe elements driving the Bush Administration. Democratic freedoms are being rolled back under the Patriotic Acts.

Operation Iraqi Freedom, which initially appeared to be a quick and easy success in April 2003, began to explode in America's face as massive car bombs became common in Baghdad and other cities. Civilian casualties mounted, US soldiers continued to die on the streets, and civil war erupted in Falluja. The UN was forced out of the country in the summer of 2003 when a truck bomb destroyed its headquarters and killed the UN representative Sergio Viera de Mello. The government and officials, Iraqi police forces and military, trained and installed by the US in 2004, continued to be targeted. It quickly became unsafe for foreigners to live and work in the country.

Short of "cutting and running" the US would be forced to keep a large number of US troops in Iraq for an indefinite number of years at a very high price to American taxpayers and the uncertainty of whether adequate numbers of soldiers could be recruited without bringing back the military draft. Meanwhile the political situation in Iraq and the prospects of holding elections and establishing a legitimate government remained extremely problematical. The Kurdish demand for greater autonomy threatened the territorial integrity of Iraq and raised fears in Turkey of an independent Kurdish state. American hubris had overshot its mark in Operation Iraqi Freedom, and America would likely be paying a heavy cost for many years to come. The cost of establishing US hegemony over Iraqi oil was proving to be great. The Greater Middle Eastern Initiative of "bringing democracy to the entire region" was launched with the actual aim improving the US image in the region and securing the economic resources for US and Israeli capital.

Today the costs of American hubris are being born not only by the people of the region but by large numbers of the American working class in the deprivation of the fruits of their hard labor. Operation Iraqi Freedom, similar to the Vietnam War a generation ago, has come to threaten America itself. In the following months the situation in Iraq would become increasingly grave for the American occupation. The US was losing the war, but not essentially because it was mismanaged and "intellectually bankrupt." The global community, as we explore in Chapter Three, is no longer ready to tolerate Hitler-like attacks on sovereign countries under the label of "preemptive war" even if it is carried out by the United States of America. With George W. Bush's White House, America's once bright image has likely perished from the earth forever.

References

1. Adeed Dawisha and Karen Dawisha, "How to Build a Democratic Iraq," *Foreign Affairs*, 82 (3), May/June 2003, pp. 36-50.
2. Fouad Ajami, "Iraq and the Arab's Future," *Foreign Affairs*, 82 (1), January/February 2003, pp. 3, 10.
3. Joseph S. Nye, Jr., "US Power and Strategy After Iraq," *Foreign Affairs*, 82 (4), July/August 2003, pp. 60-73. Nye urged that the US could not establish their foreign policy goals without the cooperation of other countries.
4. James P. Rubin, "Stumbling into War," *Foreign Affairs*, 82 (5), September/October 2003, p. 64.
5. *Ibid.*, p. 62.
6. Kenneth M. Pollack, "Securing the Gulf," *Foreign Affairs*, 82 (4), July/August 2003, p. 12.
7. Sarah Anderson, Phyllis Bennis, John Cavanagh, and Erik Leaver, "Coalition of The Willing or Coalition of the Coerced?" Part II. Institute for Policy Studies, www.ips-dc.org. March 24, 2003. The "coalition of the willing" ultimately included 46 countries comprising 19 percent of the world's population. Turkey, with a population of 66 million is included, although it is not clear that it should be, given the decision in the Turkish Parliament not to allow US land forces to be

stationed in Turkey. Of the 45 nations outside the US, only two (Britain and Australia) made significant contributions to military operations. Other countries in the "coalition" had overwhelming antiwar publics who were reassured "that being on the coalition list is basically meaningless." Little was said about the much longer list of nations that refused to join the "coalition of the willing." See Maria Tomchick, "Powell's Flimsy Evidence," www.zmag.org, Feb. 9, 2003. On the protest movements, John Pilger, "The New Protest Movement," www.zmag.org, November 4, 2002.

8. Tariq Ali, "The UN Has Capitulated," *The Guardian*, May 24, 2003.

9. David Kotz, "Neoliberalism and the U.S. Economic Expansion of the '90s," *Monthly Review*, 54 (11) 2003, pp. 15-33; Robin Blackburn, "The Enron Debacle and the Pension Crisis," *New Left Review*, No. 14, March-April 2002; Paul Krugman, "Stating the Obvious," *The New York Times*, May 29, 2003; Chalmers Johnson, *The Sorrows of Empire: Militarism, Secrecy, and the End of the Republic* (New York: Metropolitan Books, 2004).

10. The US occupation has had a strong resemblance to the racial and ethnic arrogance of classical colonial rule and this is likely to continue.

11. Kenneth M. Pollack, *The Threatening Storm: The Case for Invading Iraq*. New York: Random House, 2002. Opposing arguments can be found in Milan Rai, *War Plan Iraq: Ten Reasons Against War On Iraq*. London: Verso, 2002; and Geoff Simons, *Targeting Iraq: Sanctions and Bombing in US Policy*. London: Saqi Books, 2002. See Jason Leopold, "Wolfowitz Admits Iraq War Was Planned Two Days After 9/11," ZNET, June 2, 2003. Useful background is found in Andrew Cockburn and Patrick Cockburn, *Saddam Hussein: An American Obsession*. London: Verso, 2002. (Published in 2000 as *Out of the Ashes*.

12. Kenneth M. Pollack, "Next Stop Baghdad?" *Foreign Affairs* 81 (2) March/April 2003, pp. 32-47.
13. *Ibid.*
14. Jason Leopold, "Wolfowitz Admits Iraq War Was Planned Two Days After 9/11" ZNET, June 2. 2003.
15. Scott Ritter, *War On Iraq: What Team Bush Doesn't Want You to Know*. London: Profile Books, 2002; Research Unit for Political Economy, "Behind the War on Iraq," *Monthly Review* 55 (1) May 2003, pp. 20-49. In 1997, Rolf Ekeus, head of United Nations Special Commission (UNSCOM) from 1991 to 1997, reported that 93 percent of Iraq's major weapons capability had been destroyed. Similarly, the International Atomic Energy Agency (IAEA) certified that Iraq had no nuclear stocks and "most of its long-range systems had been destroyed." Iraq's main biological weapons facility had also "been destroyed and rendered harmless" by 1999, according to a special panel of the UN Security Council. ("Behind the War," p. 44) When Iraq submitted documents to the United Nations Security Council on its WMD in December 2002, the US rushed to get first access to the documents apparently to pull the evidence of US and European supply of WMD to Iraq. A Berlin Daily, *Die Tageszeitung,* published a list of corporations which had supplied Iraq with nuclear, chemical, biological, and missile technology prior to 1991. On the list were at least 24 American corporations, including Bechtel (chemical), Honeywell (rockets and chemical), UNISYS (nuclear and chemical), Rockwell (chemical), and so on. See Tony Paterson, "Leaked Report Says German and US Firms Supplied Arms to Saddam," *The Independent* (London), December 18, 2002. See also David Edwards, "Iraq and Arms Inspectors: The Big Lie," *Media Lens*, October 28, 2002. Many articles pointed out the deception about WMD early on. See David Edwards, "Iraq and Arms Inspectors: The big lie," *Media Lens, October* 28, 2002; Robert Jensen, "Bush's Lies And Simple Truths," ZNET, October 28, 2002; David Edwards, "Our Pravda, The BBC, Panorama and Iraq," *Media Lens*, Nov. 11, 2002.

16. Noam Chomsky, "Imperial Ambition: Noam Chomsky Interviewed by David Barsamian," *Monthly Review* 55 (1), 2003, pp. 11-19. For Chomsky, Iraq is an "easy test case" in which the US is "establishing a new norm" of ruling the world by force as laid out in the *National Security Strategy of the United States of America* (Sept. 2002). According to Chomsky, "...the 1981 Israeli bombing of the Osirak nuclear reactor probably stimulated and may have initiated the Iraqi nuclear weapons development program." (p. 15) Noam Chomsky and VK Ramachandran, "Iraq is a trial run," *Frontline*, (India) April 2, 2003.
17. Tariq Ali, "Recolonizing Iraq," *New Left Review*, No. 21, May-June 2003, 2003.
18. Noam Chomsky, "Wars of Terror," *New Political Science*, 25 (1) 2003.
19. *Ibid.*
20. Paul Street, "Down the Memory Hole With Weapons of Mass Destruction," ZMAG, April 23, 2003.
21. "Behind the War on Iraq"; Joost Hiltermann, "Who Minded Iraqi Mustard Gas In 1983?" *International Herald Tribune*, December 3, 2002.
22. Geoff Simons, *Targeting Iraq: Sanctions and Bombing in US Policy* (London: Saqi Books, 2002).
23. "Behind the War on Iraq," pp. 34-39.
24. Abu Spinoza (pseudonym), "War Crimes, US Planners And Iraq's Water Vulnerability," ZNET, June 3, 2003; Thomas Nagy, "The Secret Behind the Sanctions: How the US Intentionally Destroyed Iraq's Water Supply," *The Progressive*, (2001).
25. *Ibid.*
26. Some comments from US soldiers depict the actual situation. From Brigadier General Louis Weber, who commented about one brigade killing at least 1000 Iraqis by direct fire alone on a single road into Baghdad: "They're just dying." From Staff Sergeant Ira Mack: "At the Karbala Gap, the Iraqis put

up a good fight, but to no avail because we had the firepower. It was way too easy." From an American soldier: "For lack of a better word, I feel almost guilty about the massacre. We wasted a lot of people. It makes you wonder how many were innocent." (Quoted in the Christian Science Monitor, April 11, 2002.) Edward Herman, "From Vietnam to Iraq," Swans, April 30, 2003.

27. Jonathan Steele, "Body Counts," ZNET, May 28, 2003; Mark Engler, "Those Who Don't Count: Why it Matters To Remember Civilian Casualties," ZNET, May 15, 2003; Robert Fisk, "We Bomb, They Suffer," *The Independent*, March 23, 2003.

28. Robert Fisk and Amy Goodman, "An Anti-Colonial War Against the Americans May Have Already Begun," (Interview with Robert Fisk), *Democracy Now*, April 22, 2003.

29. *Ibid.*

30. Robert Fisk, "The Troops Are Afraid To Go Out At Night," *The Independent*, May 31. 2003. "Bush is a onetime C student- a History major, ironically enough- who couldn't care less about the difference between a Mesopotamian statue and a Mexican taco."

    Paul Street, "The Looting Of Iraq: An e-mail interview with Paul Street," *Evrensel Daily* (Turkish), May 4, 2003; Robert Fisk, "Pillage," *The Independent*, April 12, 2003. According to the 1949 Geneva Conventions, "Pillage is prohibited." Robert Fisk, "Untouchable Ministries," *The Independent,* April 16, 2003; Robert Fisk, "A Civilization Torn to Pieces," *The Independent*, April 14, 2003; Some newsmen also got in on the act of looting. There were also reports that some soldiers took part of the money found in the Presidential Palace. Possibly only the guilty know. Curt Anderson, "Media, Troops Investigated in Iraq Theft,: AP, April 23, 2003. Some of the missing items were later discovered in a vault in the Central Bank, but Robert Fisk documents how many precious items were simply smashed to pieces on the museum floor. Hamza Hendawi, "Treasures of Nimrud Found in Iraqi Vault," AP, June 7, 2003.

31. Fisk and Goodman, "An Anti-Colonial War Against the Americans May Have Already Begun." (Fisk interview)
32. *Ibid.* (Fisk interview)
33. David Espo, "Iraqis Demand U.S. Withdrawal in Baghdad," AP, April 19, 2003.
34. Niko Price, "Many Iraqis Turn Anger Toward the US," AP. April 16, 2003.
35. Robert Fisk, "War Over? George Bush has announced the end of the war. But try telling that to the Shias and the Badr Brigade." *The Independent*, May 6, 2003.

3

Preemptive War

"We must try something new, out of self-interest... as revolutionaries of sorts..." **Victor Davis Hanson**[1]

"The United States has adopted a new policy, a forward strategy of freedom in the Middle East."

George W. Bush

"All Done: Go Home."

Graffiti on the base of the statue of Saddam Hussein in Firdas Square

The George W. Bush Administration entered office with the neo-Wilsonian agenda of waging "democracy" in the Middle East in order to strengthen US global hegemony. The neoconservatives in the Pentagon exploited the 9/11 attack on New York to unleash US military might on the region. The doctrine of preemptive war was "altered" to that of preventive war and promulgated as official US national security doctrine in September 2002. The US "blitzkrieg," overthrew Saddam and occupied Iraq in only 26 days. The occupation and actions of the Coalition Provisional Authority, under Paul Bremer, resulted in the emergence of a strong insurgency in mid 2003. US forces engaged in urban warfare, leading to serious doubts about the future of Iraq as a US-sponsored neoliberal capitalist model for the Arab world. The US invasion and occupation of Iraq was at the same time a preemptive strike upon the European Union, South Asia and China, in a bid to control global energy resources vital to US economic competitors. The first preemptive war has now essentially been lost by the United States, disrupted the Atlantic alliance and given rise to grave doubts about the future of the international order.

The neo-Wilsonian "revolution," launched by the neoconservative unilateralists in the first Bush Administration, claimed as its purpose "ridding Saddam Hussein of weapons of mass destruction" and "bringing regime change" to Iraq. "Democratization" in the greater Middle East was offered as another rationale for the war in late 2003 when US Administration claims about weapons of mass destruction in Iraq were proven false. The first "preemptive war" was hailed as a brilliant success after the US invasion and overthrow of Saddam Hussein in just 26 days with a "cost of 161 dead." An early estimate claimed 3400 Iraqi civilians died in this phase of the war. By October 2004, however, estimates of Iraqi civilians killed ranged from 17,000 to 100,000 or more, with some four times as many wounded. It appears now that up to 80 percent died from the US bombing.[2] "Wilsonianism with boots" had triumphed, it appeared, and victory was proclaimed by George W. Bush from the decks of the USS Abraham Lincoln off the Pacific Coast, on May 1, 2003.

Less than six months into the US-British occupation, however, an insurgency began to emerge and grew stronger. One year into the operation, the roads and cities of Iraq became ever more deadly for American forces as the resistance to American-British occupation matured into a large scale insurrection to drive the Americans and British out. US-British forces were forced to fight battles with local militias in the major cities. The United Nations was driven out of Iraq along with a number of humanitarian organizations in the summer of 2003 by massive car bombs. The US failed to consolidate control over significant areas of the country, particularly the Sunni Triangle west and north of Baghdad. The next six months led to increasing doubts about the future of Iraq and the ultimate result of the US-led invasion. The sweeping plans of the neoconservatives in Washington had bogged down beyond their greatest fears, putting the first test-case of preemptive war in grave peril. The US military could not be defeated on the ground; but America was failing to win the "hearts and minds" of the people and secure Iraq. Serious questions now cloud the future of Wilsonian millenarianism which the Bush

White House has unleashed and pursued with almost religious zeal.[3] With the American presence on the Tigris and Euphrates, the crucial question is how long it will take for the American people to weary of the inordinate costs of the global crusade to wage democracy from the banks of the Potomac.

The Bush Doctrine

The George W. Bush doctrine of preemptive war, or more accurately preventive war, was announced in September 2002.[4] The US invasion and occupation of Iraq in March 2003 was the first test-case for the doctrine.[5] When the US was unable to obtain a UN Security Council resolution specifically authorizing a military invasion in March 2003 the US and Great Britain launched the war. The "coalition of the willing" consisted mostly of small nations participating on a largely token basis. The war was called illegal under the United Nations Charter by UN Secretary General Kofi Annan, speaking in September 2004. By November 2004, after more than eighteen months, the US occupation of Iraq had failed to secure and gain de facto control of some areas, such as the Sunni Triangle in Anbar Province. While President George W. Bush announced "mission accomplished" on May 1, 2003, events on the ground were soon to prove him wrong. Sovereignty was formally returned to an "interim Iraqi government" on June 28, 2004, by US Coalition Provisional Authority (CPA) Administrator Paul Bremer. It could not be seriously doubted, however, that the US continued to rule Iraq and that the US appointed government of Iyad Allawi remained in office only through US firepower. The de facto US occupation is likely to continue for many years. At a minimum the US seems determined to hold on to at least twelve newly established US military bases for the purpose of shoring up American power in the larger Middle East and Central Asian region. This effort grows more problematical as casualties mount, with the number of US soldiers killed well over 1400 by February 2005 and the number reaching 2600 by the summer of 2006. By February 2008, at least 3940 American soldiers had died in the war and almost 29,000 had been wounded. In 2004, efforts were underway to increase the number of US troops in the country and to "retake" "no-go areas" outside US and Iraqi Government control. A major assault on insurgents in Fallujah was carried out in November 2004 using some 20,000 US and Iraqi troops, which is explored in Chapter Four. All indications are that securing Iraq as a base of US military operations and US corporate profits will prove very costly and may possibly be a greater burden than the American people are willing to sacrifice, reminiscent of the "Vietnam quagmire" in the 1960s. Indeed, a "decade-long nightmare" had been predicted early-on, with the deaths of several thousand American soldiers as the US established itself as a permanent Gulf power.[6]

The first preemptive war has also had major repercussions for the US in terms of its relations with the rest of the world and significantly with its traditional European allies. In the view of the neoconservatives, after the Cold War, "a global empire was essentially laid at the feet of the United States." The policy of deterrence was scrapped as a Cold War relic, in favor of "compellence" or the systematic use of force. The best "defense" was seen as "offense."[7] The future of preemptive war, or more accurately, preventive war, the strategy of the neoconservatives in the Bush White House, remains uncertain. The Bush Administration drew up a lengthy list of nations which were said to be potential targets in future. At the top of the list were North Korea and Iran, designated by the Bush Administration as members of the "axis of evil."

By mid 2004, the United States had already lost the first preemptive war while gravely damaging its image around the world, particularly in the Middle East. The US presence in Iraq has continued to destabilize the region. The notion of establishing functioning democracies across the Arab world from the outside need not be taken seriously as it is not only highly problematical, but directly contradictory to US "national security objectives," as we explore in Chapter Five. The invasion of Iraq was not a "war on terrorism," but rather a colonial war for empire. Predictably, "preemptive war" has encouraged many more nations to seek weapons of mass destruction, while it has fueled the ranks of terrorist organizations in Iraq and around the globe. The United States is unwilling to cut short its losses in Iraq for several more years into the future, although the emerging failure of neoconservative foreign policy may deter the US from additional ventures in the immediate future. It is not clear if the US will seek to rejoin the global community as a law-abiding state or continue the unilateral pursuit of power through force, further endangering world peace. By the 2008 US Presidential Campaign, some US officials had begun to break the unwelcome news to the American people that the US occupation would stretch at least another ten years. Senator John McCain was probably more realistic when he said the troops would be there another hundred years. The pursuit of preemptive war has lowered the barriers to the use of force, globally, and set a precedent which gravely threatens the very future of the human species itself.

Sweet "Regime Change" on My Mind

The first George W. Bush Administration was installed in Washington by the US Supreme Court[8] with "regime change" in Iraq at the very top of its agenda.[9] The neoconservatives called for the invasion and overthrow of a sovereign government, under the false pretexts that Iraq possessed chemical and biological weapons, continued to pursue the development of nuclear weapons and had links with al-Qaeda.[10] After emphasizing that the administration would not be bound by constraints of international law, the Bush Administration was able to accelerate its predetermined agenda of overthrowing the government of Saddam Hussein after the events of September 11, 2001.[11] A policy of "preemptive war" was announced in September 2002 as the official US strategic security doctrine.[12] It was debated at the highest levels in the US Government as to whether the US should first launch an attack on the Taliban government of Afghanistan or proceed at once against Iraq.

The primary argument before the war in Iraq was that Saddam Hussein was a threat to his neighbors and the world because he possessed weapons of mass destruction (WMD). It was seldom mentioned that the US was the major sponsor and source of Iraq's acquisition of such weapons in the 1980s. The US also attempted to find evidence that Saddam had links with al-Qaeda[13] and the continuous statements of administration officials, particularly Vice-President Dick Cheney, led some sixty-nine percent of the people in the US to believe this was true.[14] The US was the only country where a majority of people believed that Saddam had something to do with planning the attacks of September 11, 2001 on New York and Washington. The Bush Administration intentionally confounded the "war on terrorism" with overthrowing the government of Iraq, which was facilitated by the practice of US TV networks, such as Fox TV, of labeling the war in Iraq as a "war on terror."[15] In fact intelligence in both the US and Great Britain failed to discover direct evidence linking Saddam Hussein and al-Qaeda. Many intelligence officials also doubted the claims about WMD[16] but the Bush Administration argued for the absolute certainty of WMD in Iraq, as seen in the presentation of Secretary of State Colin Powell to the UN Security Council in February 2003, and repeated statements by US Administration officials as well as British Prime Minister Tony Blair.[17] "We know he's got them," became practically the official mantra in the US and Great Britain.

The US had already moved quickly in the summer of 2002 to deploy troops and weapons to the Persian Gulf in preparation for the war, accelerating the build-up at a rapid rate after January 1, 2003.[18] Few could doubt that war was on tap. It was clear that the US and Great Britain were "hell-bent" on overthrowing Saddam and that deterring the neoconservatives in the Pentagon would be extremely difficult, although governments on both sides of the Atlantic insisted that no decision had been taken about going to war. As arms inspectors in Iraq came up empty handed again and again, Washington remained vigilant in the face of threatening peace.

Urged on by Tony Blair, early in 2003, the Bush Administration launched an effort to secure a second UN Security Council resolution which would provide a green light for the war. UN Security Council Resolution 1441, passed on November 8, 2002, was not originally seen as authorizing a US attack upon Iraq. Tremendous pressure was put on the other members of the Security Council and heated debates at the UN, particularly with France, attracted unprecedented global attention. These efforts failed, however, as France, Russia and Germany could not be convinced to authorize the US-British invasion of Iraq. The Bush and Blair governments forged ahead, dividing the European community into "old Europe," and "new Europe." Old Europe, countries such as France and Germany, refused to go along with the global superpower. "New Europe" included the former Communist states, such as Hungary and Poland, and right-wing regimes, such as Italy and Spain, which were willing to do the bidding of the United States in the face of massive public opposition to war. The Bush Administration, which lost the battle to keep the UN weapons inspectors from returning to Iraq, argued incorrectly that weapons inspections could never work and that time was running out. The massive build-up of war materiel and troops in the Persian Gulf states was pushed forward in preparation for "Operation Iraq Freedom," as the world looked on with grave apprehension.

Global Public Opinion and Democracy

The neoconservatives in the Pentagon preached the doctrine of "unleashing democracy" in the Middle East through "reconfiguration" of the region, while massive peace protests were organized around the globe. "What happens inside Iraq on the day Saddam Hussein is gone will reveal American intentions, capabilities, and morality," the neoconservatives suggested, not incorrectly. "Today, without the specter of a global and nuclear Soviet Union to make 'regime change' difficult and distort elections, we are once again free to promote democracy in unlikely places."[19]

Those places did not include France and Germany, presumably, where democracy seemed to be working all too well for American tastes. Dubbed, "old Europe," by Secretary of Defense, Rumsfeld, government policies here closely followed public opposition on participating in a war on Iraq.[20] Nor did the promotion of democracy apply to Turkey, where 90 percent of the people opposed the war and the vote of the Turkish

Parliament on March 1, 2003, turning down the stationing of US troops in Turkey, met with venomous anger and sharp threats from the banks of the Potomac.[21] "Washington would have been happier had the Turkish Parliament accepted the Ankara government's proposition for hosting US forces," Marc Grossman, Undersecretary of State for Political Affairs, stated. Defense Secretary Donald Rumsfeld declared that the democratic act of the Turkish Parliament was "disgraceful." US Secretary of State, Colin Powell, told the press that "there is still a level of disappointment in the United States within the administration and within the Congress over the inability to get the vote on March 1... There is a lingering sense of disappointment that we have to make sure that we do nothing more to contribute to in the days and weeks ahead as we push for the supplemental [one billion dollar funding for Turkey]." Deputy Secretary of Defense, Paul Wolfowitz, viewed the parliamentary vote as "bad news" because the Turkish military was not "forceful" enough in "leading" the Government toward a positive result for the US. Further, he suggested a lack of "Muslim Solidarity" with the people of Iraq was a "general failure of the Turkish public." What "Turkey needs to do is look into its democratic soul," and proceed to "work with the Americans" in bringing "democracy for Muslims and Arabs." He suggested that "the whole economic package could have been something more substantial."[22]

In the wake of finding the Turkish "democratic soul" so wanting in its willingness to come up with aid for the American preemptive war against Iraq, Turkish officials were duly warned of the perilous shores of flirting with such democracy and that they would "pay a price" for going against the US war effort. Being oblivious to public opinion in Italy, Spain and Hungary, on the other hand, produced no "disappointment" in Washington; quite the contrary. Support for the war in these countries was accorded high honors by those about to "unleash democracy" on the Arab world. Perhaps democracy in the Middle East would make the neoconservatives happy; democracy in Europe clearly had not.[23] George Orwell would have been amused.

Protests against the imminent war around the globe set a historical precedent. On February 15, 2003, some eight million marched. There were even 300,000 in the streets in Yemen and large demonstrations in Cairo and Amman.[24] A million people marched against the war in London. Massive protests swelled the streets of cities across the US. Public opinion polls found that most people in Europe believed that the major threat to peace came, not from Saddam, but from the US. The US President, "standing on principle," "shrugged off" reports that some 600 million around the world marched against the war. Democracy was again brushed aside in this case. "Evidently some in the world don't view Saddam as a risk to peace. I respectfully disagree," President Bush was quoted as saying; being incorrect, as future reports on the lack of WMD in Iraq were to prove.[25] Saddam Hussein and other Iraqi officials had, in fact, told the truth about not having weapons of mass destruction. But for Bush and Blair, there were no two ways about it. He had them and all who doubted were shouted down with righteous wrath from their lofty seats of power. Statements from Washington and London became increasingly belligerent as the run-up to the war continued. Saddam Hussein had "messed with Texas" and could not "outrun the long arm of the law" being laid down by the neoconservatives.

Baghdad Bound

Unable to obtain a second resolution on Iraq from the UN Security Council, the neoconservatives sent US tanks across the Kuwaiti border on the morning of March 20, 2003. The massive bombing of Baghdad, the so called "shock and awe" tactics, designed to produce panic and a quick surrender early in Operation Iraqi Freedom, continued night after night. The same B-52 bombers used to bomb Hanoi thirty-five years before took off from England with bombs bound for Baghdad. It was the most powerful nation on earth up against an embargo-ruined country with no navy, no air force, a rag-tag army, and no WMD since 1991. In fact, the US had invaded, not because Saddam was a threat, but precisely because he was not. Some CIA analysts had predicted it would be a quick and easy victory. Saddam Hussein had destroyed his chemical and biological weapons after the first gulf war, and lacked the capability to continue a nuclear weapons program. Hundreds of cruise missiles were fired at Baghdad from US ships and planes[26] as US forces pushed through the desert arriving within the vicinity of Baghdad with little resistance. Supply lines were stretched so thin that some US soldiers were attacked and taken hostage. But the weakened Iraqi regime was quickly toppled. The feared Republican Guard put up stiff resistance at points, but Baghdad was easily taken on April 9, 2003. Most Iraqi troops simply melted away without a fight.

The US President announced that major combat operations had ended on May 1, 2003 in a staged for TV appearance on the deck of the USS Abraham Lincoln.[27] In the midst of fervent triumphalism, no one seemed to suspect that perhaps the US forces had been pulled into a trap. US military officers settled down to celebrate their victory on plush divans and jovially sported big cigars in Saddam's largest palace on the banks of the Tigris. US boots were firmly planted in Baghdad. This "Bush Palace" was to serve as the US Embassy until the new $750 million US Embassy could be completed, sometime in 2008.

Keeping with the spirit of "Honest Abe," presumably, the US military stage-managed the memorable scenes filmed for American TV of the statue of Saddam Hussein in Firdas Square in central Baghdad being toppled on April 9, 2003. The event was, in fact, faked for newsmen staying in the Palestine Hotel across the street, the statue being actually pulled down by American Marines with some 150 Iraqis gathered in the park. Members of Ahmed Chalabi's Iraqi National Congress (INC) militia were shown whacking the face of the statue with plastic sandals. The US Marines actually secured the square to protect the INC from other Iraqis, while presenting the demonstration as spontaneous. US Marines climbed onto the statue and wrapped the same American flag which had been flying at the Pentagon on September 11, 2001 around the face of Saddam.[28]

Indeed it appeared that the major fighting was over in Iraq by May 1. "Coalition forces" had toppled the regime with surprisingly little resistance and the urban guerrilla warfare predicted by many critics had not materialized. Most of the regular Iraqi Army soldiers were simply captured or left the lines and went home. US forces encountered not a single whiff of poison gas, at least not from the Iraqis. The real war, which Saddam had prepared in case of US occupation, was to emerge one year later.

Post-War Spin: "Stuff Happens"

The US occupation, initially dubbed the Office of Reconstruction and Humanitarian Assistance (ORHA), was established under retired army General Jay Garner. When Garner was fired a couple of months later, the title was quickly changed to the Coalition Provisional Authority (CPA) and transferred to a new administrator, Paul Bremer.[29] The US CPA Headquarters was set up in Saddam's Republican Palace in Baghdad, which was seized for the US embassy in the country, now the largest US embassy in the world. Baghdad suffered massive structural damage and coalition authorities tolerated and even encouraged looting. Claims about WMD being everywhere quickly began to evaporate. The US and international press, which had mostly been "embedded" during the war, remained largely on board, nevertheless, positive to the results of the operation and anticipating a new "free Iraq" with a flourishing Iraqi press and oil revenues and profits in the hands of US companies. The beginning of a new era of growth and prosperity was seen, first under US occupation and then under a sovereign and democratic Iraq. While analysts laid out plans detailing how to make Iraq "democratic," others, more cautiously, waited for the emergence of an "anti-colonial war."[30] As it turns out, it was not long in arriving.

It appears that little post-war planning was done by the Bush Administration, anticipating a "cake walk." There was no "exit strategy,"[31] perhaps because there was to be no exit, at least not in the foreseeable future. The US had no intention of leaving after setting up extensive military bases. Secretary of Defense, Donald Rumsfeld, had scaled back the number troops asked for by the US military, particularly General Eric

Shinseki, who reportedly called for 400,000 or more troops. Rumsfeld called Shinseki's estimate "wildly off the mark" and cut the number of troops deployed to some one-half of this. Shinseki was later forced into retirement. Former Army Secretary Thomas White concurred with Shinseki, coming into conflict with Rumsfeld.[32] The neoconservatives had anticipated that the occupying forces could be scaled back to some 50,000 shortly after the war. Others, more prudently, predicted it would be necessary to keep a large US occupation force in place for years.

Once Baghdad fell, there was massive looting of historical libraries, museums, and even ammunition dumps, as noted in Chapter One. Some 380 tons of explosives disappeared from the al-Qaqaa military compound, near Baghdad, apparently after the Americans had arrived and viewed the stockpiles. Every government ministry except the Ministry of Oil was sacked and burned as noted before. Anarchy prevailed as American troops were sent into the streets to take over police and security duties, resulting in a large number of civilian casualties. Entire families were shot in their cars by edgy American soldiers at check points. When asked about the looting, the US Defense Secretary said that people were simply enjoying their new found freedom and "stuff happens." Paul Bremer was later to admit in October 2004, however, that the US paid a heavy price for not sending an adequate number of troops to control the looting and secure the country.

Early on, the neoconservatives in the Pentagon, led by Rumsfeld, quarreled with Secretary of State, Colin Powell, battling for unilateral control of the post-war occupation, against the US State Department, the United Nations and British Prime Minister, Tony Blair. Reports suggested that the neoconservatives considered the State Department officials, who had long experience in the Arab world, as "too pro-Arab" and wished to place members of Chalabi's Iraqi National Congress in key positions. A pro-Israeli Likud Party bias was seen in these Pentagon tactics. Rumsfeld insisted that relief and aid work come under Jay Garner, the coordinator of the Office of Reconstruction and Humanitarian Assistance (ORHA), reporting to the Chief of US Central Command, General Tommy Franks. Powell asked that the US relief work be put under the US Agency for International Development (USAID), attached to the State Department. Aid groups, on the other hand, called for the relief operations to be directed by the UN. All this reflected the Pentagon's anti-UN position, which was also challenged by Tony Blair and the European Union. France rejected having the UN subordinated under the US occupation authority. But the neoconservatives in the Pentagon insisted upon complete control of the operation.[33]

After Paul Bremer arrived to head the CPA, he immediately disbanded the Iraqi Army, adding some 400,000 to the ranks of the unemployed, and placed a ban on anyone who had been associated with the Ba'ath Party serving in the new Administration and the security forces.[34] These actions immediately brought large crowds of angry Iraqis into the streets to demonstrate against the US occupation.[35] Unemployment was to continue at some 60 to 70 percent into February 2005. With former Ba'ath Party members banned, it was not clear where the needed expertise to administer the country would be found. It also meant that the only security force to fall back upon was that of American troops, who had been told they would be going home quickly, once Saddam was overthrown. Instead, inexperienced American troops were sent onto the streets and roads around the capital on daily patrols which made them easy targets, sitting ducks, for rocket propelled grenade (RPG), improvised explosive device (IED), vehicle-born improvised explosive device (VBIED, or car bomb), and mortar attacks. Private security firms, like Blackwater USA were brought in to protect American civilians and diplomats. Saddam had ensured that the country was awash with arms and explosives. The American soldiers' tours of duty, some forty percent of them reservists, were extended by several months, creating a "back-door military draft." They would be sent back to Iraq for new tours of duty, some as many as three times or more. Casualties mounted, both American and Iraqi civilians dying in increasing numbers. The Iraqi resistance quickly perfected the method of using improvised explosive devices (IEDs) planted along the roads to blow up American convoys, killing and wounding soldiers almost daily, in trucks and Humvees. Casualty figures were swelling. In addition large car and truck bombs (VBIEDS) continued to be exploded in the centers of cities, even near the Green Zone in Baghdad, creating chaos and disrupting life for Iraqi citizens. Those with the means, simply left the country hoping normalcy would soon return. But by 2007, at least two million Iraqis had left the country, most of them living in Syria and Jordan.

The oil pipelines were continuously blown up, the line to Ceyhan in Turkey being exploded some thirty-seven times in twelve months. Oil terminals in the south were attacked at least ten times. The oil industry that once had "55,000 well-trained and highly disciplined technocrats" fell into a state of catastrophe. Two million barrels of oil a day was being lost to the world oil market[36] with at least 110 attacks on oil pipelines in the first 18 months of the US presence.

Occupation and "Appointocracy"

Bremer moved forward to appoint a 25 member Iraqi Governing Council (IGC) on July 13, 2003 with a "nine-member presidency" which was intended to stay in office until national elections could be held.[37] Meant to be representative, the IGC included 13 Shias, 6 Sunnis, 4 Kurds, 1 Turkman and 1 Assyrian. Several members, however, were former exiles, lacking a popular political base in the country. UN Security Council Resolution 1483 was passed on July 17, 2003, calling for a UN presence in Iraq, a clear timetable for the restoration of sovereignty, and specific steps for ending the US military occupation. The US needed the resolution to legitimize the US-British occupation, establish legal control of oil sales, and put into place sweeping measures to privatize the Iraqi economy.

But the lack of security continued to increase throughout the summer of 2003, as American companies began "reconstruction" operations on profit-guaranteed "no-bid" contracts.[38] US companies even received contracts to prepare the blueprint for a future "free-market Iraq" which would serve as a neoliberal model for the entire Middle East. There was stiff resistance to the occupation forces even at this time, but the problem was portrayed by coalition authorities as merely a mopping up operation to rid the country of "Saddam loyalists," "former Baathist dead-enders," and "foreign terrorists." These holdouts had not yet gained the status of "insurgents." As freedom increased, and the coalition succeeded, the American party line ran, attacks would increase up until the time sovereignty was returned to Iraq... and maybe after that too. The media banter kept repeating the line that the better things got, the worse they were going to be (because it would make the Saddam loyalists unhappy), but resistance would, nevertheless, be quelled in a relatively short period of time. Somehow this logic was not quite convincing. The situation would become increasingly hopeless by mid 2006 and deteriorate even further by 2007, in spite of the escalation of the number of troops in Iraq.

The press largely went along with this image of "staying the course." CPA functionaries conducted up-beat press briefings to ensure journalists of the progress being made. The picture on the ground told a considerably different story, however. By mid-2004, Bush administration officials could no longer pretend that the "good life" the occupation had promised was what they were actually "living today."

The "Untidy Freedom"

By the spring of 2003, the coalition, primarily the US and Great Britain, began to experience the beginnings of a more widespread insurgency in Baghdad and major cities around the country, such as Najaf and Fallujah. Bush's response to the threat of a wider insurgency on July 2, 2003, was "Bring them on." "Freedom's untidy," Rumsfeld added. A poll in Iraq at the time showed that only 36 percent of Iraqis thought that the US would help the country, only 23 percent said they would like to model their new government on the US, some 66 percent wanted the US to leave in a year or less, and 55 percent gave a negative rating to the US military in dealing with Iraqi citizens. The poll showed that Iraqis wanted the help of their neighbors, not that of the US.[39] The British, presumably forgetting their history, attempted to distance themselves from the growing brutality of the American occupation. They attempted to give the appearance of occupying a lofty plateau and claimed more friendly terms with Iraqis in the street in their Basra sphere of occupation.

Then a series of catastrophic car and truck bombings during the summer of 2003 gave the lie to CPA and US Administration assurances that they were gaining ground in improving security. The Jordanian Embassy was bombed on August 7, 2003, followed by the United Nations headquarters, which was destroyed on August 19, killing UN Representative Sergio Vieira de Mello and 23 UN staff. This was a major blow to the US, as the UN was to establish its presence in the country as a symbol of international presence and help provide a fig leaf of international legitimacy to the US-British occupation. The Red Cross building in Baghdad was also car-bombed on October 27 and the insurgents succeeded in driving all major aid agencies out of the country by the end of 2003.[40] On October 26, an American colonel was killed in an attack on the Al-Rashid Hotel, where Paul Wolfowitz was also staying. The attack wounded 18, including several US military personnel, coming from an artillery rocket launcher in the park across the street from the hotel. The Al-Rashid, Iraqi state property, was seized by the Americans during the war and used to house CPA and US military personnel. A Black Hawk helicopter had just been shot down with an RPG north of Baghdad. The Iraqi occupation was quickly turning into the larger insurgency that many had warned about and would only grow stronger through 2006 with thousands of Iraqis perishing in suicide bombings. Local Shia and Sunni militias were about to begin major battles with US forces in deadly urban guerrilla warfare.

The "Insurgency"

US CPA authorities also encountered difficulties in controlling the "perception" getting out to the world. In particular, the US had a problem with Arab stations like al-

Jazeera, al-Arabia, and Abu Dhabi TV. Tension mounted to the point of attacks on journalists in Iraq who were not putting the proper spin on the news desired by Bremer.[41] The US spent $62 million to set up its own TV station, "al-Hurra" (the free one), by all accounts a predictably dismal affair.

In the summer of 2003 the US was warned by the Israelis of their failure to secure the country and that they were in danger of losing the war unless they took drastic action and closed the border with Iran; the situation could become catastrophic. The infiltration of "foreign elements"[42] would destabilize the country and the Americans would lose control. Israel reacted by sending its own intelligence operatives into Iraq, particularly into the Kurdish areas of the north to protect what they perceived as a threat to their own interests. The Israelis reportedly began training Kurdish commando units to carry out secret operations, including assassinations in Iraq and surrounding countries.[43] American soldiers, facing the prospect of urban guerrilla warfare in Iraqi cities, were sent to Israel to be trained by the Israelis. They brought back the Israeli "rules of engagement," reportedly turned over to the Americans on the orders of Israeli Prime Minister, Ariel Sharon.[44] The US, however, failed to heed the advice of the Israelis to close the borders with Iran.

The US clearly had a huge security problem. Private security firms, such as Blackwater USA, used mercenaries to expand their services.[45] The US was struggling to secure the country sufficiently to allow construction efforts to get underway, restore adequate water and electrical power services, and simply get government employees to work and back home safely.[46] This meant that in urban areas even those who were amenable to tolerating the US occupation began to chafe under the problems of living without basic utilities, as well as the treacherous lack of security. With attacks picking up during the holy month of Ramadan in November 2003, a US Chinook helicopter was shot down killing 15 US soldiers and wounding 21.[47] Life was intolerable, except perhaps for those in Saddam's former palaces.

Democratization

With things quickly breaking down on the ground, and the search for WMD virtually abandoned, the Bush Administration shifted gear to focus upon the smokescreen of "democratization of Iraq" and the greater Middle East, in early November, 2003, as discussed more broadly in Chapter Five. This marked the beginning of efforts to convince American voters in the coming 2004 presidential election of the success and broad vision of American foreign policy in the Middle East. On November 6, 2003, President Bush spoke about a new US policy to initiate democracy in the Middle East,[48] claiming that depriving the region of the "global wave of democracy" would be "cultural condescension," that Islam was fully consistent with democratic rule, and that "sixty years of Western nations excusing and accommodating the lack of freedom in the Middle East did nothing to make us safe, because in the long run, stability cannot be purchased at the expense of liberty." Bush used the occasion to warn Iran, even though its then President Mohamad Khatami had been democratically elected. He also warned Syria, where, he said, lack of freedom had "left a legacy of torture, oppression, misery, and ruin." A "free Iraq" was to be the model for the region. Others, more accurately, pointed out that the West had never actually "excused and accommodated" lack of freedom in the Middle East. Rather, it was the West that had created it and supported autocracies for sixty years. When freedom threatened to break out, such in Iran in the early 1950s, the West restored the Shah to power.[49] In fact, military rule, under the auspices of the US was soon to be clamped on Iraq under the government of interim Prime Minister Iyad Allawi in the summer of 2004. The US, however, was just about to be embarrassed by another problem.

Gitmoization

With the increase in insurgent activity in mid-2003, Defense Secretary Donald Rumsfeld reportedly ordered a "special access program" to be put into place in which large numbers of ordinary Iraqis were arrested and incarcerated. The model for the operation was the war in Afghanistan, in which suspected members of al-Qaeda were captured by US forces and flown to the secretive US prison, Camp X-Ray, in Guantanamo ("Gitmo") Bay, Cuba. The prison at Gitmo was a legal black hole where prisoners were classified as "illegal combatants" and held in legal limbo without access to lawyers and the right of habeas corpus. Major General Geoffrey Miller, the officer in charge of the operation at Guantanamo, was transferred to Iraq to set up the programs at Abu Ghraib, Umm Qasr and other prison facilities. "Operation Copper Green" was put into play, which led to the physical coercion and sexual humiliation of Iraqi prisoners in order to gain intelligence about the growing insurgency. These secret operations were concealed from the American public, but the Iraqis knew them well.

The story broke in April of 2004, with pictures of Iraqi prisoners being tortured by American soldiers appearing in the press around the world. Private firms, such as CACI International and Titan Corp, were involved in the questioning of the prisoners in addition to Army intelligence and counter intelligence operations personnel.[50] The quality of intelligence obtained by the US military from torture was not of high quality, but the intimidation was meant to also send messages to potential insurgents outside the prisons of the dire fate of those captured. US forces were operating other secret prisons in Iraq, where torture was reportedly authorized by top Pentagon officials. These practices, particularly the alleged sexual abuse of women, led to an investigation in the US Congress, the results of which were quickly hushed up and the issue essentially disappeared from the mainstream press. The US military instituted heavy handed damage control, carrying out a few token courts-martial, while expediting administrative measures, such as discharges and transfers of personnel to dispense with most cases.[51]

Seymour Hersh has shown that this damaging scandal resulted from a CIA system that was put into place at the highest level in the Pentagon. The exposure of the abuses led to the release of thousands of Iraqi prisoners, over the next few months. Most, it seems, were completely innocent. Most of the evidence which US officials feared would emerge seems to have been buried and quickly disappeared from the media. Nevertheless, the security situation on the ground in Iraq only grew worse.[52] A similar scandal of British abuse of prisoners in Iraq was revealed in January 2005.

The New Iraq: Handover and "no-go areas"

On March 1, 2004, four American civilians working for Blackwater USA, a US Security firm, were killed and hanged from a bridge near Fallujah in the Sunni Triangle.[53] The US military promised to find those guilty and bring them to justice, along with Abu Musab al-Zarqawi, a Jordanian terrorist thought to be a mastermind of the resistance and said to be hiding within the city. Indiscriminate artillery attacks were launched by the US Marines, along with air strikes. House to house searches were carried out resulting in mass arrests, with plastic restraints being used to bind prisoners' hands. US Marine snipers reportedly took up positions in the minarets of a local mosque and shot a number of innocent residents. These actions became a further rallying cry for the insurgency. US forces were first ordered to attack the city, then after a few days were ordered to pull back, turning the city over to the Fallujah Brigade, reportedly to avoid a blood-bath.

The Fallujah Brigade was made up of 1600 former members of Saddam's special security forces and former members of Saddam's Republican Guard. Some 800 residents were killed in the spring assault, the majority reportedly women and children, but a US military spokesman claimed that 95 percent were military-aged males. The attempt to reach a political solution by installing the Fallujah Brigade seemed to work for about a month. The force was equipped and paid by the US Marines but it became clear that many of those on the payroll were actually working for the insurgents, while the manufacture of car bombs continued inside the city. In September 2004, the brigade was disbanded, the US admitting that its establishment had been a fiasco. The US military was unable to recoup the weapons, vehicles, uniforms, and other supplies given to the brigade. It was clear that most likely the disbanded brigade members, out of work, would rejoin the Sunni insurgency.[54]

The official handover of sovereignty to Iraq was conducted on June 28, 2004, two members of the IGC chosen as interim Prime Minister and President. Iyad Allawi, a Shiite, was chosen as the new interim Prime Minister and Ghazi al-Yawar, a Sunni, as the President. The handover took place clandestinely two days early. Paul Bremer was on a plane and out of Iraq by the time news of the fiat accompli was announced and footage of the event appeared on international TV. The IGC had previously approved a new temporary constitution on March 8, 2004, the Transitional Administrative Law (TAL), which made Islam the official religion of the state, but tended to exacerbate Sunni unrest by politically marginalizing Sunni Iraqis. The document also gave the Kurds a veto over a permanent constitution to be approved by an elected parliament. The Kurds feared they might not be guaranteed semi-autonomy and special minority rights. In fact, the problem of political accommodation of major groups remained a thorny problem for the future.

Interim Prime Minister Iyad Allawi was the leader of the Iraqi National Accord (INA), a group of former Baathist officials who broke with Saddam, and provided misleading information to the Bush Administration. He was criticized for having been on the payroll of a number of foreign intelligence agencies, including the CIA and the British MI5. He reportedly carried out terrorist activities against Saddam's regime as a US CIA employee. He had at one time been a spy for Saddam Hussein before defecting. A report emerged in July 2004 that he had shot six prisoners in cold blood at a police station in Baghdad a few days before the handover. The murky past of the new leader, however, was largely left unexplored in the mainstream Western press.

The weakness of the US sponsored Iraqi government was suggested by a public opinion poll taken in May 2004 indicating that 67 percent of Iraqis supported the radical Shia cleric Muqtada al-Sadr and 70 percent supported the Shia Grand Ayatollah Ali al-Sistani, while only 23 percent supported Iyad Allawi for office. The poll showed that 78 percent had "no confidence" in the CPA, while only 11 percent expressed some confidence and two percent expressed strong confidence. Only 28 percent had confidence in the IGC at the time.[55]

In the summer of 2004, US forces battled the Mehdi Army of radical Shia cleric Muqtada al-Sadr in the holy city of Najaf and Sadr City in Baghdad, a slum with one-million inhabitants. A "peace plan" negotiated by Ayatollah al-Sistani on August 26 ended the siege of Najaf and helped to contain the influence of the younger Muqtada al-Sadr. The US program of buying up weapons provided some needed cash for residents but could not permanently quell the insurgency. The Iraqi resistance controlled hundreds of square miles of territory around Baghdad with government authority largely confined to the capital city. Fallujah, and even parts of Baghdad, continued to be "no-go areas" for American forces and al-Sadr's militia was in control of Najaf. According to an agreement with al-Sadr, the US army could drive only on roads agreed to by the Mehdi Army and had agreed to remain on a US base.[56] American forces were being attacked up to 80 times a day by mid-2004.

In the run up to the November 2004 Presidential elections, a major assault was prepared to retake the Sunni Triangle and allow for Iraqi elections scheduled for January 30, 1995 as nightly bombings were being carried out by US aircraft. Planes from the USS Kennedy in the Gulf were reportedly bombing Iraq some 20 times a day. The Major assault to clear Fallujah of insurgents was delayed until after the US elections while some 850 British troops from First Battalion Black Watch were transferred from Basra to near Baghdad to free up American soldiers for this major battle, which is explored in Chapter four. A US military spokesman expressed the military's view that the only choice the insurgents had was to "submit or die."[57] In the event, the US has been charged with war crimes by critics, given the massive use of force and unknown number of civilians who died in the assault on Fallujah in November 2004. Most residents of the city of some 300,000 became refugees as some 70 percent of the buildings in the city were destroyed. While the US claimed to have killed some 1200 insurgents at the time, it is also acknowledged that many fighters fled to other cities to carry on the insurgency.

Kidnappings of foreigners had become endemic with al-Zarqawi's Tawhid and Jihad movements increasingly active in 2004. By October some 150 foreigners had been kidnapped with many beheadings shown on Internet websites. At least 30 foreigners had been killed, including the beheadings of three Americans. Security became the overriding immediate problem. The country lacked an Iraqi army and a national guard. The private company, Vinnell Corp, which had trained Saudi security forces, had been awarded a contract to train 9000 men but more than half of the first 900 deserted in December 2003, after which the US turned the training over to the Jordanians.[58]

At the same time, the US found itself increasingly isolated internationally. As the insurgency and kidnappings began to take a higher toll, there were more frequent attacks, not just on US forces, but on Iraqi police stations and national guards as new Iraqi personnel came on duty, including the massacre of some 50 police trainees from the Kurkush Military Camp on October 24, 2004. Assassinations of Iraqi officials also increased and officials were even abducted from offices in Baghdad.

The coalition charade, largely symbolic from the start, continued to unravel. After Prime Minister Jose Marie Azner lost the election in Spain in early 2004, the Spanish pulled out their 1300 troops. Next to bolt were Honduras, the Dominican Republic, and Nicaragua, with small numbers of troops. The Philippines pulled out under populist pressure to prevent the killing of a worker taken hostage. Then Norway pulled out 140 of its 155 troops. Next New Zealand and Thailand announced they were leaving. The Netherlands and Poland were considering getting out by mid-2005. Estonia announced pullout plans, while Singapore pulled out all except 33 of its personnel. Moldova recalled all but 12 of its contingent.[59]

The Sunni Question

While the insurgency was broadly a response to the occupation, embracing both Sunnis and Shias, the political marginalization of the Sunnis was at the root of the insurgency in the Sunni triangle and a crucial question was how the Sunnis could be accommodated in the new constitution and state to be finalized in 2005. It has been pointed out that the Sunnis enjoyed prominence in Basra and Baghdad, historically, under the Ottomans. Sunni hegemony was maintained in the monarchy of King Faisal set up by the British in the early twentieth century. While there was considerable support for the removal of Saddam Hussein among the Sunnis, the de-Baathification carried out by the CPA targeted the Sunni community. Consequently, Sunnis saw themselves being disempowered by the new institutions set up by the occupation forces. The Sunnis were given only four of twenty-five seats on the IGC, and no Sunni member enjoyed popular grass-roots support. The community was marginalized in the writing of the interim constitution, so Sunnis realized that in the new state they would be dominated by the Shias. This continued to feed the Sunni insurgency and grew stronger; threatening the break up of Iraq. It also fed regional instability as regional powers feared the strengthening of the Shia and Kurdish communities in Iraq, especially after the elections of January 2005.[60] Political accommodation of all ethnic and religious groups remained a major challenge in the writing of a new constitution in 2005.

Staying the Course

The US is now and will be a major Gulf power for at least the next half century. Iraq promises a significant power base, "stupendous prize" of oil, and continued profits for US and British corporations.[61] On the other hand the costs were starting to mount. The continuing insurgency indicated that establishing a legitimate and stable government was extremely problematical. In fact, going against history and tradition in marginalizing the most coherent force for rule in the country, the Sunni tribes, appears to be a serious miscalculation. In launching the war, the neoconservatives disregarded the warnings of most experts. The US resorted to force to repress the traditional secular Sunni ruling class, while promoting the interests of shiites who threatened the rise of a theocracy. Ultimately, it seemed that the US might be driven out of the country by popular resistance to the occupation. The only question was how long it would take before the American people would be willing to call the occupation a failure and cut their losses. Even with the disillusionment of the American people it was clear that the US Government would not listen to the democratic grassroots and pull the troops out.

The real reasons for going to war in Iraq had nothing to do with weapons of mass destruction, a link between Saddam Hussein and al-Qaeda, the threat that Iraq might develop nuclear weapons, nor the fact that Saddam was a dictator. The US went to war in Iraq because of the "stupendous prize" that Iraq was deemed to be, leading not only to the control of oil, but power and a basis for the control of the larger Middle East region. Saddam was effectively skirting the UN-US sanctions in 2003 and would have soon begun to market large quantities of oil in Euros, militating against the US dollar. Many of the oil contracts were in the hands of France and Russia, which militated against US companies.[62] The US would have lost the chance to establish huge military bases in Iraq for the purpose of controlling the massive oil and natural gas reserves of the Middle East and Central Asia. US firms would have lost out on lucrative contracts for the "reconstruction of Iraq" worth many billions of dollars. Controlling Iraqi oil was also calculated to give the US leverage over its growing rivals, The European Union, China and India, with rapidly expanding economies. The US also saw Iraq as a basis for projecting power over Iran, Syria and Lebanon. Eventually, with large oil revenues, an autonomous Saddam could have rearmed, militating against the interests of Israel. The overthrow of Saddam was seen as a golden opportunity to extend the American Empire, which was unlikely to ever come again.

Saddam Hussein was overthrown, not because he was strong, but because he was weak. Overthrowing Iraq was seen as a way of significantly increasing US hegemony, and an action, albeit illegal, that the US could get by with as a result of the terrorist attacks of 9/11/2001. The Bush "fossil-fuel" Administration, after all, was top heavy with Texas oil men. That the American people would swallow the bait and that the operation would be relatively trouble-free was a gamble the neoconservatives were willing to take.

American Hubris and the Failure of Preemptive War

The first preemptive war, "a war of choice," had by 2004 become a catastrophe of world historical proportions, the magnitude of which was yet to be determined by history. The US had been pulled into a trap in Iraq of its own making and faced a growing, mostly indigenous, insurgency. The US had spent some 200 billion dollars by February 2005 on the war and lost more than 1500 US soldiers, with over 7500 combat related wounded. Total American casualties were in the vicinity of 32,000 by November 2004, according to accounts of those at US medical facilities in Germany. Up to a hundred thousand Iraqi civilians had lost their lives. The neo-Wilsonian ideology of the neoconservatives, allied with tough-talking religious fundamentalists, about the war on terrorism, making the world safer for Americans, and strong belief in Biblical prophecy, had provided an ideological cover for the US drive to increase its hegemonic power over the world and challenge any country that posed a potential threat to this goal. The neoconservatives had alienated and frightened much of the world, while their Iraq policy had collapsed in disarray. The neoconservatives were unable to successfully contain other members of the "axis of evil" such as North Korea and Iran. In fact Iran had been greatly strengthened its influence in the Middle East. US credibility had been badly damaged after the false rationales for launching an illegal war in Iraq. The root problem of political instability in the Middle East, the Israeli occupation of Palestine, was largely left to the self-defeating policies of Ariel Sharon and later Ehud Olmert. This would become clear by 2006 as Hezbollah strengthened its power in Lebanon. Afghanistan remained a hot bed of Taliban activity and Pakistan was a tender box of anti-Americanism and sentiment for Osama bin Ladin. The US had weakened international law. Resentment toward US unilateralism threatened to militate against the IMF, World Bank and WTO regimes constructed over the last half century. On the positive side, this opened opportunities for developing countries to challenge the encroaching neoliberal order and demand greater economy autonomy over their own economic development and a degree of equality and social security for their people. The reckless hubris of the neocon "revolutionaries" has threatened the entire global community. Other nations, such as Russia, have logically adopted similar policies of preemptive war, and this trend is likely to accelerate. The neocons have ended the elite consensus within the United States, bitterly dividing ruling elites. The American people have been stampeded by trumped-up fear into giving up significant constitutional civil liberties, while preemptive war has endangered them as never before. The gains of preemptive war are likely to fall far short of those anticipated by the neoconservatives, while the costs are certain to be far greater. The magnitude of the unfolding tragedy of the ill-conceived and illegal preemptive war in Iraq has yet to be realized or understood by the majority of the American people. No one knew how long it would go on as the country prepared for the relatively successful exercise of "demonstration elections," staged on January 30, 2005. As in the Vietnam War, Americans must ultimately come to grips with what their nation has wrought and its implications for the decay of the global order. As we see in Chapter Four, in spite of carrying out elections, the insurgency continued to spiral out of the control of the Americans. The assault on Fallujah, after the killing of four Blackwater USA security guards, did nothing to curb the trend toward the ensuing mayhem.

References

1. Victor Davis Hanson, "Democracy in the Middle East," *The Weekly Standard*, Vol. 8, No. 6 (21 October, 2002). Hanson is Shifrin professor of military history at the United States Naval Academy.
2. Max Boot, "The New American Way of War," *Foreign Affairs*, Vol. 82, No. 4 (July/Aug. 2003), p. 44. Boot compared the US invasion to the German blitzkrieg in 1940, the US and Britain shattering Hitler's "gold standard of operational excellence" and "making fabled generals such as Erwin Rommel and Heinz Guderian seem positively incompetent

by comparison." On civilian deaths see "Iraqi Victims of War: Fact Sheet," Aljazeera.net, 16 March 16, 2004; Les Roberts, et. al., "Mortality before and after the 2003 invasion of Iraq: cluster sample survey," *The Lancet*, Vol. 364 (20 November, 2004), pp. 1857-64.

3. Herbert P. Bix, "The Faith that Supports U.S. Violence," www.zmag.org, (1 September, 2004).
4. "National Security Document," (September 2002). Useful background to the 2003 US-British invasion and occupation of Iraq can be found in Andrew Cockburn and Patrick Cockburn, *Saddam Hussein: An American Obsession*, London, Verso, 2002; Kenneth M. Pollack, *The Threatening Storm: The Case for Invading Iraq*, New York, Random House, 2002; Geoff Simons, *Targeting Iraq: Sanctions and Bombing in US Policy*, London: Saqi Books, 2002; Milan Rai, *War Plan Iraq: Ten Reasons Against War on Iraq*, London, Verso, 2002; Scott Ritter and William Rivers Pitt, *War On Iraq*, London, Profile Books, 2002; Richard A. Clarke, *Against All Enemies: Inside America's War on Terror*, New York, Free Press, 2004; Kenneth M. Pollack, "Next Stop Baghdad," *Foreign Affairs*, Vol. 81, No. 2 (March/April 2002); Kenneth M. Pollack, "Securing the Gulf," *Foreign Affairs*, Vol. 82, No. 4 (July/August 2003) pp. 2-16; Fouad Ajami, "Iraq and the Arabs," *Foreign Affairs*, Vol. 82, No. 1 (Jan./Feb. 2003); Kenneth M. Pollack, "A Last Chance to Stop Iraq," *New York Times* (21 Feb., 2003), p. A27. Former CIA analyst Kenneth M. Pollack was one of the strongest advocates of the US invasion, arguing that the US could easily overcome the opposition, "ensure the free and stable flow of oil from the region" and "stabilize the price of oil." The US, he argued, needed to keep everybody else out of the gulf region, gaining the ability to "influence events elsewhere" and keeping Saddam Hussein from developing nuclear weapons. A ground war would be "cheap" and would "make success almost certain." The military operation would be "straightforward." The US would "own" the country and "get to decide the composition and form of a future Iraqi government..." Simons argued that the long regime of UN/US sanctions against Iraq during the 1990s was criminal. Ritter and Pitt argued correctly that Saddam

could not have many weapons left, as he had destroyed most of them after the 1991 Gulf War. Milan Rai made a case for the global peace movement to prevent the US-British invasion and occupation and a large number of Iraqi civilian casualties. Clarke stressed the overwhelming goal of the Bush White House to take out Saddam, with the September 11, 2001 attack on New York providing the green light.

5. There is a legal distinction between "preemptive war" and 'preventive war." Preemptive war is "waged in an attempt to repel or defeat an immanent offensive or invasion, or to gain a strategic advantage in an impending (usually unavoidable) war." In general, to justify a preemptive war, a state needs to show that the threat is (*a*) "clear and imminent," (*b*) "direct, that is, threatening ... in specific concrete ways," (*c*) "critical," likely to cause "unacceptable harm and danger" to "vital interests," and (*d*) "unmanageable," that is it cannot be "deterred or dealt with by other peaceful means." Preventive war is waged against a country that is merely a "potential challenge" and so might attack in future; "and is generally considered to violate international law." (http://en.wikipedia.org) The US National Security Document (Sept. 2002) lays out the Bush Doctrine on "preemptive war" in Section V. The document argues that deterrence as practiced in the cold war will not work against "terrorist enemies" who do not care if they die. It points out that the concept of preemptive war in international law has long held that states may take action when enemy forces "present an imminent danger of attack," such as "a visible mobilization of armies, navies, and air forces preparing to attack." The document then states that "we must adapt the concept of imminent threat to the capabilities and objectives of today's adversaries." This means that the US can attack another country "even if uncertainty remains as to the time and place of the enemy's attack." In other words, the document simply redefines "preemptive war." The new definition is that of "preventive war." It then proceeds to refer to de-facto preventive war as "preemptive war." It seems clear that from a legal standpoint, Operation Iraqi Freedom" was a "preventive war," as the case cannot be made that an attack upon the

United States by Iraq was clear and imminent, direct, critical, and unmanageable. The National Security Document, however, also stresses that other nations should not follow the US example. Other nations should not "use preemption as a pretext for aggression." Thus, the doctrinal concept of "preemptive war," in the Bush Doctrine, can be seen as giving the US the exclusive right to engage in de-facto preventive war. See Paul W. Schroeder, "Iraq: The Case of Preemptive War," *The American Conservative*, http://www.amconmag.com/10_21/iraq.html.

6. Scott Ritter, "The Saddamist/Islamist Resistance Will Win," www.zmag.org., (24 July, 2004).
7. Jay Bookman, "The President's Real Goal In Iraq," www.informationclearinghouse.info, (29 Sept., 2002).
8. George W. Bush lost the popular vote in November 2000 by some 500,000 votes. The US Supreme Court's decision, 531 U.S. (2000), halted the disputed recount in Florida and allowed Bush to "win" when the Electoral College cast ballots. That is the presidential vote that actually counts. See Greg Palast, *The Best Democracy Money Can Buy*, London, Plume, 2003, Chapter 1.
9. On January 21, 2001, George W. Bush's first full day in office, CNN International aired a documentary, "The Unfinished War." Curiously, the program cleverly built up the case for a US invasion of Iraq, perhaps sending a strong suggestion from corporate America and signaling the media's eagerness to play an accommodating role in conditioning people for the event. Jason Leopold, "Wolfowitz Admits Iraq War Was Planned Two Days After 9/11," www.zmag.org, (2 June, 2003); "Former Insider Says Bush Planned Iraq Invasion from Beginning," *The New Standard*, http://newstandardnews.net., (2 February, 2004). Paul O'Neill, who was Bush's first treasury secretary, claimed that removing Saddam Hussein was discussed ten days after Bush took office and eight months before 9/11 in a Security Council meeting. President Bush reportedly said: "Go find me a way to do this."
10. Paul Wolfowitz admitted that the alleged Iraqi WMD was decided upon as the justification for the war simply because

it was the only issue the security bureaucracies could agree on.

11. As early as 1963, the United States claimed the right to launch strikes against Cuba outside of international law, when Secretary of State Dean Acheson argued that no legal issues could arise when the prestige and authority of the United States were at stake. However, the doctrine of preemptive war was not raised to the level of official policy at the time.
12. See "National Security Document," (Sept. 2002); Noam Chomsky and VK Ramachandran, "Iraq is a trial run," *Frontline India*, (2 April, 2003). Chomsky argues that the US is seeking to establish a "new norm" in international relations if Operation Iraqi Freedom is successful. That new norm is the right to launch "preventive war." Indeed, establishing the new norm seems well advanced. Few analysts bother to mention that the US attack on Iraq was clearly illegal.
13. It appears that much of the false reporting about the alleged link between Saddam Hussein and al-Qaeda came from suspect evidence from the Information Collection Program, an operation of the Iraqi National Congress (INC), run by Ahmed Chalabi. The INC supplied stories to the major western press and intelligence services. Much of this later turned out to be wrong. The INC reportedly received some 33 million US dollars from the US government between March 2000 and May 2003. See Douglas McCollam, "Ahmed Chalabi's List of Suckers, *Columbia Journalism Review,* Alternet, (12 July, 2004).
14. A Washington Post poll showed that 69 percent of Americans thought it was at least likely that Saddam Hussein was involved in the attacks on the World Trade Center and the Pentagon. Bush continued to link al-Qaeda to Saddam in almost every speech on Iraq. Vice President Cheney said it was "pretty well confirmed" that Mohamed Atta, who planned the attacks, met with a senior Iraqi intelligence official in Prague in April 2000. Evidence of this was never provided. The neoconservative newspaper, *The Weekly Standard,* published an article which the author

claimed was based on leaked classified information, a top secret US government memorandum, which the paper had obtained. The paper claimed that the document, which came from Undersecretary of Defense for Policy, Douglas J. Feith, showed that "Osama Bin Laden and Saddam Hussein had an operational relationship from the early 1990s to 2003 that involved logistical support for terrorist attacks, al-Qaeda training camps, safe haven in Iraq, and Iraqi financial support for al-Qaeda. Feith is a member of the neoconservative circle. Dick Cheney later cited this article as the "best source of information," on the alleged link between Iraq and al-Qaeda. Increasingly, the war in Iraq was labeled "the war on terror." Stephen F. Hayes, "The U.S. Government's secret memo detailing cooperation between Saddam Hussein and Osama bin Laden," *The Weekly Standard,* (24 November, 2003); "Hussein Link to 9/11 Lingers in Many Minds," *Washington Post*, (6 Sept., 2003). The central figure in the link between Saddam and al-Qaeda was considered to be Abu Musab al-Zarqawi.

15. The neoconservatives continued to insist that the Iraq war was a "war on terror." They claimed that the war was necessary to prevent terrorists from getting their hands on WMD and "finding a home" in Iraq. In fact, it appears that the US invasion may have assisted the terrorists far more than Saddam. It was discovered in October 2004 that part of the dual use potentially nuclear related equipment, such as milling machines and electron beam welders, had been stolen from a facility near Baghdad. The terrorists have most certainly found a home in Iraq and have pursued their own efforts to develop crude chemical weapons. One group, the Al Abud network worked with local chemists to try to produce mustard gas, ricin and tabun. Another group, Jaish-e-Muhammad (Army of Muhammed), was reported to be trying to manufacture chemical-filled mortar rounds. Daniel McKivergan, "Was Iraq a diversion from the war on Terror? Bush and McCain remind us that the answer is: No," *Weekly Standard,* (6 October, 2004); Bob Drogin, "The Other Weapons Threat in Iraq," *Los Angeles Times,* (10 October, 2004). The links between Washington and al-Qaeda have been manifold since Osama bin-Laden was

recruited as an American agent against the Soviets in Afghanistan. See "Michel Chossudovsky, "Links Between the Bush Administration and al-Qaeda," *World Affairs*, Vol. 8, No. 2 (April-June 2004), pp. 66-86.

16. David Sirota and Christy Harvey, "They Knew Despite the Whitewash, we now know that the Bush administration was warned before the war that its Iraq claims were weak," *In These Times,* (3 August, 2004); Michael Kinsley, "Ours Not To Reason Why," *Washington Post*, (27 September, 2002), p. A23. The late British scientist, David Kelly, assessed the probability that Saddam had WMDs as thirty percent. Stephen Gardner, "Goodby 'Hot Preemption," *Spiked Online, (*6 August, 2003).

17. Iraq was required to submit a 12,000 page declaration on the destruction of its stock of weapons of mass destruction in early December 2002. Barton Gellman, "U.S. Suspects Al Qaeda Got Nerve Agent From Iraqis," *Washington Post,* (12 December, 2002), p. A 1. The claims made by Powell on February 5, 2003, many of them outdated, quickly unraveled. Powell claimed that Iraq attempted to buy Uranium yellow cake from Niger, that aluminum tubes found in Iraq were for use in nuclear centrifuges and that Iraq was using mobile bioweapons laboratories mounted on trucks. "Inspections will not work, Powell says," *Boston Globe online,* (22 January, 2003); Robert Fisk, "Powell's Presentation," 6 February, 2003, www.zmag.org. At the end of May, 2003, the CIA claimed that the US had discovered "Mobile Biological Warfare Agent Production Plants," one near Mosul and another at the al-Kindi Research, Testing, Development, and Engineering facility in Mosul. "Iraqi Mobile Biological Warfare Agent Production Plants," May 28, 2003, www.cia.gov. The US President declared, "We found the weapons of mass destruction." This CIA white paper began to unravel at once and appeared to have been in response to intense pressure to find the missing WMD. It was pointed out by Iraqi officials that the equipment was used to produce hydrogen for artillery weather balloons. The CIA claimed that this was just a "cover story." Doubters among the intelligence community pointed out the technical problems of using the equipment for production of biological

weapons. Judith Miller and William J. Broad, "Some Analysts of Iraq Trailers Reject Germ Use," *New York Times,* (7 June 2003); Jamil Ahmad, "Mobile labs found in Iraq are NOT capable of producing biological weapons," *Houston Independent Media Center*, (2 June, 2003); Imad Khadduri, "Mobile Lies," YellowTimes.org. In fact, it appeared that the US was not looking very hard for the alleged WMD. Donald Rumsfeld said on April 17, that he didn't think the US would find anything, but "we'll discover people who will tell us where to go find it." David Corn, "War on Iraq: Where Have All the WMD-Hunters Gone?" 28 April, 2003; "Blair in Iraq as row brews in London over 'embellished' weapons dossier," Agence France Presse, 29 May, 2003; Tom Raum, "Bush Brush Asides Failure to Find Weapons [sic]," AP, 9 June, 2003. Rumsfeld had set up the "Office of Special Plans" a secret Pentagon committee, in October 2001. It was headed by Deputy Secretary of Defense Paul Wolfowitz, Undersecretary of Defense for Policy, Douglas Feith, and other hard line neoconservatives. This group supplied "intelligence" to the National Security Council, Vice President Dick Cheney, National Security Advisor Condoleezza Rice and Rumsfeld on WMD which turned out to be wrong. Jason Leopold, "CIA probe finds secret Pentagon Group manipulated intelligence on Iraqi threat," www.onlinejournal.com. (25 July, 2003); Jason Leopold," White House Silenced Experts Who Questioned Iraq Intel Info Six Months Before War," www.scoop.co.nz, (12 June, 2003). When Congress held hearings on the faulty intelligence, Republicans refused to allow an inquiry into whether the intelligence had been "manipulated" to justify the war. Senator Robert Byrd and many others criticized the action. Blair, on the other hand, tried to silence his opponents with the Hutton inquiry, which turned out to be a white wash. "Leading Democrat slams Republican move to close hearings on US' Iraq intelligence," June 12, 2003, AFP; Robert Byrd, "War on Iraq: Time to Come Clean, Mr. President," Alternet, (6 June, 2003). Of course, the weapons were never to be found, and the CIA concluded that they had not existed since the early 1990s. The Iraq Survey Group's final report, authored by Charles Duelfer was released in October 2004. Bob Drogin and Greg Miller, "Iraq's Illicit Weapons Gone Since Early '90s, CIA Says," *Los Angeles Times,* (7 October, 2004); Scott Ritter, "Duelfer's Report," *The Independent,* (11 October, 2004). This climb down was a radical shift from earlier CIA claims. Director George Tenet had been fired. Not only had intelligence been "cooked" under Tenet, the CIA's Center for Weapons Intelligence and Arms Control had deliberately falsified the data such as rotor testing to falsely prove that the aluminum tubes sought by Iraq were for the purpose of developing a nuclear weapon. Ray McGovern, "The Corruption of Intelligence," TomPaine.com, (12 July, 2004).

18. Robert Burns, "U.S. Sending Iraq Battle Staff to Gulf," Yahoo.com, 7 Jan., 2003; Duncan Campbell and Richard Norton-Taylor, "Allies speed up deployment to Gulf," *The Guardian,*(13 Jan., 2003).
19. Hanson, "Democracy in the Middle East
20. Geir Moulson, "Rumsfeld Comment Sparks Angry Responses," AP Europe, (23 January, 2003). The anti-war stance of France and Germany was called a "problem" by Rumsfeld. "New Europe" included countries in Eastern Europe which supported the US-British war, despite overwhelming public opposition.
21. The term "democracy," is used here in its generic meaning, as following the will of the people, as opposed to the doctrinal definition generally used by US officials. US officials, in general, consider democracy to mean rule by a class of elites who are expected to follow the current dictate of a neoliberal economic agenda and policies which serve the "national security interests of the United States." The US, of course, does promote democracy around the world, in the doctrinal sense.
22. "Grossman Discusses Turkish Vote on U.S. Troops with Turkish TV," http://usinfo.state.gov/xarchives, (4 March, 2003); Noam Chomsky, "Turkey and the US War on Iraq," www.zmag.org, (3 April 2003). In the words of Chomsky, "Turkey taught the US a lesson in Democracy. That is regarded as criminal... I do not recall ever having seen such a demonstration of intense hatred for democracy on the part

of elite opinion in the US (and to some extent Britain)."; "Powell Briefs Press on Iraq, Turkey En Route to Ankara," http://usinfo.state.gov/xarchives, (1 April, 2003); "Deputy Secretary of Defense Paul Wolfowitz Interview with Cengiz Candar and Mehmet Ali Birand of CNN Turk," DOD News Briefing, http://istanbul.usconsulate.gov/pressoff/1p0508.html, (5 May, 2003).

23. The neo-Wilsonian campaign launched pro-Israeli neocons on a campaign to "democratize" the Middle East. "Bush shares dream of Middle East Democracy," *Asia Times Online,* (28 Feb., 2003); Jay Bookman, "The President's real Goal In Iraq," www.informationclearinghouse.info, (29 September, 2002); Gabriel Kolko, "The Age of Unilateral War: Iraq, the United States and the End of the European Coalition," *Counterpunch,* (2 May, 2003). Neoconservative activists and groups include: American Enterprise Institute (AEI), Project for a New American Century (PNAC), Center for Security Policy (CSP), Jewish Institute for National Security Affairs (JINSA), Defense Policy Board (DPB), and Freedom House (a neoconservative think tank). Sympathetic publications include *The Weekly Standard,* the *Wall Street Journal,* and Fox News. The neocons have been associated with the right-wing Likud Party in Israel. Prominent figures include John Bolton, Undersecretary of State for Arms Control and International Security; Richard Perle, Donald Rumsfeld, Lynne Cheney, Jeane Kirkpatrick, and Deputy Defense Secretary Paul Wolfowitz. Many, such as former CIA officer Marc Reuel Gerecht, want to cut US ties with Saudi Arabia totally. Founding members of the Project for a New American Century include: Dick Cheney, Donald Rumsfeld, Paul Wolfowitz, Jeb Bush, Zalmay Khalilzad, Elliot Abrams, Dan Quayle, Francis Fukuyama, Midge Decter, I. Lewis Libby, Donald Kagan, and Norman Podhoretz. Neocons in the Bush Administration include Wolfowitz; John Bolton, Undersecretary of State for Arms Control and International Security; Eliot Cohen, a member of Rumsfeld's Defense Policy Board; I. Lewis Libby, Chief of Staff of Vice President, Dick Cheney; Dov Zakheim, Undersecretary of Defense and Chief Financial Officer for the Pentagon; and Stephen Cambone, head of the Office of

Program, Analysis and Evaluation at the Defense Department.

24. Calvin Woodward, "Protesters Massing Against the War on Iraq," Associated Press, 17 Jan., 2003; Tariq Ali, "Recolonizing Iraq," *New Left Review*, No. 21 (May-June 2003); Robert Fisk, "Arab Response to War," *The Independent,* (19 Feb., 2003).
25. Steve Holland, "Bush Shrugs Off Global Antiwar Protests," Reuters, (18 Feb., 2003).
26. Eddie J. Girdner, "Operation Iraqi Freedom: The Bush Doctrine and the Projection of US Power into the Middle East," *Mainstream Weekly,* Vol. 41, No. 35 (16 August, 2003), pp. 23-30.
27. David Gun, "Bush's Top Gun Photo-Op," *The Nation,* (2 May, 2003). Only 128 Americans died in combat in the initial phase of the war. Once again, US officials pointed out that they would not do body counts of Iraqis who died.
28. The World War II image of the US Marines raising the flag over Iwo Jima was also faked. Ted Rall, "War on Iraq: How We Lost the Victory," Alternet, (16 April, 2003).
29. Daren DeYoung, "U.S. Sped Bremer to Iraq Post," *Washington Post*, (24 May, 2003), p. A1.
30. Adeed Dawisha and Karen Dawisha, "How to Build a Democratic Iraq," *Foreign Affairs,* Vol. 82, No. 3 (May/June, 2003); Robert Fisk, "Anti-Colonial War," www.zmag.org., (17 April, 2003).
31. Ruth Rosen, "What's the Exit Strategy?" *San Francisco Chronicle,* (10 July, 2003). Colin Powell clashed with the neocons on many fronts. A criterion for military intervention for Powell was a clear exit strategy.
32. Dave Moniz, "Ex-Army boss: Pentagon won't admit reality in Iraq," *USA Today*, (3 June, 2003). Meanwhile, not all the "coalition of the willing" was willing to pay the bill. The US agreed to pick up the tab for "peacekeeping troops" from Poland, Ukraine, Nicaragua, El Salvador, Honduras, and the Dominican Republic. The cost of the war appears to have exceeded $8 billion per month for the first 18 months.

Paul Richter, "U.S. Enlists More Countries in Iraq at Taxpayer Expense," *Los Angeles Times*, (22 June, 2003). By $2007, the real cost of the war was estimated to be $720 million per day

33. Jim Lobe, "Who Will Rule Iraq," Alternet, (7 April, 2003); Erik Gustafson, "Congress to Pentagon: Iraq Is All Yours," Alternet, (16 April, 2003).
34. Jim Krane, "Many Baathists Banned From Iraq Gov't," Associated Press, (16 May, 2003). This included up to 30,000 Baath Party officials who had been "able administrators." The US Office of Reconstruction and Humanitarian Assistance claimed to be "putting a stake in the heart of Saddam Hussein." In fact, de-Baathification was later seen as a serious mistake which prevented establishing a functioning administration in a reasonable time.
35. "US abolishes former Iraq army, assurances given on postwar contracts," Agence France Presse, (24 May, 2003); Kareem Fahim, "The New Man in Baghdad," *The Village Voice,* (18 June, 2003).
36. Youssef Ibrahim, "Iraq's Oil," www.znet.org, (6 October, 2004).
37. The nine members were: Ahmad Chalabi, Founder and head of the Iraqi National Congress; Jalal Talabani, Secretary General of the Union of Kurdistan; Abdul Aziz al-Hakim, leader of the Supreme Council for Islamic Revolution in Iraq; Masood Barzani, President of the Kurdistan Democratic Party; Ebrahim Jafari Al Eshaiker, the main spokesman of the Islamic Da'wah Party; Seyyid Muhammad Bahr ul-Uloom, a Shiite clergyman; Adnan Pachachi, President of the Iraqi Independent Grouping; Ayad Allawi, Secretary General of the Iraqi National Accord; and Mohsen Abdul Hameed, Secretary General of the Iraqi Islamic Party (IIP). Originally the interim government was to have been chosen by a national conference of 300 Iraqis from a range of groups. The Iraqi National Council would in turn nominate Iraqis to serve in senior positions in ministries. A convention was planned which would work out guidelines for a national constitution to be approved in a national referendum. John Daniszewski, et. al. al., "U.S.

Increases Role in Picking Iraqi Leaders," *Los Angeles Times,* (2 June, 2003).

38. Kenny Bruno and Jim Valette, "Cheney and Halliburton: Go Where the Oil Is," *Multinational Monitor,* (May 2001); Jason Leopold, "Defense Dept. Secretly Tapped Halliburton Unit to Operate Iraq's Oil Industry in November," www.zmag.org, (13 May, 2003); Josua Kurlantzick, "Iraq Reconstruction Spells Opportunity," Entrepreneur.com, (14 April, 2003).
39. Carol Brightman, "It Wasn't Supposed to be Like This," Alternet, (14 July, 2003); James Zogby, "What Iraqis Think About the Occupation," Alternet, (27 October, 2003).
40. Slobodan Lekic, "U.N. and Aid Groups Pull Out of Baghdad," AP, (30 October, 2003). US Administration officials stated that the security situation in Iraq was steadily improving. Medicins Sans Frontiers announced they were pulling out the same day.
41. Michael Wolff of the New York Magazine was attacked by a civilian employee of the Pentagon for questioning the usefulness of the military and CPA briefings. Fox TV attacked Wolff for "lack of patriotism" and right-wing radio host Rush Limbaugh organized a campaign of hate mail against the reporter. The question asked was: "Why are we here? Why should we stay? What's the value of what we're learning at this million dollar press center?" Press freedom took hits in the war from the beginning. Peter Arnett, who had been a CNN star reporter in the first Gulf War, was fired from NBC at the beginning of the war for granting an interview with Iraqi TV. Early in the war, the Pentagon asked Al-Jazeera to remove its reporters from Baghdad. There was pressure on reporters to become "embeds" (600 reporters including 150 foreign did). The independents or "unilaterals" were at risk of being shot. By June 15, fifteen media people had died and two were missing. Some claimed that members of the press had been targeted by the US military. On April 8, 2003, three war correspondents were killed at the Palestine Hotel. An American tank fired a shell into the 15th floor and a cameraman for Al-Jazeera was killed by the US bombing of the channel's office in Baghdad.

French TV channel, France 3, filmed the tank turret swiveling, aiming and firing. American soldiers fired on the offices of Abu Dhabi TV in Baghdad. In the US, Clear Channel radio group organized pro-war rallies through their stations. Philip Knightley, "Turning The Tanks On The Reporters," *The Observer,* (15 June, 2003). In Sept. 2003, the interim Iraqi National Council threatened the press, aiming at al-Jazeera and al-Arabia, warning that Iraqi or foreign press and TV news organizations could be shut down for advocating the return of the Baath Party or issuing any statements that represented the Baath directly or indirectly. The restrictions were meant to prevent Iraqis from hearing Saddam's voice (as stations had broadcast Saddam's tapes). Some 106 newspapers emerged in Baghdad after the war. The restrictions were approved by Bremer's legal advisors who drew up the censorship rules. Fisk pointed out that even reporting deaths from an American missile could be interpreted as "incitement to violence." Robert Fisk, "Against the Press," *New Zealand Herald,* (24 Sept., 2003). Al-Jazeera TV was forced to answer a series of questions in 24 hours as demanded from Bremer's office. Meanwhile, the television and radio stations in Baghdad were operated by a private American company, SAIC. The 357 journalists working for the American stations complained of censorship and went on strike twice for more pay. The stations gave news that was a "miserable affair." Robert Fisk, "Iraq's Press," www.zmag.org, 23 November, 2003. *Al Hawza,* a radical Shiite weekly, which spoke for Muqtada al-Sadr, was closed down for 60 days in March 2004. American soldiers tightened chains around the office door. Iraqis gathered to protest this action and shouted "No, no, America" and "Where is Democracy now?" Bremer signed the order to close down the paper, among others. Jeffrey Gettleman, "G.I.'s padlock Baghdad newspaper," *New York Times*, (29 March, 2004). In August 2004, the editor of al-Basaer, Dr. Muthana Harith al-Dhari, was arrested as he was coming from an interview with the Lebanese Broadcasting Company. He was media officer for the Association of Muslim Scholars, a Sunni group. "US Forces arrest leading

Iraqi editor," Aljazeera.Net, 2 August, 2004. Generally, American journalism was caught up in the ideology of "American exceptionalism" and relied upon official sources of information. Embedding reporters, except in rare cases, served the needs of the US Administration and the US military. Robert Jensen, "The Failure of US Journalism," Aljazeera.Net, March 15, 2004. Dima Taareq Tahboub, "The War on Al-Jazeera," *The_Guardian,* 6 Oct., 2003. Dima's husband was killed when the US bombed Al-Jazeera's office in Baghdad. The station was bombed because it reported the suffering of the common people in Iraq, according to the article.

42. As if Iraq was a colony of the United States, Americans, British, Israelis, and troops from other member countries of the "coalition" in Iraq are not treated as "foreigners" by the press and official commentators.
43. Seymour M. Hersh, "Plan B," *The New Yorker,* (28 June, 2004).
44. "Submit or Die: The Siege of Fallujah and Beyond," www.zmag.org., (14 April, 2004).
45. Brendon O'Neill, "Outsourcing the Occupation," Spiked on Line, Posted on Alternet on 20 April, 2004. At least 20,000 soldiers for hire were operating in Iraq. The International Institute for Strategic Studies in London estimated that 500,000 troops were needed to stabilize Iraq. Ray McGovern, "More Troops Later," TomPaine.com, Posted on Alternet, (29 Sept., 2004). The other two firms contracted by the State Department to work in the north and south of the country were Dyncorp and Triple Canopy. Blackwater USA had some 1000 mercernaries, called "contractors" in official Orwellian terms, in Iraq in 2007 when their tactics of shooting civilians in cold blood on the streets of Baghdad began to receive attention in the Western press.
46. Christian Miller, "Iraq Power Grid Shows U.S. Flaws," *Los Angeles Times,* (12 Sept., 2004). Instead of using Iraqi personnel to restore the existing system, the emphasis was on upgrading with new equipment from Bechtel, Siemens and General Electric. This was much slower than under Saddam.

47. Tini Tran, "Chopper Shot down in Iraq, killing 15 GIs," AP, (2 Nov., 2003). By February 2005, US forces had lost at least 33 helicopters in Iraq, some 20 of them shot down.

48. The speech was delivered at the US Chamber of Commerce on the twentieth Anniversary of the National Endowment for Democracy. The NED was set up in the early 1980s after negative revelations about the US CIA in the 1970s. Some previous activities of the CIA were shifted to the NED through which US government funds are secretly given to organizations such as the Center for International Private Enterprise, which distribute them around the world to support centrist and rightist labor and political organizations, especially during elections. They shore up the needs of US business and the government while claiming to encourage "pluralism." In short, the organization manipulates elections to get right-wing groups elected. Bush stated: "I appreciate the bipartisan, the nonpartisan spirit of the National Endowment for Democracy." Nonpartisan, however, it is not. See William Blum, *Rogue State: A Guide to the World's Only Superpower,* London, Zed, 2002, Chapter 19.

49. "Bush Demands Mid-East democracy," news.bbc.co.uk, 6 November 2003; "Middle East Democracy," Online Newshour, (7 November, 2003); Robert Fisk, "How We Denied Democracy to the Middle East," *The Independent,* (8 November, 2003).

50. See the series of articles in *The New Yorker* by Seymour M. Hersh: "The Battle between Donald Rumsfeld and the Pentagon," (17 April, 2003); "Chain of Command," (May 17, 2004); "The Gray Zone: How a Secret Pentagon Program Came to Abu Ghraib," (24 May, 2004); and "Plan B," (28 June, 2004).

51. It has been reported that while some in the lower ranks of the US military were made scapegoats, at least two generals were in line for promotion for their work in the Abu Ghraib prison where torture was used and the same private corporations involved have been awarded huge new contracts from the US Government. "Pentagon Rewards Generals, Corporations Tied to Abu Ghraib Scandal," *The New Standard,* (19 October, 2004).

52. Stan Goff and Derek Seldman, "Bring the Troops Home Now," *Left Hook,* www.zmag.org, (11 Nov., 2003). The morale of the soldiers in many cases seems to have hit rock bottom.
53. How the system works is explored in Jeremy Scahill, *Blackwater: The Rise of the World's Most Powerful Army.* New York: Nation Books, 2007.
54. Alissa J. Ruben, "Ineffective Iraqi Force in Fallouja disbands," *Los Angeles Times*, (11 Sept., 2004).
55. Stephen Soldz, "Iraq: What Went Wrong?" www.znet.org, (26 July, 2004).
56. Robert Fisk, "The Government Rules Only in the Capital," *The Independent,* (22 July, 2004).
57. "Submit or Die: The Siege of Fallujah and Beyond," www.zmag.org., (14 April, 2004).
58. Steven Rosenfeld, "Vinnell's Army on the Defensive," TomPaine.com., (21 Jan., 2004).
59. Phyllis Bennis, "The Coalition Unravels," www.zmag.org, (20 July, 2004). Australia had only 920 troops. By this time the so-called "coalition" was, for all practical purposes, a coalition of two: the US and UK.
60. Gareth Stansfield, "The reshaping of Sunni Politics in Iraq," Aljazeera.net., (18 March, 2004).
61. Estimated US-British profits from Iraqi oil over the next fifty years range between $600 billion and $9 trillion.
62. Florence C. Fee, "Russia and Iraq: The Question of the Russian Oil Contracts," *Middle East Economic Survey,* Vol. 46, No. 14 (7 April 2003); Carrie Satterlee, "Facts on Who Benefits From Keeping Saddam Hussein in Power," WebMemo #217, http://www.heritage.org; "Iraq awards oil contracts to Russia," *POE News*, http://www.poe-news.com., (21 January, 2003).

4

Mother of All Mayhem: Operation Phantom Fury, the Electrions and the Continuing Morass in Iraq

"Mr. President, Iraq is sovereign."

US Secretary of State, Condoleezza Rice, June 28, 2004

"It is the megalomaniac US policy since 9/11 that has very largely destroyed the political and ideological foundations of the former hegemonic influence and left the US with little to reinforce the heritage of the Cold War era but an admittedly frightening military power.

Eric Hobsbawm[1]

"We don't want elections, we want electricity."

An Iraqi in Baghdad

While Operation Iraqi Freedom accomplished the US goals of removing Saddam Hussein from power, destroying the possibility of autonomous economic development in Iraq, gaining American control over Iraqi oil resources, and generating vast profits for major US corporations, the first preemptive war also precipitated major problems for US regional and global control. It is by no means certain that in the long term the establishment of US hegemony in Iraq will prove to be a positive gain in terms of the chief objective of the neoconservative Bush Administration, that of maintaining an unchallengeable US global dominance.

The US operation has, in fact, strengthened Iran, economically and politically, spurring the further development of nuclear weapons programs in Iran, North Korea and other countries. It is not clear if the agreement made with North Korea in 2007 to close down its nuclear reactors will prevent the country from becoming a nuclear power in future. The war has brought Iraq to the point of a de facto civil war between the Sunnis and Shias and rapidly accelerated the Kurdish goal of an independent Kurdish state. While a clear objective of the war was to give the US greater control over the economies of the European Union, China, Russia and India, as we have noted, these areas may actually assert greater economic independence as a result of US superpower overreach. The war has greatly strengthened Islamic fundamentalism in Iraq, produced huge US structural deficits, increased global terrorism, and irreparably damaged the image of the United States in regional and world opinion. Further, the patience of the American people, with increasing war casualties, and lack of credibility of Pentagon and Government claims, began to grow thin as the war and occupation dragged on with no notable progress from the American perspective.

The US operation in Iraq, after going badly off track in the summer of 2003, continued to confound US planners, and "snatch defeat from the jaws of victory" in the events throughout 2004 and 2005. While the US attack on Fallujah, Operation Phantom Fury, and the elections of January 30, 2005, were portrayed by the Pentagon and the American press as major successes, they were actually part of the same catastrophic pattern. Contrary to popular opinion, both Operation Phantom Fury and the elections seriously militated against US goals in Iraq and the greater Middle East region. These events failed to crush the "insurgency," brought the Shiites to power, greatly increased terrorist violence throughout the country, greatly strengthened the national interests of Iran in the region and failed to create the stability needed to send a significant number of American troops home.

While the elections were hailed as an enormous victory, justifying the American invasion and occupation, and bringing a windfall of freedom for the Iraqi people, the results actually proved to be a major disaster on the ground, with the insurgency moving from strength to strength in the face of futile American efforts to stem the mayhem, the rot, and the chaos that continued to engulf the country. The war in Iraq is most likely to go down in history as a failure of world historical proportions, probably surpassing even the precedent-setting American blunder in Vietnam, a generation before.

While American officials began to boast about their accomplishment of bringing "democracy" to Iraq, in reality, they were forced, against their wishes, by Ayatollah Ali al-Sistani and the Shiite community to hold the January 2005 elections. Having no choice, the US put the best face on an unavoidable situation. Seriously alarmed about the coming Shiite rout at the polls, the US Administration panicked, and carried out a secret CIA operation, with limited success, to rig the elections. In the event, the US ability to control events in Iraq only continued to weaken. While creating problems for the US, the elections were a significant victory for the Shiites in Iraq and more significantly for Iran. Not only had Operation Iraqi Freedom not turned out as anticipated by the neoconservatives in Washington, the ongoing debacle was destabilizing the larger Middle East region. With the American military increasingly bogged down in the quagmire, the US was unable to accelerate its withdrawal of US troops contributing to the mounting costs and troop casualties. By mid 2006, sectarian violence led the US to increase the level of troops to 140,000, with seemingly little gain. The numbers would increase again by some 20,000 in 2007. The attempt to secure a major beachhead for US military strategic power and US capitalist profits based upon the control of Iraqi oil was beginning to turn sour. While it was clear that Congress and officials in Washington were divided over the way forward, no one could say just when there would be "light at the end of the tunnel" or how it would come. What none could deny was that the war had fueled unprecedented mayhem, as seen by the increase in terrorism in Iraq and around the world. By late 2005, the war in Iraq had become the mother of all mayhem.

Desert Mirage: The Elusive Security

When Paul Bremer, the Coalition Provisional Authority (CPA) Chief, claimed to turn over the reigns of power to the Iraqis at the end of June 2004, this act was supposed to usher in a new peaceful and prosperous Iraq. Instead, it marked the beginning and escalation of a major "insurgency." More accurately, it spurred on Iraqi resistance to continued US occupation. The US had banked not on "sovereignty" for Iraq, but on keeping tight control of the political and economic situation. The US installed a former Baathist and former CIA employee, Iyad Allawi, to allow continued American rule from behind the scenes. This was to continue, at the least, until a new constitution, based upon the US authored Transitional Administrative Law (TAL), could be clamped upon the country. Allawi, the US hoped, would be elected as the new Prime Minister. The US plan was derailed, in the event, when Ayatollah Ali al-Sistani and the Shiite community demanded direct elections. The US was forced to make the best of a bad situation and allow the elections to go forward. US officials claimed later, incorrectly, that it was the Bush Administration that had pushed forward the direct elections.

This development was highly problematical for the Americans in the country. The "insurgent" war continued to increase after Bremer left, with the situation in the Sunni Triangle, particularly in Fallujah, spinning out of control. Moreover, unable to control the borders with Syria, Iran and

Jordan, the US faced the catch 22 that the more they attacked resistance fighters, the more they spurred the recruitment of "foreign fighters" coming into Iraq. While the Bush Government sought to convince the world that the "insurgency" was "in its death throes,"[2] nothing worked to quell the resistance; not the turnover of sovereignty, not the battle of Fallujah, not the elections, and not the formation of a new government following elections.

By October 2005, the resistance continued with undiminished strength across the country, with the US still bombing in the north near Tel Afar and planning large scale military operations across a wide area. In early July 2005, London was hit with a wave of terrorist bombings linked to the British co-occupation army in Iraq. European countries geared up massively, following the United States, to greatly restrict people's freedoms in order to deal with the growing threat of terrorism from those angered by the US-British presence in Iraq. The fallout from Operation Iraqi Freedom was becoming a depressing spectacle for the entire globe. The western media mostly played it safe, largely clinging to the party line, but some dissent began to emerge. As in the Vietnam War, a generation ago, US and British officials claimed to see "light at the end of the tunnel." Most of the rest of the world was left wondering if they were living on a different planet, as this wretched train of disasters hurtled on through the thick screen of obfuscations thrown up by obsequious American and British officials to an unknown fate.

The Battle of Fallujah: "Operation Phantom Fury"

When the going gets tough for the American superpower, history instructs us that one can likely expect a large scale massacre. Operation Phantom Fury was not an exception in this regard. As in the tragic destruction of the ancient city of Hue in Vietnam in 1967, the people left behind in Fallujah were slaughtered in November 2004, followed by a predictable deep amnesia in the press and the American public.

The Western press has established the fiction that the Battle of Fallujah was the suppression of an "insurgency." It should not be forgotten, however, who are the insurgents in Iraq. They are based not on the Tigris and Euphrates but on the Potomac in Washington. The insurgency against the legitimate government of Iraq, illegal under international law, was launched by the neoconservatives in the Bush Administration. Those fighting the US occupation comprise an army of resistance against the US neoconservative de facto insurgency. Since this factual construction of reality was unacceptable to the US and British ruling classes, the western press devised an Orwellian construct, as part of the American ruling class ideology, and agreed to the convention of referring to the Iraqi resistance as an "insurgency." The fighters in Fallujah, a large city west of Baghdad, reinforced by fighters from other countries, were actually a counter-insurgency force against the US insurgency and occupation. Analogously, Americans would probably be surprised to find domestic resistance to the take-over of the United States by Cuban soldiers referred to as an "insurgency,' and American patriots who resisted described as "anti-American."

The crushing of the resistance in Fallujah was the continuation of the illegal attack and occupation of a sovereign nation by de facto "foreign troops," namely the Americans. It should be noted that in the US Orwellian construction, American troops are not considered to be "foreigners" in Iraq. On the other hand, those Iraqis fighting the US occupation are seen to be "anti-Iraqi." From the standpoint of international law, however, these so-called "insurgents" have a legal right to defend themselves from an illegal foreign occupation. While they greatly contributed to the death, destruction and mayhem in Iraq, this, of course, is what they were doing. To see this truth it is necessary to think outside the U.S. doctrinal framework, which is practically unthinkable in both the mainstream press and academia in the United States.

By mid 2004, it was clear that the worst fears of the critics of Operation Iraqi Freedom had been realized. Iraq seemed to be turning out to be the worst failed occupation in history. The US, was fighting an "insurgency" from both the Shiites and the Sunnis. In late summer 2004, the US was able to stem the forces of the Mahdi Army of Muqtada al-Sadr only by buckling to demands from Ayatollah Ali al-Sistani for direct elections and persuading al-Sistani to reign in al-Sadr. The US plan was to delay elections until officials were better able to control the results, but with their hand forced, they had little choice but to move ahead. This, however, only tended to inflame Sunni resistance in the Sunni triangle in Anbar Province. By late 2004, the US was ready to move in a major assault on Sunni hold-outs. Officials were only waiting to nail down a second term for President George W. Bush in the November 2004 elections before launching the assault on Fallujah, seen as the major stronghold of the resistance. It would not be the first, nor the last, time evens in Iraq were geared to political considerations in the United States.

Fallujah had been the place earlier in the year where four Americans, working for an American security firm in Iraq, Blackwater USA, had been killed. Their bodies were burned and then hung from a bridge. The US then launched an assault on the city, killing an unknown number of fighters and civilians, and at one point turning security over to local militias. The US also supplied arms and equipment. This arrangement fell through in the summer of 2004, however, as it became clear to the Americans that fighters resisting the US occupation were being sheltered in the city. The US strategy had failed to gain control of the area and stop the production of car bombs, much less "win hearts and minds."

Consequently, on the eve of the November 2004 Presidential elections, American troops were poised, waiting for the green light to attack on the city. A US military commander lectured American troops, telling them that the battle would go down in history as "another Hue," the historical battle in the Vietnam War. The US military had made the famous statement that Hue must be "destroyed in order to save it."[3] In the wake of the battle of Hua, there were at least 2000 dead civilians with 80 percent of the buildings destroyed.[4] Cleaning the "insurgents" out of Fallujah was seen as a pre-requisite to conducting the elections in Iraq scheduled for January 2005.

As for the US strategy, some in the press observed perceptibly that the US meant to "instill fear" in the local population, fighting for minds only, not hearts.[5] The operation would tend to terrorize people into voting in the upcoming election. The US "narrative," on the other hand, claimed that the operation was for the purpose of expelling the "foreign fighters" and "restoring local control." The US claimed that there were at least 3000 insurgents in the city, some 20 percent of them foreigners under the control of Abu Musab al-Zarqawi.[6] Control of information was clearly a priority for the US military and using embedded reporters served this purpose. The western press reported that the operation was under the charge of interim Prime Minister, Iyad Allawi, giving it the appearance of an "Iraqi operation." Most of the western press attempted to distance the operation from similar atrocities in Vietnam, although the US Military reference to Hua clearly established the link and signaled the Americans' intent to "kick ass" in a major way. Local civilian deaths were to be downplayed or not mentioned at all.[7]

While the US Army warned women and children to get out of the city before the US attack, it has been estimated that some 30,000 to 100,000 people stayed in Fallujah as the attack was launched.[8] General George Casey, the top US commander in Iraq, claimed that 50 to 70 percent of the residents of the city had left. Some 14,000 residents, who had the means, fled to a lake side resort called Habbaniya Tourist City, on the Euphrates River, many expressing anger at the US operation. Many who were poor simply had no place to go.[9] With martial law in effect, except for Kurdish areas, all highways leading into the city were closed allowing only government and emergency vehicles to come and go. All weapons in the city were banned. Airports were closed and the borders with Syria and Jordan sealed. Fallujah was about to become, in Vietnam terms, a strategic hamlet, or an indigenous concentration camp.[10]

After the first week of November, with the US elections safely in the bag for President George W. Bush, and the Administration claiming a sweeping mandate for continuation of the Iraq operation, the assault on Fallujah began. On November 8, 2004, US warplanes carried out some two dozen sorties, dropping massive bombs, ranging from 500 to 2000 pounds. US military gun ships "indiscriminately raked the city." Some of the ordinance consisted of cluster bombs and phosphorus weapons that burned right through the skin of those who survived the blast. It was clear that napalm, which is outlawed by international convention, was also used. Some 20,000 US troops stood by, ready to invade the city, while 800 British troops had been brought north from Basra to take up American patrol duties in the area.

US Army and Marine units fought their way into the heart of the city on November 9, 2004 with fierce street battles which destroyed US tanks and damaged at least one helicopter. US jets proceeded to fire missiles into crumbling buildings, wreaking havoc in most of the city. House to house searches were carried out in the Jolan and Askari neighborhoods, considered to be insurgent holdouts. US troops tightened a "security cordon" around the city for the purpose of killing or capturing "insurgents" rather than allow them to escape.[11]

Press reports of the resulting carnage described Fallujah as in "utter destruction." There were "gutted buildings, crushed cars, charred bodies, flattened concrete houses, ruined mosques, downed telegraph poles, hanging power and phone lines, piles of rubble, and burned and bloated bodies. The utter destruction had turned parts of the city into a ghost town. Some reports claimed that most fighters had already fled to other towns before the assault.[12]

In the total absence of respect and trust for the local people, residents, lacking food, water, and medical help, had been largely left to their own to attempts to survive. US troops had cut off electricity and water, closed shops, closed or destroyed hospitals, and declared a round the clock curfew. There were reports of ambulances being targeted by the US military as they attempted to save lives.[13] It was also reported that the US captured the doctors and arrested the medical staff at the hospitals, sealing medical supplies so they could not be used. Most of the wounded would simply be left to die. It was claimed that two hospitals were bombed, the al-Hader Hospital and the Zaid Mobile Hospital. A week later, a Red Cross official reported that at least 800 civilians had died, based on Red Crescent aid workers in Fallujah and refugee reports. But the US refused entry to the Red Cross into the city. The US also refused to allow in medical supplies, as requested by Red Cross and Red Crescent. And no supplies were allowed to go to Fallujah General Hospital, even though a convoy was waiting to enter the city. There were also reports that the Iraqi Ministry of Health had stopped supplying hospitals and clinics in Fallujah two months before the attack. It was said that the plan was to attack and close down the hospitals.[14] Another report said that US soldiers stopped an operation in the hospital and left the patient to die.[15]

US soldiers sat on roof tops, staring down at the grizzly ruins. Bodies with heads blown off lay among up market homes which had been utterly destroyed. The call to prayer from the mosques had ceased as the stench rose from dead bodies. "Allahu Akbar" was occasionally heard from a minaret when a large bomb exploded. Thousands of terrorized residents remained trapped inside homes, while corpses were piled like cordwood in the streets. Many civilians lay dying after being wounded with no access to food, water, or medical aid. Many women and children were killed by bombs and flying shrapnel.

American soldiers proceeded to destroy every remaining car on the streets. There was widespread use of chemical weapons, including napalm, as noted above, in the form of Mark 77 firebombs. The US admitted that napalm, internationally outlawed, was previously used in capturing Baghdad. The *Sunday Times* reported that artillery guns fired white phosphorus rounds, laying down a screen of fire that could not be put out with water and which melted peoples' skins. Doctors reported that many corpses were "swollen, yellowish and without smell."[16] Reporters noted graffiti on the walls which read "Long live the Mujahedin." At least 120 mosques were destroyed, half by US bombing and shelling from US tanks, amid a scene of utter devastation. The tactics of the Mujahedin, or resistance, included sniping from rooftops, using bicycles to escape, firing mortars from behind abandoned buildings, attacking US tanks with RPGs, and ambushing Bradley fighting vehicles.[17]

The numbers of "foreign fighters" in Fallujah were fewer than expected and no "top-notch leaders" were found.[18] Some locals said the "foreign fighters" escaped to Baghdad even before the battle began. Americans claimed the insurgents had been crushed, but the US military continued to bomb the city for weeks after the assault. Extensive attacks began to spring up in other parts of Iraq, however, suggesting that many "insurgents" simply dispersed to operate in other areas.[19] The operation was carried out mostly with American troops and the 36th Iraqi Battalion

(Kurds), said to be the only effective Iraqi unit. Most Iraqi military units were unwilling to fight in Fallujah. Former weapons inspector, Scott Ritter, predicted accurately that the battle would be the beginning of a long and bloody phase of the war, but that in the end, US could not win. The insurgency was to continue long after the battle of Fallujah.

By the first night, hundreds of houses had been destroyed. The night skies were lit up by artillery barrages. Donald Rumsfeld, US Defense Secretary, emerged to ensure Americans, erroneously, that there would be no "large numbers of civilians killed."[20] Yet UN Secretary General Kofi Annan warned of the wider possible consequences of the assault. "The threat or actual use of force not only risks deepening the sense of alienation of certain communities, but would also reinforce perceptions among the population of a continued military occupation," he said.[21] Some analysts predicted that the assault would go down as a "war crime," in contravention of the Geneva Conventions. It was a "crime against humanity, morally indefensible by any civilized standard or for that matter, by the Statute of the International Criminal Court." The assault was compared to the Wehrmach in Warsaw in 1944 and the assault of the Russian Army on Grozny in 1999.[22] It is illegal for a military force to attack the civil infrastructure and neglect to take precautions to protect civilians. But in Fallujah, the water treatment plant was attacked, two main libraries burned, electrical plants destroyed, two main hospitals targeted, medical clinics attacked and schools destroyed.[23] Reports claimed that at least 6000 civilians were killed in the battles. The reaction of US troops was said to be "out of all proportion" in "devastation" as buildings were leveled.[24]

Horrible stories of death and suffering began to emerge in subsequent days, while most could never be told. The battle trapped at least 50,000 residents in the city. Some residents made a futile attempt to flee the city into the desert when the US attacked. Both Sunni and Shia Mosques collected food and relief but these supplies were not allowed into the city. In Khama, a small city near Fallujah, houses were bombed killing a family of five,[25] typical of hundreds of such bombings since the first days of the war.

The major assault on Fallujah lasted about two weeks. The city was devastated. The BBC reported streets full of sewage, rabid animals, and hundreds of corpses. US forces stored hundreds of corpses in a potato warehouse while dogs fed on those still to be collected. US tanks were used to pull dead bodies to the soccer stadium where they were burned. Bodies of others were simply dumped into the Euphrates.[26]

Indeed, further alienation of the Sunni community was immediate. The Iraqi Islamic Party pulled its cabinet member, Industry Minister, Hajan al-Hassani, out of the government, as a protest against the assault. Across Iraq, police stations were attacked, as at Baqouba. The US, declaring victory once again, claimed to have killed 1200 insurgents, but a resistance leader said that only some 100 of these were actually fighters.

Deeply alienated, the resistance fighters were ready to allow "Iraq to sink into a quagmire of death and destruction in order to bog down and eventually expel the American occupier."[27] Even US officials acknowledged that the "insurgency" could mean many more years of conflict. US public opinion was running at about 70 percent in favor of the war at the time of the Fallujah Battle but was soon to decline, not surprisingly, as the US dug in for the long haul and American soldiers continued to die. Life in Fallujah had been turned into something akin to that of the West Bank in Palestine. American occupation of Iraq indeed followed the brutal pattern pioneered by the Israelis in their continued occupation of Palestine, which Ilan Pappe has concluded constitutes "genocide."[28]

It was clear at the time that the resistance was strong and unified throughout the country. A network operated through mosques with several groups involved, including the Ansar as-Sunah, al-Jayshas-Siri (Secret Army), ar-Rayat as-Sawda (Black Banners), The Lions of the Two Rivers, the Abu Baqr as-Sidiq Brigades, and the al-Tawhid wal-Jihad (Unity and Holy War), said to be controlled by Abu Musab al-Zarqawi.

The Sunni Association of Muslim Scholars (AMS) immediately announced that it was boycotting the elections as the Fallujah assault got underway. Sunni Iraqi resistance was characterized by one writer as "a full-fledged revolution."[29] Fallujah resistance was not confined to the city but extended to Baghdad, Ramadi, Samarra, Latifiyah, Kirkuk, Mosul and other cities. The Mujahedin was said to now control all the greater Baghdad area for the first time since the fall of Baghdad in April 2003. Suicide bombings flared up in Mosul following the battle. Two churches were attacked by car bombs in Baghdad, while a terrorist blast at a hospital killed 9 and wounded 80.[30] Thousands of other bombings would follow in coming weeks, months and years across the country.

At the time of the Fallujah Battle, it was reported that unemployment was running at around 70 percent, and at least 75 percent of Iraqis were fully dependent upon the food ration program set up by Saddam during the sanctions. US appropriation of the economy continued through illegal orders promulgated by the CPA, giving the US a monopoly over the reform and reconstruction of the economy. For example, Order No. 39 allowed the privatization of Iraq's 200 state-owned enterprises, 100 percent ownership of Iraqi businesses, "national treatment," meaning no preference for local firms, unrestricted, tax-free remittances of all profits and other funds and 40-year ownership licenses. The hiring of local Iraqis was not required.[31]

From the viewpoint of US officials, America now owned Iraq. The old programs of social assistance would be cancelled under a free market economy, food rations would be eliminated, and an IMF program brought in to ensure privatization and economic austerity.[32] The infrastructure was being put into place to secure the "stupendous prize" of Iraqi wealth in the service of US corporate capitalist accumulation. The slaughter of human life in Fallujah, as in Hua a generation earlier, was simply another necessary sacrifice to the gods of Wall Street and neoliberal capital.

Return to Fallujah

To return to their city and demolished homes, Fallujah residents would be subjected to iris scans and fingerprints, virtual Gestapo conditions which treated people less than human. On December 23, the first 200 people were allowed to return to Fallujah while the battle was ongoing. Bombs continued with tanks shelling buildings and F-18 fighter bombers striking targets in the area. Reports filtered out which began to expose the tip of the deep anger of the thousands expelled while mostly being ignored by the western press. Those able to return faced winter cold, no medicine, spreading disease, diarrhea, contaminated water, closed schools, continuing house searches, dire poverty, and sporadic fighting. By December 30, 2004, it was reported that about 8000 people had been allowed back into the city, but some 60 to 70 percent of the houses had been completely destroyed.[33]

Under the US plan, the city was now to be turned into a "benevolent and functional metropolis," a "model city." There would be "a huge effort to carry out social and physical engineering," Many viewed this as the setting up of a US-controlled "police state." All residents would be fingerprinted, photographed by the US military, and have their retinas scanned for IDs. They would live under strict curfews. No car would be allowed to move within the city. No child or elderly person was allowed to cross the street. Reminiscent of the city of Grozny, the US brought in a work brigade of some 800 men to clear piles of rubble. While one report claimed that 60,000 residents had returned by January 11, this seemed highly questionable.[34]

The Bush Administration predictably claimed that, "foreign fighters brought the destruction and ultimately are the ones to blame" for the destruction and loss of life. This was technically true, when one considers that most of the "foreign fighters" were the Americans and British. Local residents were to get a pitiful $100 up front, a paltry $500 of aid later on, and a laughable (up to) $10,000 for a damaged home. A May 2005 report on progress claimed that the US had allocated $200 million for reconstruction but there had been little progress on this front. The report claimed that half the residents had returned, but there was still no sewage system, no adequate electricity, and no running water. At least 30,000 houses remained damaged with 5000 houses totally destroyed, along with 8500 shops. Some 60 mosques and 20 government offices needed massive repairs.[35]

Bassel Mahmoud, director of Fallujah's Reconstruction Project, reported less than $50 million released for aid. The main hospital had been repaired, but only three out of 40 schools were operating, with some schools being used as military bases. Some classes were being held in tents. Only four government buildings out of 20 had been rebuilt.

The US promised $40 million for a new general hospital. But only corruption, it seems, reached the promised celestial heights of success. Some half of all oil revenues during the US occupation, some 8.8 billion US dollars in all, simply went missing.[36] The fallout from the war in Iraq showed that the US made a major miscalculation. Operation Phantom Fury brought great destruction but proved to do little to curb the "insurgency" that guaranteed that a large US force would remain in the country for no one knew how long. On the other hand, the occupation was never intended to be short-term. The promise of a quick withdrawal of troops was merely a selling point in the war. The Americans had come and they were not about to get out of town any time soon.

Iraqi Elections: Purple Fingers and the Ghost of Ayatollah Khomeini

With the loudly trumpeted Iraqi elections on January 30, 2005, Ayatollah Khomeini's dream of Shia rule in Iraq was finally realized. The Supreme Council for the Islamic Revolution in Iraq, founded by Khomeini as a resistance in Iran, was duly installed in power by none other than the enemy of the Iranian regime itself, the United States of America. Ironically, the Iraqi elections, while hailed as a great milestone on the road to democracy in Iraq, were actually a disaster in the eyes of many in the US Government. The neoconservatives in the White House apparently failed to foresee that elections in Iraq would bring pro-Iranian Shias to power. The elections also foiled US plans to keep former Baathist and former US CIA employee, Iyad Allawi, as the Prime Minister and US puppet ruler. Highly unpopular, Allawi was known locally as "Saddam without a moustache," and commanded the support of only three to four percent of the electorate.

In fact, the "demonstration elections" were not about bringing democracy or freedom to Iraq, but rather intended to justify the US invasion and occupation. They would also provide a pretext for retaining US soldiers in the country over the long term.[37] As noted above, the US agreed to the elections as a bargain with Ayatollah al-Sistani to quell the Shia uprising in the summer of 2004. In a larger sense, the poll was actually something other than an election. Unable to see the lists of candidates before voting, voters had little to go on except religious and ethnic identity, encouraging voting along communalistic, that is religious and sectarian, lines.

Even if they had risen to high standards of conduct, however, the Iraqi elections could be seen as "democratic" only in an extremely marginal and questionable sense, being carried out under the occupying power which had overthrown the Iraqi government illegally. Needless to say, there were many other undemocratic procedural elements. It is not even clear whether the elections were legal under international law. The "Bremer laws" under the Transitional Administrative Law (TAL), seemed to contravene the Geneva and Hague Conventions. Under the Hague Regulations of 1907, an occupying country cannot change the laws of a country.[38] Another question is whether a free election could be held under foreign military occupation and be managed by those occupying the country.[39] It was not possible to have an international committee of oversight given the security conditions and the country remained under martial law. The neoconservatives never cared much for international law and this election was no exception.

Beyond the above fundamental questions, the Bush Administration, itself, guaranteed that the elections would not be "free and fair." The Bush Administration made a secret decision to go outside official channels, "off the books," and subvert democracy by rigging the election. While it has not been proven, there is strong evidence that US underground operatives arranged for the massive stuffing of ballot boxes in favor of Iyad Allawi.[40]

It should be noted here that it is standard procedure for the US to manipulate elections around the world through arranging to funnel money to favored parties which serve US corporate interests. Normally this is carried out through the National Endowment for Democracy, which funnels money through a series of so-called non-governmental organizations, as explored in Chapter Five. These are the National Democratic Institute for International Affairs, the International Republican Institute, and the International Foundation for Election Systems. Ostensibly for the purpose of promoting democracy, these institutions actually subvert democracy in favor of parties which will promote the interests of US capital and large corporations abroad. Attempts to swing the Iraqi elections went beyond these operations, however, when it was clear that the preferred US candidate would be routed on Election Day. The US government panicked when officials could not sway the elections through these normal operating procedures.

Ignoring all advice from Congress and the above institutions, which feared the public fallout from rigging the elections, the Bush Administration made the decision to hire former US CIA employees and civilians to carry out an "operation." They "did an operation," a covert operation, which appears to have included voter intimidation, ballot stuffing, bribery, and falsification of election returns.[41] In addition, the US provided massive funds to Allawi and flooded the airwaves with his campaign messages, all of which seemed to backfire. The US preached democracy, while rigging the elections, but in the end its operatives were simply outflanked by Shias who reportedly proceeded to stuff ballot boxes massively in the south of the country. The Kurds, who were allowed to let voters vote twice, as part of an agreement in which US officials would look the other way and the Kurds would not ask for an independent state.[42] An election, no matter how crooked, was nevertheless an election and nothing was going to stop President George W. Bush, the US media, and the neocons from bragging about the great American achievement. "Democracy or Bust" could have been an appropriate motto for the ensuing fiasco. Democracy or not, Iraq was busted and the cost of the war would soon ship the American economy south as well.

Knowing before the election that their candidate was facing a disaster, US officials decided they had no choice but to engage in vote rigging. Perhaps, they simply decided to take a page out of the Florida election in 2000. By Florida standards, perhaps, the Iraqi election could be chalked up as a success.

It was a dead give away that the Shias would walk away with the election and that this would divide, rather than unite the country. The Sunnis would be the big losers, whether they went to the polls or not. Following the US assault on Fallujah, the major Sunni group, the Association of Muslim Scholars, which represented 300 mosques, immediately called for the boycott of the elections. A poll conducted by the State Department Bureau of Research and Intelligence between Dec. 12-26, 2004, showed that among Sunnis, only 32 percent were "very likely," to vote, and only 12 percent considered the election legitimate. On the other hand, 87 percent of Shiites said it was "very likely" that they would vote. There were strong dichotomies between Sunnis and Shiites on other dimensions. When asked if it was important to take part in the elections, 93 percent of Shiites agreed, while only 50 percent of Sunnis thought it was important. Sixty-one percent of Sunnis were concerned about family security, while only 24 percent of Shiites expressed a concern. When asked if the election would be "completely free and fair," 52 percent of the Shiites agreed, while only 12 percent of Sunnis thought so.[43] Another poll showed that Iyad Allawi had only three to four percent of popular support. A Zogby Poll showed that 82 percent of Sunnis and 69 percent of Shias wanted the US to leave Iraq, either immediately or after a government was in place.[44]

Keeping with the new-found spirit of Iraqi Democracy, presumably, Ayatollah Sistani issued a fatwa for all Shias to vote for the United Iraqi Alliance, or otherwise, they would go to hell. Being even more enthusiastic about their new democratic freedom, presumably, many Kurds reportedly voted, not once, but twice. This was seen to be acceptable, under the circumstances and far better than not voting at all, and, by all indications, made the Americans proud of them...as long as they voted for the right party... twice. The turnout, initially said to be 72 percent, was later rolled back to 60 percent, some eight million voters in all.

It was also reported that many voted out of fear of having their food rations cut off, as the ration cards were being stamped at the polls. Election Day was surprisingly peaceful, according to the Western press, with some nine suicide bombers and deaths of 20 voters, and fifty killed in the country, after a British military plane crashed near Baghdad. Ironically, the Shiites said they were voting to rid Iraq of the American occupation.[45]

Some areas were clearly unsafe. In Ninevah, 150,000 Christians claimed they were denied the vote because ballot boxes arrived late.[46] There were curfews, border closures, and country-wide travel restrictions. With the banning of cars, many people had to walk to the polls. Major groups in the elections included the Shiite United Iraqi Alliance (UIA), which included the Dawa Party of Ibrihim al Jaaferi and the Supreme Council for the Islamic Revolution in Iraq (SCIRI). The Kurdish coalition put together its own slate of candidates.

Robert Fisk warned that with the elections, "the law of unintended consequences, writ large," would set in. The result of Iraq being the first Arab nation to be ruled by Shias would bring deep fears among the Arab governments of the Middle East. This was likely to change the geopolitical map in ways that the Americans could not imagine. Shias elsewhere would want their proper share of power. King Abdullah of Jordan warned that this could destabilize the Gulf. Another worry was that Shias lived in the areas with the most oil, in Kuwait, Saudi Arabia and Iraq.[47]

The press reports, both in the Arab world and the West, were generally highly positive about the elections.[48] But behind the electoral façade, with long lines of voters in front of TV cameras, the reality was rather different and did not indicate that control had been turned over to the people. The US controlled $24 billion in reconstruction funds along with the neoliberal rules for the new Iraqi economy. The US had appointed the auditors and inspector generals in every Iraqi ministry for five-year terms. They had sweeping authority over contracts and regulations. There had been moves to open the Iraqi National Oil Company to privatization and foreign investment, as US corporations continue their salivation over Iraqi resources. The surface machinations of ongoing Iraqi politics could not obscure one's vision of where real power lay in Iraq. As of late 2008, the US had declined to announce any time table for even beginning to withdraw troops from Iraq.[49] This was to continue as it became an article of faith among Republicans and leading Democrats, including Hillary Clinton, that announcing a timetable for withdrawal was a threat to US national security.

Of the 275 members of the National Assembly, the United Iraqi Alliance ended up with 146 seats. The Kurdish Alliance had 77 seats, leaving the remaining seats to other parties. It took some three months to form the government with Jalal Talabani as President and Ibrahim al-Jaafari as Prime Minister. The wrangling over the draft constitution, continued till mid-September and its fate remained unclear in an upcoming referendum, scheduled for October 2005.[50] Washington sent mixed signals about how long it would keep large numbers of troops in Iraq, indicating that it would take years for the Iraqi security forces to be on their own, and at other times speaking about sharp withdrawals. Members of the US Congress began to grow increasingly restless as America sank deeper in the quagmire and US soldiers continued to die.

In the summer of 2005, Cindy Sheehen, the mother of a soldier killed in Iraq, protested the Iraq war and occupation by setting up a camp outside George W. Bush's ranch in Texas, where the President spent his summer vacations. She protested the war in Iraq along with several hundred other protestors, making plans for large demonstrations in Washington. As the antiwar movement geared up, and the President's ratings fell to new lows, Hurricane Katrina hit

New Orleans. While this catastrophe diverted attention from Iraq, the media lashed out at the Bush Administration for spending lavishly in Iraq, under the name of a "War on Terrorism," while thousands perished at home. The linkage of the growing needs of the people in America with the failure and massive squandering of resources in Iraq seemed to be a potential turning point, in which the Administration would finally have to level with the American people about where the country was going. It seemed that a majority had come full circle since September 11, 2001 and begun to doubt that the real threat to America came from Iraq or the Middle East. Indeed, the war had divided both countries.

US Strategy: A Failure of Vision

Planning for the war in Iraq, US policy makers envisioned a range of hefty benefits at a very marginal cost of some fifty billion US dollars. On the drawing board, the US would control vast oil resources and greatly enhance its global empire. The United States, similar to the debacle in Vietnam, quickly accomplished the major goal of destroying the country. The US dismantled the infrastructure, ensuring that the country could develop significantly only through US-controlled capital and in such a way that US corporations would reap huge profits. This would accelerate corporate capitalist accumulation. It would also ensure that a neoliberal economy would be established to ensure future access and profits for US corporations. As in Vietnam, the US might technically lose the war but gain the most critical of its overriding objectives, global reach and capitalist accumulation at home.

In the event, this adventure went badly off track in critical respects. The model the US envisioned to control the country largely broken down, creating major dilemmas. First, the US plan of running the country through a US sponsored client, such as Iyad Allawi, until a US-controlled constitution, based upon the TAD could be established quickly failed. Instead, Ayatollah Ali al-Sistani forced elections, which the US wished to put off for some years. This quickly brought the Shiites to power, raising Sunni resistance, and greatly fueling the "insurgency." Moreover, the fundamental goals of the Shias and Kurds were contradictory in critical ways. By mid 2005, short of a break-up of the country, Iraq had become practically ungovernable.

This presented a major problem for the Bush Administration. Politically, it was getting more difficult to stay, but reducing the 130,000 troops could not be done due to the lack of trust in the Iraqi Army and security forces. By 2006, the number of troops would be increased by some 30,000. The dream had also soured significantly for US corporations, which could not proceed with "reconstruction" as they had planned. Still, they reaped their massive war profits by sub-contracting to local firms. The cost of the war had ballooned to more than $300 billion by mid 2005, badly affecting the balance of payments deficit and the swollen US budget deficit in the United States. As in Vietnam, this began to take its toll on the once almighty dollar. This trend was to continue to shrink the greenback.

To Washington's dismay, the further crippling of Iraq had the effect of strengthening Iran and autonomous development there, particularly in the area of nuclear technology. The hard liner former Mayor of Tehran, Mahmoud Ahmedinajad, came to power in relatively democratic elections, at least as democratic as those staged by the US in Iraq. Iranian influence soared in Iraq and strengthened in Syria as a result of the US misadventure.

Stress on the US armed forces also grew, some troops serving three tours of duty by 2005. In the country, the US was forced to practically abandon land transport to supply the troops due to the danger of roadside bombs. The US was forced to stretch its troops thin on the ground and fight further battles similar to that in Fallujah in towns on the

Syrian border in Western Iraq. This meant the bombing and destruction of entire towns and villages. This only increased the resentment of the local people who were often caught between the "insurgents" and the Americans. Iraqi military participation was minimal in these actions. These battles had the effect of making it easier to recruit more foreign jihadis and fueled terrorism around the world. Countries which still kept troops in Iraq were potential targets. Fundamentalism in the South of Iraq strengthened, even as "democracy" took hold. It was possible to intimidate most people into going along with the militants. In the north, the Kurdish Workers' Party (PKK) was able to infiltrate into Turkey and carry out more terrorist actions, due to a safe sanctuary across the border and access to a vast supply of explosives stolen from stockpiles in Iraq. This situation would come to a head as more Turkish soldiers were being killed by 2007 and lead to large-scale Turkish military operations along the border with Iraq.

The US had failed to "pacify" the country and by the fall of 2005 large unanswered questions lay ahead. Would the draft Constitution, adopted in a referendum, be accepted by the Sunnis, Kurds and Shias, and how long would it endure? Would the Sunnis accept their subordinate role after being the traditional ruling group? How far would Iraqi ties go with the hardening fundamentalist government in Iran? How many more jihadis would be recruited and enter the country as a result of the ongoing US mis-adventure? What would be the reaction in the US and Europe if the insurgency continued into another year, with the danger of increasing of terrorism? What impact would President George W. Bush's Greater Middle East Initiative have, when public opinion in the region had turned so anti-American? Greater democracy in any country in the region would likely result in the strengthening of political forces opposed to US interests. This seems to have already happened in Iran in the 2005 elections. When would the American public balk? This seemed to be the crucial question.

Further, from a global strategic viewpoint, the US invasion and occupation had strengthened the drive for nuclear capabilities elsewhere in Iran and North Korea. The US "war on terrorism" most certainly increased the danger of WMD proliferation. In the longer term, the illegal invasion in Iraq might also militate against the major global financial and trade regimes, IMF, World Bank and the WTO as previously mentioned. While the Bush Government spoke of the expansion of democracy, it was clear that the fallout from the US misadventure had made democracy more difficult and that a genuine expansion of democracy in practically any country of the world would prove to be a direct threat to the US Empire.

Except for Halliburton and a handful of American corporations, who engaged in war profiteering, the balance sheet seemed exceedingly thin. Almost 2700 American soldiers had died by mid-2005. Some 30,000 had been badly injured. Iraq had been destroyed. Over a hundred thousand Iraqis, maybe more, had died. America was becoming more divided as during the Vietnam days of the 1960s. President George W. Bush became more unpopular by the day all across the US. And, in spite of optimistic statements from Government officials, no one knew exactly how it would all end. There was no light at the end of the tunnel. Would the US, as in Vietnam, eventually be blown out of Iraq? The attempt to breathe new life into the corpse of western imperialism had singularly failed up to this point. People around the world had little time or patience for the US brand of imperialist brutality the Bush Administration was perpetrating. It was only a question of time and more wasted lives, both American and Iraqi.

Conclusion: From Victory on to Defeat

While the US quickly carried out regime change in Iraq, the result for the global position of the United States must be looked at more closely. In major goals, the US had not been entirely successful in the Middle Eastern region and the world in its major goals, and the US adventure seemed to have badly backfired. Looked at from a class perspective, however, the ruling class had reaped the profits while the working class had paid the costs and would be billed for generations in future. Huge profits had accrued to the ruling class at least in the short run in its bid to build empire and buck up corporate capitalist accumulation.

But in the larger historical context, it is a question of how long the empire can be sustained, because of the inordinate cost to the US economy and to other societies around the globe. Moreover, the reputation of the United States around the world now lay in utter devastation, reminiscent of Fallujah itself.

On balance, Operation Iraqi Freedom had been a failure of world historical proportions by any reasonable measure. America may never recover from this misadventure of vast scale and inordinate folly. Indeed, one is at a loss to imagine how Osama bin Laden could have done such inordinate damage to the superpower, had the US totally ignored any threat from his quarter. It appears that US President George W. Bush was vastly more talented in diminishing the superpower status and image of the United States of America than bin Laden could ever have been in his wildest imagination.

There were many wise and courageous prominent US citizens who began to acknowledge that the continued US occupation of Iraq had become a hopeless and costly boondoggle. Unfortunately, the neoconservatives in the White House and Pentagon were made of exceedingly stern stuff, refusing to acknowledge their mistakes and failures. It seemed that they were robots. Either they had either not heard of democracy, or had no use for it, in their callous disregard for public and global opinion. Indeed, the neoconservatives had no use for democracy, either at home or abroad, except as a cover story for their pursuit of imperialist goals. They had massively squandered the wealth of their nation, which belonged to the people and was not theirs to squander. They had proceeded to strip citizens at home of freedoms and civil liberties, while further deeply impoverishing the majority of them. They wasted vast wealth, leaving US citizens threadbare when the real tragedy, Hurricane Katrina, hit the US. Not only did they trashed the world but their own country as well, with their greed for wealth and imperial power. When the people of the United States of America would arise from their inexplicable stupor and toss this cabal of rulers upon the trash heap of history, at long last, only history could tell. What was abundantly clear was that real freedom in Iraq would mean not only token but actual independence from the United States and Great Britain. But it was certain to be a long historical struggle as the Americans were dug in on the banks of the Tigris and Euphrates with the largest US embassy in the world being constructed in the heat of the Iraqi sun.

The problem of the rise of the Shias and what to do about Iran would lead to a new war in 2006, which was planned between the US and Israel as a way to crush the rise of Hezbollah in Lebanon and pave they way for regime change in Iran. As it turned out, both the US and Isreal were in for a surprise as the war unfolded in Lebanon in the summer of 2006. This episode is explored in Chapter Six. Before moving on to the war in Lebanon, it will be useful to examine the roots and operational logic of George W. Bush's "Greater Middle East Initiative," announced early in the war, as it became abundantly clear that the weapons of mass destruction were never going to be found in Iraq.

References

1. Eric Hobsbawm, "War, Peace and Hegemony at the Beginning of the Twentyfirst Century," Mainstream 43 (13), March 19, 2005.

2. Vice-President Dick Cheney repeatedly asserted that the insurgency was in its "last throes," being forced later to admit that his predictions were wrong. In July 2007, in an interview on "Larry King Live," Cheney stated, "My estimate at the time...turned out to be incorrect." Matt Spetalnick, "Cheney admits was wrong about 'last throes' in Iraq," Reuters, July 31, 2007.
3. Tony Kevin, "All the makings of a war crime- with Australia Silently onside," Sydney Morning Herald, Nov. 9. 2004.
4. Danny Schecter, "Selling the War," Alternet, MediaChannel.org, Nov. 11, 2004; For the full account, see Stanley Karnow, *Vietnam: A History* (New York: Viking Press, 1983).
5. Jonathan Schell, "A Heartless War," The Nation and TomDispatch.com, Nov. 20, 2004.
6. Jim Krone, "U.S. Forces Push Into Heart of Fallujah," AP Dispatch, Nov. 9, 2004.
7. Schecter.
8. Michael Georgy and Kim Sengupta, "Falujah, a City in Ruins," UK Independent, Nov. 16, 2004.
9. Yassir Faisel, "Residents Anxious to Return," Boston Globe, Dec. 14, 2004.
10. Erik Leaver, "The Quagmire Deepens in Fallijah," Foreign Policy in Focus, Nov. 9, 2004. Dahr Jamail, "Outrage in Baghdad," Znet (*www.zmag.org*), Nov. 9, 2004.
11. Krone.
12. Georgy and Sengupta.
13. Jamail, Nov. 9.
14. Dahr Jamail, '800 Civilians Feared Dead in Fallujah," Znet, Nov. 16, 2004.
15. Dahr Jamail, "Unuseal Weapons Used in Fallujah," IPS, Znet, Nov. 27, 2004.
16. Mike Whitney, "Firebombing Falluja," Znet, Dec. 10, 2004,
17. Pepe Escobar, "A Thousand Fallujahs," Asia Times Online, Nov. 14, 2004.
18. Georgy and Sengupta.

19. Scott Ritter, "Squeezing Jello in Iraq," Znet, Nov. 13, 2004.
20. Krone.
21. Leaver. The Secretary General spoke as if the Iraqis would not be able to see the occupation in front of their eyes, had the battle not taken place. Their view of the American occupation was quite concrete with practically every family having one or more members killed and one wonders what could have created an alternate perception. There was not much danger that they were going to stop seeing the occupation for what it clearly was. That is, an occupation.
22. Kevin.
23. It must be said that the US policy of destroying the civilian infrastructure was not new, going back to the 1991 Gulf War.
24. Georgy and Sengupta; "Disease Risk Stops Fallujah Return," BBC, Dec. 10, 2004; Mike Whitney, "Fallujah and the Disappearing Media, Znet, Dec. 29, 2004.
25. Jamail, Nov. 16.
26. Disease Risk Stops Fallujah Return," BBC, Dec. 10, 2004
27. Ritter
28. Ilan Pappe, "Palestine 2007: Genocide in Gaza, Ethnic Cleansing in The West Bank," *The Electronic Intifada,* Jan. 12. 2007.
29. Escobar.
30. Krane.
31. Jamail, Nov. 10.
32. Naomi Klein, "No, You don't own it," Znet, Dec. 28, 2004.
33. Nick Wadhams, "Casualties Reported After Fallujah Clashes," AP Dispatch, Dec. 23, 2004; Fadel al-Badrani, "Fallujah's displaced grow angry in harsh conditions," Reuters, Dec. 6, 2004; Joseph Kay, "Fallujah Residents return to a destroyed city." WSWS.org., 30 Dec. 2004.
34. Kay; Adam Shoop, "Falluja and the New York Times," Jan. 5, 2005.
35. Abdul-Qadir Saadi, "Fallujah Residents Angry Over Destruction," AP Dispatch, Jan. 11, 2005; "Iraq: Focus on Reconstruction in Fallujah," Reuters, 24 May, 2005, IRIN.

36. Robert Scheer, "Now U.S. Must Get Out of Iraq's Way," Los Angeles Times, February 1, 2005.
37. It was not until near the last year of the George W. Bush Presidency that US officials, such as Defense Secretary Robert Gates, began to admit that US troops would stay in Iraq for at least another ten years from 2007. With the institutional framework in place and US military bases established, neither political party would be able to make significant inroads in rolling back US imperialist plans, regardless of what they promised the American people. Indeed, the tight institutional system in the US would ensure that no presidential candidate could be elected who had a serious intent of doing such a thing. The US corporatocracy had the means of protecting and furthering future war profits. That, in part, consisted of the control, through political donations, which candidates could "go the distance" in a US presidential campaign. Only US corporations can supply the hundreds of millions of dollars required.
38. Dahr Jamail, "Iraqi Critics Speak Out on Occupation, Elections," *The New Standard*, Nov. 22, 2004.
39. Robert Jensen and Pat Youngblood, "Iraq's Non-Election," *www.zmag.org*, Jan, 28, 2005; Phyllis Bennis, "Iraq Elections," *www.zmag.org*, Dec. 20. 2004; Frank Broadhead, "Reframing the Iraq Election," *www.zmag.org*, Jan. 21, 2005. Kenneth Katzman, "Iraq: Elections, Government and Constitution," CRS Report for Congress, June 15, 2006.
40. Seymour M. Hersh, "Get Out The Vote," *The New Yorker*, July 25, 2005.
41. *Ibid.*
42. Voting twice in the same election would prove beyond a doubt, presumably, that the Iraqis had really fallen in love with democracy and voting.
43. AFP, "Internal US poll shows Sunnis not likely to vote in Iraq election," AFP, Jan. 6, 2005.
44. Sheer.
45. Robert Fisk, "Triumph and Tragedy For Iraq," *The Star*, Feb. 1, 2005.

46. Juan Cole, "Election Fallout," *Informed Comment*, Feb. 1, 2005.
47. Robert Fisk, "The Shia will inherit Iraq," *The Independent*, Jan. 29, 2005.
48. Mohamad Ozeir, "Arabic Media Call Election Historic," *Pacific News Service*, Feb. 1, 2005.
49. Dahr Jamail, "What they're Not Telling You About the 'Election,' *www.zmag.org*, Feb. 1, 2005.
50. Edward Wong, "Major Parties in Iraq Agree on President and 2 Vice Presidents," *New York Times*, April 15, 2005; Kim Sengupta, "After nine weeks of wrangling, Iraq has a new Government," *The Independent*, April 6, 2005; Pepe Escobar, "The Shiites Faustian Pact," *Asia Times Online*, Feb. 11, 2005. The Constitution was approved in the referendum.

5

The Greater Middle East Initiative: Regime Change, Neoliberalism and US Global Hegemony

"..The United States has adopted a new policy, a forward strategy of freedom in the Middle East."

(George W. Bush, Nov. 6, 2003)

"We are always threatening the Middle East with Democracy..But there is another kind of freedom they would like, and that is freedom from us."

(Robert Fisk)

"The Alternative to the old realpolitik is a brand new strategy oriented toward ending the entire apparatus of autocracy and creating in its place the conditions for future political legitimacy and economic growth."

(Victor Davis Hanson, 21 October 2002)

"..I don't think in any reasonable time frame the objective of democratizing the Middle East can be successful...and in the process of trying to do it you can make the Middle East a lot worse."

(Brent Scowcroft, National Security Advisor under George H.W. Bush)

"Where democracy appears to fit in well with US security and economic interests, the United States promotes democracy. Where democracy clashes with other significant interests, it is downplayed or even ignored." **(Thomas Carothers)**

When the United States failed to find the promised weapons of mass destruction in Iraq after the invasion in 2003, the George W. Bush Administration changed tactics and began to argue that the military operation in Iraq was primarily about bringing "democracy" to the Middle East. This rationale, however, had scarcely been suggested before the war. It is useful to consider this turn in the rationale for the war and whether it can be taken seriously as a plank of contemporary US foreign policy in the Middle East.

In fact, an analysis will show that The Greater Middle East Initiative (GMEI) for "democratization" is not about increasing freedom and democracy for people in the region but instead about increasing freedom for Western capital and ensuring continued US political control of the region. Military force, along with other US foreign policy instruments under occupation, continues to be employed to secure the resources of Iraq for US global hegemony and corporate profits.[1] It is an integral part of the colonial war launched by the Bush Administration against Iraq and the larger Middle East. Since maintaining economic and political control over the entire Middle East through military force would prove too costly, and logistically impossible, taking control through clandestine political and economic control, under the rubric of a "democracy initiative," was to be pursued in cooperation with the European Union. The institutions for such control, through a partnership between US Government, private US capital, US corporations operating in the region, and local comprador elites, have been in place for some time. They have been pioneered, in part, through the US economic and political control in Latin America.

With the neo-conservative perception that the US policy of supporting authoritarianism in the Middle East had outlived its historical usefulness, renovation of politics and consolidation of US hegemony was now to be carried out through a combination of force and guile, namely incentives purporting to create a free and democratic society. As can be easily understood, at root, neoliberalism is neither free nor democratic. It is the prevailing form of corporate-capital-authoritarianism being locked upon countries and societies around the entire world today. It is not certain if the neo-conservatives believed their rhetoric that terrorism can be suppressed through Western corporate control of the region. The bottom line of the neoconservative drive was the control of the politics and capital of the Middle East region through a combination of military force, the Central Intelligence Agency (CIA) and new institutions working in league with or under the cover of US corporations.[2] The mechanism is explained in some detail below. The GMEI is nothing other than the vehicle and blueprint for the extension and consolidation of neoliberalism in the Middle East. It is, of course, the most recent form of neo-colonialism fashioned for the region and indeed, the wider world. In the neo-conservative vision, anything which presents a barrier to this agenda must be ruthlessly rooted out and destroyed.

Since World War II, the United States has largely followed a policy of realist politics around the world in the interests of serving the interests of its domestic ruling class and political constituency, the owners of corporate capital. The core of the US domestic political constituency is the corporate class. Under capitalist logic, it was necessary to secure the control of resources, raw products labor and markets, of the entire globe as a source of capitalist accumulation. To some extent, benefits would filter down to other classes of the population within the US domestic political economy.

Nevertheless, this agenda, under Cold War containment, counterinsurgency, and subversion of uncooperative regimes, was carried out under the cover of various ideological devices, such as "preserving freedom and the American way of life," "freedom and democracy," and spreading "freedom .[3] The well established Wilsonian millenarianism, often with a crusading zeal, served as an appropriate ideological cover for the US enterprise of global hegemony and pursuit of the interests of the domestic ruling classes, once the US took on the role of global hegemon after World War II.[4]

Consequently, under this rubric, the US carried out the cold war, conducted counterinsurgency against potential social democratic governments, supported authoritarian governments in Latin American and elsewhere, or supported more democratic states as well, depending upon whether this was deemed to serve its interests. National interests were calculated primarily in terms of the needs of and benefits to the corporate class in the pursuit of global capitalist accumulation.[5]

Within this framework, the US approach to the Middle East was relatively simple and straight forward, having been essentially settled at the end of the Second World War. Democracy was not considered to be on the charts, under the rubric of Middle Eastern exceptionalism, and the Unites States would support the autocratic and dictatorial regimes which were in place as long as the oil flowed through the US capitalist corporate structure. The US would be the regional hegemon with ostensibly independent states. This arrangement was referred to as the "Arab façade." The US would sponsor local "cops on the beat," Israel and Turkey, to help keep order in the region. This was part of the deal which was struck at the end of World War II. "Security" referred to the preservation of the system of capitalist accumulation in the interests of the ruling classes of the US. This "security" arrangement would be enforced by regional arrangements with Iran, Iraq, Pakistan, and so on. This often precluded democracy, as with the overthrow of Mohamad Mossadegh in Iran, and put the US at odds with more democratic states, such as India.

Consequently, while lip service was often paid to "democratization," in actual practice, democratic regimes were supported only in cases in which it was clear that this would protect capital and serve the US corporate class. In practice, US foreign policy was generally one of "deterring democracy," in which scores of regimes were overthrown by the US CIA. These regimes held the promise of the emergence of local democratic autonomy, which was deemed to militate against the needs of the US corporate ruling class.[6]

The history of US foreign policy since World War II has been fairly consistent and significant shifts in the policy of support for authoritarian regimes, such as in Latin America in the 1970s, have been compatible with the bottom line of a rational calculus about what served the domestic ruling class, rather than any abstract ideals about freedom and democracy. There is no reason why one should expect any radical shift in this historical approach in the near future trajectory of US foreign policy.

Prior to the US invasion and occupation of Iraq in March 2003, and following the destruction of the Twin Towers in New York, some of the neo-conservatives in the Bush Administration declared that the US policy of appeasement of authoritarian regimes in the Middle East had failed and that the US must move quickly to remove these regimes and establish democracy across the region.[7] "Regime change" emerged as a new buzz word in the neoconservative White House.

Nevertheless, the Iraq war was not launched upon the rationale of the establishment of democracy, but rather upon the rationale that Iraq possessed weapons of mass destruction and that Saddam Hussein had established links with al-Qaeda. When the Iraq War began to go badly and encounter stiff resistance from indigenous forces, in the fall of 2003, it became clear that the US was in for a long hard slog. The Bush Administration fell back upon the position of presenting "democratization" as the center plank in the "War on Terrorism." George W. Bush made his famous

November 6, 2003 speech at the American Enterprise Institute (AEI), where the National Endowment for Democracy (NED) is located, announcing a US "forward strategy of freedom." Bush called for $40 million for the NED budget to be targeted for the Middle East alone.[8]

The idea of the Greater Middle East Initiative (GMEI), developed by the US State Department was to be another tool of imperialist control which could be used to secure the resources, labor and markets of the region to beef up US global hegemony and secure corporate profits in the region, while theoretically, ending any incentives for terrorism. It is not clear if the neoconservative ideologues took this argument seriously, but the rational of "democratization" went forward under the same rubric as the invasion of Iraq. The program was said to be part of the "War on Terrorism." In fact, as will be argued below, both enterprises were of a piece with pushing forward the logic of serving the US ruling class in consolidating the global rule of neoliberalism and increasing global power and corporate profits. Under sleight of hand, the same mechanisms developed and used in Latin American would be brought in, opening the channels and floodgates for a massive flow of new CIA money into the region on behalf of US capital.

The Greater Middle East Initiative: Emergence and Profile

One might reasonably expect that the GMEI would be taken with a huge grain of salt, given the history of US foreign policy since World War II. Nevertheless, it has largely been taken at face value by most analysts and commentators.[9] The original US State Department document was leaked in February 2004 to the Arab newspaper, *al-Hayat.* The initiative was to cover 22 Arab nations plus Turkey, Israel, Pakistan, and Afghanistan. The modified document actually promulgated at the Sea Island, Georgia meeting of the G-8 in June 2004, was a greatly modified version of what was leaked to the press. The GMEI was the third initiative to be launched by the US since September 11, 2001. In December 2002, a US-Middle East Partnership Initiative was launched and in February 2003, the US-Middle East Free Trade Area was proposed.[10]

The Greater Middle East Initiative was first developed in the US State Department, Bureau for Near East Affairs. The 2002-2003 UN Arab Development report was used to provide demographic and economic background data to underpin the thrust of the initiative. Also the Helsinki Agreements of 1975, which were seen to encourage the reforms in the governments of Eastern Europe, were seen to provide a model for the process of political reform which was envisioned.

The 2002-2003 UN Arab Human Development Report (AHDP) highlighted "three deficits" in Middle Eastern societies: Freedom, Knowledge, and Women's Empowerment. The logic forwarded was that these deficits contributed to a pool of disenfranchised individuals and led to an increase in extremism, terrorism, international crime, and illegal immigration to Europe and beyond. The thrust of the initiative was the argument that to address these deeper problems, which bred terrorism and other ills, political reform and democratization was a priority.

The AHDP presented a profile of the region in which the GDP of the 22 Middle Eastern countries had a combined GDP less than that of Spain, 40 percent of adult Arabs (61 million, 2/3 women) were illiterate, six million new jobs needed to be created per year, only 1.6 million had access to the Internet (the lowest proportion in the world), women held only 3.5 percent of seats in the parliaments of Arab countries (compared to 8.4 percent in sub-Saharan Africa), and some 51 percent of Arab youths wanted to emigrate, mostly to the EU or America.

There was also said to be a "freedom deficit," in which Israel was the only country in the region rated "free" by the

2003 report of Freedom House. Only four countries in the region were rated "partly free." Of the seven world regions, the Arab world had the lowest freedom score in the late 1990s. Empowerment of women ranked only slightly above sub-Saharan Africa. On the other hand, it was reported that democracy was rated high among the peoples of the Middle East as the most desirable form of government.

The launching of the GMEI was problematical, after the leaking of the initial document, and the negative image that the US had suffered in the Middle East after the invasion of Iraq and the Abu Ghraib prison torture scandals. The "sharp crisis of confidence" was reflected in the image of the US as a neo-colonial power in the region.[11] Further, the US failed to consult with the governments of the countries to be targeted and failed to mention the Arab-Israeli conflict in the document.[12] It was recognized that Middle Eastern governments would see such a "patronizing" initiative as a "new form of economic and cultural hegemony." They would also understand that Washington wished to extend the programs of the National Endowment for Democracy (NED) from Eastern Europe and the Balkans to the Middle East.[13] The NED uses taxpayer money to fund favored US-favored political parties in elections around the world, a practice which would be illegal in the US. The US Office of Management and the Budget (OMB) had announced the allocation of $458 million for "democracy promotion" in Iraq for the first six months of 2004 alone in Iraq. It was subsequently revealed that the US carried out a secret operation to rig the January 30, 2005 elections in Iraq, as noted in Chapter Four. Therefore it was realized that the launching of the program would need to be compromised by the views of the Europeans and the Arab leaders.

The Americans would have to link the GMEI with the NATO Mediterranean Dialogue and the European program known as the Barcelona Process, launched in 1995. The first includes Israel, Egypt, Jordan, and four North African states in a "security partnership." The Barcelona Process adds Syria and Lebanon to the other countries and is supposed to lay the foundation for an economic partnership and a free-trade area starting in 2010. The European program speaks of "modernization" rather than "democratization." Unlike the original GMEI proposal, the European program agreed upon the need to address the Israel-Palestinian problem and the ongoing crisis in Iraq. The European program also put considerable emphasis upon addressing poverty and underdevelopment.

The US would have to use a "clever" approach and get the regional leaders engaged, "gain local acceptance" by "providing them with the necessary safety net," and "put serious money into the region."[14] It was never pointed out that since the GMEI would be patently illegal in the United States, perhaps the leaders of the Middle East had legitimate reasons for questioning the initiative.

In brief, the initiative was based upon five core components. First, the initiative would provide a venue for discussion of reform goals and programs; encourage cooperation between states; and bring business and civil society leaders into the process. Secondly, there would be a Greater Middle East Democracy Assistance Group to coordinate the American and European groups "promoting democracy." On the American side, this would include the National Endowment for Democracy (NED), and its four major organizations as discussed below. In Europe it would involve the affiliated *stiftungs* associated with German political parties and the Westminister Foundation in the UK. Thirdly, the initiative would establish a multilateral foundation modeled on the NED to focus on political change in the Middle East. Fourthly, there would be a Greater Middle East Literacy Corps. Fifthly, it would establish a G-8 microfinance pilot project, based upon an existing French proposal, fund new small businesses, and contribute to building an Arab "middle class." Other elements of the program included "civic education" programs, technical assistance with voter registration, parliamentary exchanges and training, women's leadership workshops, legal aid, media training, "anti-corruption" efforts, strengthening NGO's (which may actually only masquerade as NGOs), and support for certain labor unions.

One can get a better picture of what is intended here by noting the emphasis upon business initiatives, business education, civil society, human rights, and training political party leaders. The document suggested that the Bahrain Institute of Banking and Finance, with an American director and a partnership with several US universities, could serve as a model for other countries. The program would provide an avenue for US universities to market their educational programs, tailored to corporate needs, to the Middle East region. It was said that the "key" to the program was "unleashing the region's private potential", under the auspices of Western and American capital. This, of course, has always been the formula from the US perspective for developing a region of the world. The initiative also emphasized the growth of an "entrepreneurial class" to "help democracy and freedom flourish." This also gives a clue as to the type democracy that the program would foster. A neoliberal capitalist framework that provides freedom for Western capital and defined as "democracy," was the desired final product. In fact, it is widely recognized by serious political economists that in today's global political economy, there is a sharp contradiction between capitalism and democracy, between corporate profit and democracy, and between corporate control and democracy. The GMEI is clearly concerned with freedom for capital, rather than freedom for human individuals.

The GMEI also called for the establishment of a Greater Middle East Development Bank (GMED Bank), a "partnership for financial excellence," and an emphasis upon "removing barriers to cross-border financial transactions."

In other words, neoliberal financial liberalization, which has been the cause of many financial crises around the world in recent years, was given a high priority. Financial services would be liberalized, to allow the marketing and control of local financial institutions by Western capital. There would be promotion of intra-regional trade, a push for WTO accession for countries, export processing zones, which were referred to as Business Incubation Zones (BIZ), and special trade zones. This would increase the process of the maquiladorization of the Middle East. Maquiladoras are primarily labor-added assembly plants in Mexico along the US border where products are assembled after the parts have been shipped from the US or elsewhere. These plants primarily add labor, taking advantage of the sharp difference in wages between the US and Mexico for large profits. Of course when small business enterprises succeed through US taxpayer dollars, the big sharks, Western corporations, will be there to buy them up and broaden the foundation of firms for capital accumulation on a global scale. From the above, we see that the GMEI was clearly the thin edge of a wedge to transform the entire Middle East under the banner of neoliberal global corporate control. The Arabs were not being unrealistic when they charged that the program was designed for imperialist control of the region. That is certainly what it was for.[15] But generally, analysts have been observed to dismiss such charges out of hand as they are not considered to be in good taste in today's global business environment.

At the same time, this is not to say that there is nothing positive about the program. For example, literacy and women's education could be a positive contribution. In a dialectical way, capitalism often develops the tools for potential human liberation. The rub, of course, is that it would have to get rid of capitalism itself in order to succeed. On the other hand, we are not to see the "invisible hand" of the CIA that is driving this program in the interests of the domestic ruling class in the interests of US and Western capital. This is to remain hidden.

One can readily discern that the elements laid out here are in fact those already established in the NED model that have been pioneered outside the Middle East region and which serve as mechanisms of control by the US Government through concealed arrangements with private corporations. The mechanism and operative principles of this regime, promulgated from the bowels of the CIA in Washington, is laid out in some further detail below.

While the initial reaction in Arab countries was negative, it has been argued that the document had some immediate positive results in forcing governments to take some reform initiatives, however halting. In Egypt, the Legal Committee of the Government appointed a National Council for Human Rights (NCHR). This committee proceeded to recommend that the state of emergency be rescinded. In Libya, Colonel Gaddafi pledged to cancel the Emergency Law. The Palestinian Authority announced that elections would be held. In Saudi Arabia, Crown Prince Abdullah hosted a series of "National Dialogue Forums" and promised that municipal council elections would be held. To some extent these were efforts to pre-empt pressures which these nations expected from the West. In fact, the measures were mere window-dressing to put Washington off while the effort was underway. The feeling among many was that the proposal would not be accepted as long as US troops occupied Iraq. Probably regional leaders were betting that the US was bluffing about human rights, which essentially turned out to be the case.

More negative opinions were held in Syria by President Bashar al-Asad and in Tunisia by President Sine El Abidine Ben Ali. Prime Minister Sheikh Khalifa bin Salman al-Khalifa of Bahrain, where the US Navy Fifth Fleet is home-ported, also rejected the initiative. Subsequently, the Arab League came forward with the "Tunis Declaration" on May

22, 2004, which expressed a "commitment to the humanitarian principles of noble values of human rights... freedom of expression, thought, belief, and the independence of the judiciary." Twenty-two Arab governments pledged to pursue reform and modernization; consolidate democratic practices; enlarge participation in political, economic, social, cultural and educational fields; and reinforce the rights and status of the above in their societies.[16] It was merely more of the same window dressing but the countries played along, helping Washington to save some face over the lack of weapons of mass destruction in Iraq.

In Egypt the "chronic indifference" to reform and moving toward "democratization" was apparent. Members of the ruling National Democratic Party defended the Government and criticized the US initiative. Mohamed Abdellah, former head of Parliament's Foreign Affairs Committee called the GMEI a "smokescreen." Abu Zejd, Chairman of the Parliamentary Arab-Affairs Committee said the Arab-Israeli conflict, which breeds terror, must first be solved. Foreign Minister Ahmed Maher said "reform must come from within the Arab world" and claimed that Egypt had already made democratic achievements, such as democratic reform, women's emancipation, human rights, and educational reforms. Gamel Mubarak, the son of the President and Chairman of the NDP Policy Secretariat, argued that the Party is truly open to reform. Others, such as Secretary General Hussein Abdel-Razeg of the leftist Tagammu Party, stated truthfully what everyone knew, that the NDP was "dragging its feet" and would be subject to more pressure from the US. Egypt had yet to "appease" the US in the area of democratization because the ruling party considered it so dangerous. The Secretary General of the NDP, Safwat El-Sharif had announced that amending the Constitution was not on the agenda of political reform in Egypt. Many other members of the opposition in Egypt were seen to be supporting the US pressure for reform as the ruling party had refused to make any reforms over a 22 year period.[17] In practice, however, as Patrick Buchanan has pointed out, opening up the system had perils for Washington too, as it would likely bring the Islamist fundamentalists to power. This was soon to happen in Palestine and provoke a sharp reaction from both the United States and the European Union.

At the G-8 Summit in Sea Island Georgia, after considerable modification, two documents were actually approved, designated collectively as the "Broader Middle East and North African Initiative (BMENAI). Many leaders, including Egyptian President Hosni Mubarak, refused to attend the Sea Island meeting. Leaders came from Afghanistan, Algeria, Bahrain, Jordan, Tunisia, Turkey, Yemen, and Iraq. Documents approved were a 12-point "Partnership for Progress and a Common Future With the Region of the Broader Middle East and North Africa" and the "G-8 Plan of Support for Reform." Unlike the GMEI, the actually agreed upon BMENAI received little attention in the press, after being watered down to pass muster with European and Middle Eastern Nations. The original document was modified in significant ways.

First, the BMENAI acknowledged the Arab-Israel conflict and called for support for reform in the region to go "hand in hand" with "support for a just, comprehensive, and lasting settle to the Arab-Israeli conflict. Secondly, the revised document stressed that reform should not be imposed from the outside but depend upon countries in the region. Third, governments should not necessarily be expected to change. Fourth, there would be no universally recognized standards. Diversity of countries should be respected. Fifth, each country would decide upon the 'pace and scope of change." Sixth, the idea of organizing an NGO to monitor reform progress was rejected. Seventh, government to government meetings would be held as a "Forum for the Future." Conferences would be arranged for exchanges between business and civil society leaders.[18]

American academics and analysts, rather than analyzing the roots of the initiative, generally took the initiative at face value as one can see from a number of academic exchanges which have taken place concerning the initiative and the larger question of democratization in the Middle East.[19]

The ideological Neo-conservative Perspective:

The hard vision was laid out by Victor Davis Hanson in the *Weekly Standard.*[20] This was a crusading vision which rejected both those who argued that it would be difficult to establish democracy in Iraq after the US invasion and occupation, and those who argued that the best course would be for the US to fall back upon pro-US despotism. Hanson rejected the notion that lack of a democratic tradition and a middle class militated decidedly against the establishment of democracy. He extended this vision to the subsequent reconfiguration of the Middle East, across a wide region. He also had little patience with the arrangement of supporting the pro-US despotism of General Pervez Musharaf in Pakistan. He urged the US to decide upon a course of action before the invasion and stick to it, regardless of the cost.

Hanson argued that this is the "practical" course of action because legitimate governments have power over dictatorships. He argued that past US policy had failed, such as the "appeasement of [Yassir] Arafat" and the Palestinians, while pushing for democratic reform with no significant results. He saw this as a process, not the installation of "Jeffersonian Democracy" at once. The first step would be to "remove the dictator," and this would most likely have to be done with a war or at least considerable force. He was apparently not concerned about the illegality under international law of such use of military force. He was also not concerned that "regime change" by the US might create chaos. Even chaos, in the neoconservative view, was seen as better than what currently exists. What emerged would be flawed, to be sure, but this was not to deter the US. The emergence of a flawed democracy was considered better than the status quo because eventually the people would realize that it was up to them to make things better, he argued. "Better to deal with a subverted democracy: At least its people will soon realize they, not the United States, are responsible for their disasters." The people are responsible. The model, he suggested, would be something like Panama, Grenada, Serbia, and the Philippines. Regardless of the risks, the venture was necessary because it was not possible to leave the Middle East alone, after September 11, 2001. The Middle East was "pathological" and would only get worse, so the US really had no choice.

Hanson argued that Americans had been told that there are two types of regimes in the Middle East, except Israel, which is "democratic." The first type included "sponsors of terrorism," such as Afghanistan (before the removal of the Taliban), Algeria, Iran, Iraq, Libya, Syria and Yemen. The second type included the "moderate dictatorships," such as Egypt, the Gulf states, Jordan, Morocco, Saudi Arabia and Tunisia. But on balance, after the bombing of the New York twin towers, there was not a lot of difference between these regimes for Hanson. They were all sick societies, breeding terrorists. He argued that both kinds of governments "seek to survive through bribery, oppression, and censorship, and by scapegoating Israel and America." There is an absence of elections, no free speech, lack of any public audit of government finances, and use of the "bogeyman of the West" as an excuse for all their ills.

Nevertheless, in the end, he argued that the Arab masses hate their own governments more than they hate the US. The last two decades of ruined economics had "brought nothing but disaster." He sited the Arab Human Development Report 2002, as the best evidence for this. There was a high population growth leading to 38 percent of the population being under fourteen years of age. The minimal GNP in the region meant that 22 Arab countries had a combined GDP of less than that of Spain. On the other hand, the wealthiest 85,000 Saudi families had $700 billion in overseas assets.

Hanson neglected, however, to explore how the US encouraged this situation, selling useless arms, and recycling petrodollars through US banks so that some seven percent of the US economy was now owned by the Saudi Royal Family. Some billions of dollars of Saudi money were invested in companies controlled by the Bush family themselves. It was also not explored how well global capitalism had done in developing the world in general. Also not mentioned were the needs of Western capital in the region for continued profits? Would the profits stay in the countries of the region or go to US, Israel, and Europe. These were larger questions that needed to be addressed in a historically realistically critique. Labor productivity in the Middle East had actually fallen between 1960 and 1990, Hanson noted, and even Africa had outperformed the Middle East in economic growth. Too few foreign books were being translated into Arabic. Half of the youths wished to emigrate, most often to the US and Europe. Rather facetiously, Hanson presented the US as a country that had tried everything in the Middle East, and was now "exasperated" at the lack of cooperation and progress.

In other words, with things so bad and getting worse, the US really had nothing to lose in going after the Middle East with a meat cleaver. The idea that whatever the result, the situation could not get worse was at the heart of the neoconservative logic. In any event, according to Hanson, there was really no choice. Supporting these regimes in the past, he argued, did not address the problem of "Arab development." In the past, it had failed, but now there was little to fear. Without the USSR, the US was free to do what it wanted in the region. Great progress had been made in Afghanistan, he argued. He dismissed the critics. They were wrong about Japan, Italy, and Germany after WWII, he said. The US overcame all the predicted difficulties, so there was no reason why this should not happen in the Middle East as well. It is not known if Hanson would still defend this pre-Iraq invasion version of events after the chaos which the US has encountered there, as predicted by those most knowledgeable about the region.

And, in any event, for Hanson, "democracy" was the only game in town. For the neoconservatives, it had no rivals. Hanson did not define clearly what he meant by "democracy" but it was obviously entailed the US vision of "neoliberalism." It was Francis Fukuyama's liberal utopia of the "last man". What was really being forwarded was the thesis that "there is no alternative." This was because "democracy" has no rivals. The US need not fear competition from "French Marxism," "communist nostalgia," "Baathist nonsense," nor "Islamist fundamentalism." On the other hand, the US "has an ally in global popular culture." It becomes obvious that Hanson was talking about the type of "democracy" which exists in the United States, in which the actual constituency is the corporate ruling class and the myth prevails that the people rule. He does not recognize the possibility of a popular democracy in which the constituency would actually be the masses or majority of the people. So this tied in nicely with the Fukuyamian thesis that liberalism, or rather neo-liberalism, was the end of history and nothing else could challenge this paradigm. Neoliberalism had become the global totalitarian ideology and we could all be happy that we lived in such a totalitarian world. Now we just had to make sure that the Middle East went along with the program.

But there were dangers too, for Hanson. "Establishing lawful rule in lawless places entails costs and dangers," he quickly added. He argued that either war or the threat of force must be used. "Military power must be decisive." Another price the US must be ready to pay was for "the lengthy presence of American troops." Not everyone would be happy. "We must expect and not fear anti-Americanism."

So for Hanson, the old game of "propping up strong men in the name of stability" was over. This was to "flout the aspirations of long-suppressed peoples and forget our national principles." The world had changed since the end of the Cold War, and "in our own national interest, we must make sure that our policies evolve with it." The old option was no longer there and "the Islamic world lost the privilege of being different."[21] They too were now to be brought into the neo-liberal totalitarian world to carry out their proper role of serving the needs of global capitalist accumulation. Having committed the sin of defying their masters, in the New York twin tower bombings, they would now be taken to the woodshed and taught their proper place in the world. This vision was indeed consistent with the prevailing racist and neocolonial world view of the neo-conservatives on the Potomac.

The Real key: The Model, which is the Basis of the GMEI, and how it Works

Philip Agee, a former US CIA employee, has explained the evolution and functioning in practice of the institutions which the US has set up to control the politics and economies of countries around the world. The GMEI sought to extend this system to the whole of the "greater Middle East."[22] Disguised as activities to "promote democracy," "resolve conflicts," and "strengthen civic life," the United States spent some nine million US dollars in 2005 in the attempt to remove President Hugo Chavez Frias from power in Venezuela. This was up from two million dollars spent in 2001, when a failed coup, backed by the US, was carried out. The United States provided money, training, counsel, and direction to a network of political parties, NGOs, mass media outlets, trade unions, and businessmen to end the democratic reforms being carried out by Chavez. One can readily see that this is the same model which was to be applied to the Middle East. In other words, to call such a program of regime change against the democratic wishes of the local people "democratization" is, to say the least, the epitome of Orwellian doublespeak.

The coup being carried out from behind the scenes in Venezuela was directed by the US State Department (the architect of the GMEI), the Agency for International Development (AID) and the Central Intelligence Agency (CIA). The primary organization is the National Endowment for Democracy (NED) and its four subsidiary organizations. These are the National Democratic Institute (NDI) of the Democratic Party, the International Republican Institute (NRI) of the Republican Party, the Center for International Private Enterprise (CIPE) of the US Chamber of Commerce, and the American Center for International Labor Solidarity (ACILS) of the American Federation of Labor-Congress of Industrial Organizations (AFL-CIO). The last organization was formerly called the American Institute for Free Labor Development (AIFLD) which "worked hand in glove for many years with the CIA."[23] A contractor for AID for the insertion of these programs into Venezuela is the US consulting firm, Development Alternatives, Inc. (DAI). There can be no doubt that similar contracts exist in other countries around the world.

Philip Agee has traced the history of these operations, which began shortly after the founding of the US CIA in 1947. In October 1947, the CIA began an operation in Italy to prevent the Communist Party of Italy (PCI) from winning the election held in April 1948. President Harry Truman provided the CIA with $10 million dollars for the operation. Teamed up with the Vatican, secret operations were launched to discredit the PCI and support the Christian Democratic Party (CDP). Over the years, these secret electoral operations became routine in many countries.[24]

The US secretly penetrated political parties; trade unions; student and youth organizations; cultural, professional and intellectual societies; women's organizations; religious organizations; the communications media; and civil society organizations. Money was funded through third foundations, often foundations set up for the purpose by the CIA. These programs became important for Latin America in the 1970s, under President Jimmy Carter, when the US shifted its policy from supporting dictatorships in Latin America.

These US CIA operations ran into trouble in 1967, when the CIA cover was blown and the operations revealed to the public. Over the next few years, the system was revamped and put back on track through a new set of organizations which appeared to be above board and legitimate. What was put in place was primarily the set of organizations which operate under the National Endowment for Democracy (NED) today, and which are to be a very vital part of the GMEI. NED was established by Congress in 1983 and put under the control of the State Department. Money would be funneled to political parties and organizations abroad which supported policies which strengthened "US national interests." Today political parties and civil society organizations are supported which promote neoliberalism, privatization, deregulation, control of trade unions, reduction of social welfare, elimination of tariffs, and free access to markets. In other words, these operations are very much an integral part of US foreign policy operations.

While the NED is legally an NGO, this is not actually the case, and USAID and the CIA fully participate in these programs to "promote democracy." For all practical purposes, NED functions as an arm of the US State Department. In 1984, USAID established the Office of Democratic Initiatives (ODI), renamed as the Office of Transition Initiatives (OTI) in 1994. Along with NED, these organizations channel funds abroad through a network of US Foundations, consulting firms, and public relations firms, in order to conceal the US Government connection. While the official line is that these organizations work to "strengthen civil society," they merely support the groups that support US interests and oppose those which do not. This, of course, is again Orwellian, as it promotes US control, not democracy. Undermining local democracy is promoted as "democratization."

These organizations were used to defeat the Sandinista Government in Nicaragua in the 1990 elections and similar operations are now being conducted against President Hugo Chavez in Venezuela. It is believed that the cost of the Nicaragua operation in 1989 was some $20 million.[25]

Today, the consulting firm, Development Alternatives, Inc., has carried out development projects in some 150 countries including a number of countries of the Middle East. The corporation is considered to be an ideal corporate structure for inserting CIA officers and agents. Contracts with USAID, operating in Venezuela, have been obtained and posted on the Internet. It is clear that these operations are designed to carry out the precise programs outlined in the GMEI. They conduct "workshops, seminars, conferences and training courses to develop political parties. They form political party coalitions, run programs to register voters, and conduct programs to get out the vote.[26]

Can Turkey be a Model For Democracy in the Middle East?

Some analysts have made the case that for the US and European approach to democratizing the Middle East, the current Turkish Government under Prime Minister Recep Tayyip Erdogan can serve as an instructive example.[27] The Justice and Development Party Government (*Adalet* ve *Kalkinma Partesi* or *Ak Partesi*) shows that "religious political movements in the Muslim world can take the lead in introducing greater social, political and economic freedom to their societies." It is claimed that in Turkey's case "the evolution of a modernizing Islamist political force was facilitated by external pressures for reform." "Turkey has been cajoled, pressured and encouraged by the West in its journey toward full and mature democracy." The conclusion is that "if Western governments hope to see this evolution take place across the Middle East, they would do well to study closely what is happening in Ankara."

It is true that Turkey has taught the West, particularly the United States, something about democracy, in the recent past, but it is not what is suggested by this argument. In fact, Turkey taught the US a lesson in democracy when in 2003, the Turkish Parliament voted to refuse permission for the US army to cross Turkish soil in its invasion of Iraq, This was met with an angry reaction from US authorities who upbraided the Turkish military for not carrying out their duty and ensuring that the bill would pass. The US threatened to cut aid to Turkey. In the Spring of 2005, the US Ambassador, Kenneth Adelman, requested that Prime Minister, Recep Tayyip Erdogan, request the Turkish Newspaper, *Yeni Safak (New Dawn)*, not to publish articles critical of the US in Iraq. Over and over, the US Embassy in Ankara has made moves to counter the emerging spirit of democracy in Turkey, especially in relation to the unpopularity of the US invasion and occupation of Iraq.

In the realm of civil society, on the weekend of 24 June, 2005, the world tribunal on the Iraq war was being held in Istanbul. The criticism harshly militated against the image of the US in the region. This is part of democratization, of course, and the events were widely covered by TV in Turkey, while being boycotted by the supposedly "free press" Western press outlets like BBC and CNN. In other words, the United States has expressed hostility to democratization in Turkey in a number of ways, as democracy is seen to militate against US interests. That is probably not the case, but it most certainly does militate against the interests of the neoconservatives in Washington. This should not be at all surprising, following the historical script.

The above argument made by Thomas Carroll about Turkey under the Ak Party as a model is misleading in a number of ways. Most significantly, it is not very convincing that the Turkish experience is relevant to the Arab countries of the Middle East. It does not seem very profound that Turkey shows that democracy can co-exist with Islam, as this has been shown in a number of countries, for example, India with one of the largest numbers of Moslems of any country in the world.

In the case of the Ak Party Government in Turkey, first, it is incorrect that Prime Minister Erdogan's program for further democratization and entry into the European Union has been driven primarily by outside pressure. In the past, traditional Turkish leaders simply dug in their heels when confronted with outside pressure from Europe. Erdogan knew that the desire to move forward on democratization and entry into the European Union was broadly popular in the country at the time he took office and used this to gain votes in the November 2002 election. Secondly, political modernization for the Ak Party means greater freedom for Moslems and peasants in rolling back control by the secular Kemalist elite which has ruled Turkey since the beginning of the Republic. It also means efforts to undermine secularism by allowing students to wear Islamic headscarf in schools and universities. It is the introduction of political Islam for the consolidation of political power and would tend to gradually limit the freedoms of the secular elites. For example, Ak Party governments put high taxes on wine and beer and try to restrict drinking of alcohol, especially in rural towns. The party also tries to fill administrative posts and the bureaucracy with graduates of religious (Imam) schools. While this could be seen as a form of political modernization, and democratization, it is generally seen by secularists as regressive, rather than progressive, in the social arena. There is no doubt that many in the Ak Party would institute authoritarian measures against secular freedoms if they were not checked by secular establishments such as the Constitutional Court and the Turkish Military.

Secondly, there is no other country in the Middle East where the people are driven by the historical desire to be part of Europe and today see the possibility of actually joining the European Union.[28] Thirdly, most secular elites in Turkey do not see the Ak Party agenda as a modernizing force at all, but rather a party pursuing an agenda in which a religious party in secular clothing pursues a hidden agenda and is rolling back the modernizing secular reforms of Mustafa Kemal Ataturk. Secular elites feel threatened by the wide scale staffing of state institutions, including culture and education ministries, with Islamists educated in religious schools. Fourth, it is not clear that the Ak Party is, in fact, a modernizing regime. In the economic field, the agenda is one of neoliberalism and privatization, while at the same time considerable state benefits are being provided to the poor and to the rural areas. While this may be seen by some as "freedom" it is not generally the case for workers and trade unions, nor those who want Turkey to have some democratic economic autonomy from the IMF neo- liberal agenda.[29] In the changing of the laws to conform to the European Union, this is not always seen as modernization in the Turkish context as it opens the way for greater freedom for religious movements. Ruling Turkey, as well as the rest of Europe, from Brussels is not "democratic" as it surely strips the local people of most control over their own lives. In Turkey, it seems that roads and shopping centers are being modernized but not necessarily culture and society. Fifth, people voted for Erdogan in 2002 not because he was a "modernizer" but mainly because they were fed up with every other political party in the country for failing to provide a stable economy and government. The other parties were accurately seen as either corrupt or incompetent. Moreover, Erdogan had promised to largely keep the state and government secular. People wanted to throw the old leaders out and get beyond the series of economic crises. Sixth, the extent of reforms which have been achieved should not be exaggerated. The state security courts have been officially abolished, but states are creative in finding new ways to continue the same old practices in new ways.

Seventh, the United States is not happy with the Ak Party Government as noted above. Erdogan's government does not fit the mold of what the US would like. Moreover, the Government is pursuing many programs which depart significantly from neoliberalism in giving opportunities to the downscale in the country. These include subsidized loans for low-income housing and so on. Erdogan has sometimes sharply criticized US policies in Iraq and foreign policy more generally a number of times, which has not gone down well with the United States.[30] Further, the United States has pointedly let the Government know that it is not happy with the level of anti-Americanism in Turkey after the invasion of Iraq. The United States has criticized the Government for not doing more to influence public opinion. This is surely a shocking and shameful attack upon Turkish democracy. Appealing to the Turkish Government to crush public opinion regarding US foreign policy in the region is not likely to enhance the US as a country which promotes democracy. The Turkish public has enough examples to get the picture. It is not clear exactly what the Turkish Government is supposed to do to control public opinion. Considering these facts, the Turkish model could sink US hopes in the Middle East quite decidedly.

Finally, rather than enhance the image of the Western democracy, European Union and American pressure on the country has actually caused a backlash of public opinion, with more and more people saying that they do not really care if Turkey enters the European Union or not. So external pressure may in fact be doing more harm that good.[31] While enthusiasm about the European Union was very high in 2002, by 2007, thanks to demands upon Turkey from Brussels, there was a sharp reaction. Demands that Turkey take such action as recognizing the 1915 Ottoman conflict with the Armenians as "genocide" caused sharp nationalistic reactions and the positive image of the European Union plummeted to around 25 percent. The West still largely believes it can practice a colonialist approach to the rest of the world with no negative reaction.

Given the operational plans of the US, however, the argument misses the point. The US has no desire to transfer the Turkish model, which is defective in many ways from the US standpoint. For example, it would be difficult for the US to tolerate such a nationalistic society under democratic conditions, as shown by Turkey's opposition to the US attack on Iraq. It is not the Islamist element that the US opposes, but the courage of those in the Government to refuse to toe the US party line. On the other hand, the US has tried and true methods to create the sorts of US engineered "democratic" systems that will serve its purpose, as we see above. This makes the argument quite irrelevant and shows that it misses the point of what is going on, rather badly. Part of the problem is that Western journalists have to fit countries into stereotypes, whether they belong or not.

What is Democracy?

It appears that nowhere in the documents and discussion of the GMEI is there a working definition of democracy. There are at least two different categories of definitions of democracy. One is the plain English, generic, definition of democracy. Second is the doctrinal definition of democracy which might be used by a regime to define "democracy." In the US context, the doctrinal meaning has very little to do with the generic meaning. Democracy may be defined as "a government by the people, especially rule of the majority. A government in which the supreme power is vested in the people and exercised by them directly or indirectly through a system of representation usually involving periodically held elections."

On the other hand, there is the doctrinal definition of democracy. This is what is used by the Bush Administration.

In this sense, "democracy" is that which serves the US "national security interests." This can be further clarified by noting that it is what serves to insure and protect capitalist accumulation and power. It serves both US global hegemony and capitalist accumulation. It will be seen that within this context, the rigged elections carried out under US occupation in Iraq, as on January 30, 2005, are "democratic." On the other hand, the June 2005 elections in Iran are not "democratic." Elections in Venezuela, which continue to keep Hugo Chavez in power, by large majorities, are not democratic since they do not serve the interests of US and global capital.[32] For the US, genuinely democratic elections which bring popular leaders to power, but which militate against the interests of capital, are, by definition, not democratic. What democratic elections are to protect is capital and not the people. They are to bring to the fore governments of capital, by capital and for capital.

We can see that in the US context, democracy also involves rigging the system. There are many ways in which this is accomplished in the US. The first past the post system, the redistricting and gerrymandering, elimination of sections of the population who are not desirable voters, and so on, are actually ways to rig elections. A narrow political spectrum exists, which also effectively precludes democracy. Neoliberalism, perhaps is the most pointed mechanism today for the elimination of democracy on a global scale, as it precludes allowing people to make democratic decisions about matters, such as jobs and benefits, that most affect their lives.

In Japan, after WWII, the US set up the desirable type of system, from the point of view of capital, where a conservative pro-business party was the only party which could actually win elections. This means that in such a "liberal system," a pro-capital party, such as the Japanese Liberal Democratic Party (LDP) is going to end up controlling the system in the interest of US capitalist accumulation.

As has been pointed out by Chalmers Johnson, Japan, South Korea and Taiwan could not have been democratic, even if they had not been so authoritarian, as they were essentially satellites of the United States in the post World War II order, equivalent to the countries of Eastern Europe for the Soviet Union.[33]

The de facto system of "democracy" in the US also means that it eliminates any group or party that would serve to help the poor. Any voices that might militate against the agenda of capitalist accumulation will be eliminated. This is also seen in the approach to Venezuela. When genuine democracy emerges, it must be denied that it is democratic and destroyed. This is the historical pattern. Traditionally, when the masses raise their heads to participate, political scientists in the US have treated this as a "crisis of democracy." It signifies the problem of too many demands on the system or "too much democracy." What this means is that participation of the masses does not serve the agenda of accelerating capitalist accumulation.

Democracy in the Middle East and US National Interests

As noted above, since WWII, the US has operated covert election operations. These essentially subvert "free elections" around the world. This started with Italy after WWII to prevent the Communist Party from coming to power. This activity continues today. It is clear that if the US was really interested in supporting free and fair elections, there would be a sharp break from this standard operating procedure. But it is simply not plausible that the neo-conservatives in Washington would be interested in opening up electoral systems in the Middle East to genuine democracy.[34] As Robert Fisk has pointed out, the US has not tolerated undemocratic regimes. It has actively promoted them for more than 50 years.[35] Given the record and the objectives of the neo-conservatives to control the entire world as the global hegemon, it is simply not plausible that they would take their chances in an area so vital to US national security interests. We can understand this by briefly considering the possible scenario in a number of countries in the region.

Egypt: While the Bush Administration pays lip service to democratic change in Egypt, there is no sign that the US government is serious about opening up the system if it would bring Islamists to power. The US has praised Mubarak for changes, but these have so far been only cosmetic. In the September 2005 Presidential election, some 23 percent of eligible voters went to the polls. Bush called Mubarak and congratulated him on his victory, although the outcome was never in doubt. The White House put out the statement: "This election represents an important step toward holding fully free and fair competitive multiparty elections and both supporters and opponents of the government have told us that it has occasioned a vigorous national debate in Egypt on important issues."

There is not much evidence that the system is actually becoming democratic to a significant extent. The Muslim Brotherhood and the new movement, *Kifayah* (Enough) continue to be suppressed. Muslim Brotherhood protests have been stopped. Hundreds of members and leaders remain in prison, including at least 754 for peaceful protests. Ayman Nour, leader of *al-Ghad* (Tomorrow) was kept in prison for 45 days on trumped up charges. In December 2005, the Muslim Brotherhood won 88 seats in Parliament, some 20 percent of the seats. There were reports that President Mubarak closed the polls in other areas where it appeared that the Muslim Brotherhood might win.

Nevertheless, it is hypocritical for the West to accuse these states of lack of democracy. The West never encouraged democracy when they could have, such as during British control from 1882-1922. The regime engages in "goat barrel politics" and the ruling National Democratic Party (NDP) might still get a majority in fair elections. Even with many unhappy, Egyptians do not want Western interference in the elections.[36]

Iran. In the early 1950s the US overthrew Mohammad Mossadegh, restored Shah Reza Pehlavi to power, and kept the Shah in power until the Islamic Revolution in 1979. The US overthrow was a case of ending a regime which had come to power democratically. Is it plausible that the US will support popular democracy today in Iran, given the level of anti-Americanism?

In the elections of 24 June, 2005, the hard-line former mayor of Tehran, Mahmoud Amadinejad was elected President. Even though there were clear irregularities, it can be seen that this was basically a democratic process, at least as democratic as that in Iraq on January 30, 2005. The US has recently called the Iranian elections "illegitimate." The turn out was more than twice that in Egypt, however. If the candidates are controlled, then by the same token, there is a quite tight controlling of the candidates in the US elections as well. It is true that while there were dirty tricks in the Iranian election and that liberal candidates were disqualified, democracy is working to a significant extent. The poor Muslim masses were mobilized through the mosques and promised greater social welfare from the more conservative clerics. The critical remarks of George W. Bush about the Iranian election also seem to have backfired and increased support for Ahmadinejad. Here again, the result of democracy is the opposite of what Bush and the neo-conservatives wish see.[37]

Israel: The changing nature of the political regime in Israel has been noted by some scholars who argue that it is difficult to refer to Israel as a democracy for a number of reasons.[38] The state of Israel has no constitution. It is democratic by definition, but not when one looks at the actual content and practices in how the system operates. The United States will not demand that democratic reform take place in Israel, which is already rated as a free and democratic state.

Iraq. The US sought to guide a process in which genuinely free elections, which were risky, were avoided. The US was actually in favor of postponing elections until the situation would be less volatile and easier to control. But the US was compelled to go ahead with the January 2005 elections because of Grand Ayatolloh Ali al- Systani. Even so, the US was pressed to control the results, staging a large-scale election rigging operation so that the Shiites would not get an absolute majority and control the writing of the new constitution. In the event, the elections could not be rigged well enough, and the situation was made more difficult for the US. Nevertheless, the US has attempted to capitalize on the results of the election. The de facto situation after the elections has been much worse, in terms of the "insurgency." Resistance to the US occupation increased. It is unknown as to what extent the referendum on the Iraqi Constitution was manipulated in October 2005, but it is well known that the US has pumped hundreds of millions of dollars into the country for the "promotion of democracy." One cannot have a great deal of faith that the elections were "free and fair' to say the least. Elections held under military occupation are not generally considered to be legitimate. It is possible that democratization will lead to the regime becoming a theocracy, and Iraq may break up into three countries.[39] In the December 2005 elections the US spent hundreds of millions of dollars under occupation to promote its favored candidates, namely Iyad Allawi and Ahmed Chelabi. The US balked at allowing al Jaaferi to remain as Prime Minister demanding that he be replaced. Nouri al-Maliki was then chosen as Prime Minister after several months of wrangling without a government. Whether such elections can be considered democratic under the occupation of a foreign power is controversial. Given the level of chaos and violence prevailing in the country, it is difficult to agree with the Bush Administration that the overthrow of Saddam Hussein has resulted in "democracy." Or perhaps, one might at best call it "improvised explosive democracy."[40]

Palestine: The US would not allow elections to be held in the territories as long as Yassir Arafat was living, as he would have won. After his death, the US pushed for "democracy" but had the problem of the popularity of Hamas and the danger of this group winning the election. Nevertheless it was thought that Fatah could win. When elections were held and Hamas pulled off a surprise win, the United States and the Europeans rejected the result and cut off aid to the Palestinians. This threw the Palestinian territories into a crisis. It appeared that the Palestinians were being punished for voting for the wrong party. This was a very instructive case in which the will of the United States and the European Union to support democracy from the ballot box was put in the spotlight and both parties failed to support democracy under the pretext that Hamas would not renounce violence and recognize Israel. On the other hand, it would be unheard of to apply the same test to the Israelis and demand that the Israelis renounce violence and respect equally the democratic rights of the Palestinians.

Saudi Arabia. Would the US be willing to see the system here opened up to genuine democracy? The radical Wahhabis could actually come to power if free and fair elections were to be held. Their base is in the poor and Islamist communities, as well as stretching up into the ruling family. It is not likely that US interests would actually prevail in an election, given the amount of Anti-American sentiment in the region. Elections could well militate against US interests.

According to Milan Rai, in some sense, the Wahhabis are actually in power in the Kingdom as the al-Saud family is the "guarantor and promoter" of Wahabbism around the world. It is the "state religion" and is enforced by "force and largesse." But free elections could also lead to the overthrow of the House of Saud because of corruption. So according to this view, terrorism is not being controlled. It would be too dangerous for the present rulers to open up and allow women to vote and drive.[41]

Pakistan. The US has a long record of supporting military rulers in Pakistan. It must be said that US policy in the region is primarily the cause of the political disintegration of Pakistan today. The Taliban Movement grew out of the Koran schools in Pakistan. Former military ruler Zia-ul-Haq, supported by the US, played a major role in the US organization and sponsorship of the mujahadeen in Afghanistan to defeat the Soviet Union in Afghanistan. This tended to strengthen the Islamists in Pakistan. The US has remained firmly behind the military dictatorship of General Pervez Musharraf, after he seized power on October 12, 1999, who claims that Pakistan is under democratic rule. Prime Minister Nawaz Sharif was arrested and exiled to Saudi Arabia, returning on November 25, 2007.

The late Benazir Bhutto was also living in exile for most of the time since Musharraf came to power. Now the country is seething with opposition to the dictatorship, but the US needs a stable Pakistan to shore up the war against the Taliban in Afghanistan. Osama bin Laden is thought to be hiding somewhere in or near Waziristan and the Pakistani military has fought major battles with Islamist groups in the Swat Valley in 2007. The US claims the right to strike targets in Pakistan and has done so in 2007 and early 2008.

During 2007, President Musharraf maintained a constant struggle against the Pakistan Supreme Court, which he feared would rule against his re-election as President. Chief Justice Iftikhar Chaudhry was dismissed by General Musharraf in March 2007. This action was legally challenged and a 13-member bench reinstated Chaudhry to the Pakistan Supreme Court in July 2007. However, after petitions were brought against Musharraf's re-election, the

General declared a state of emergency on November 3, 2007, suspended the Constitution and dismissed almost all of the Supreme Court judges, including Chaudhry. Leaders of opposition parties were jailed or put under house arrest and some prominent individuals were charged under anti-terrorism measures. After appointing new judges to the Supreme Court, the court ruled on November 20, 2007, to dismiss the petitions against the General.

This cleared the way for President Musharraf's re-election for another term as President by the provincial legislatures. Having won another term, General Musharaf resigned from the military in late 2007 and called for parliamentary elections which were set for January 9, 2008. In the resulting political chaos, former Benazir Bhutto returned to the country to campaign for the Pakistan People's Party (PPP), but was tragically assassinated on December 27, 2007. Elections were rescheduled to be held in early February 2008, but not many believed that conditions in the country would allow these elections to be free and fair.

It is clear that while the US wished to make the regime appear to be moving toward democracy, while maintaining the war against Talibanization in the country, this is a distortion of the real situation. In fact, the country is today one of the most violently anti-American countries. Osama bin Laden is a local folk hero among large masses of the people. People in Pakistan genuinely desire democracy, but free elections in the country are very problematical for the United States and would not likely serve US national security interests. The US and Britain had backed an arrangement between President Musharraf and former Prime Minister Benazir Bhutto which would have allowed the leader of the Pakistan People's Party to become the Prime Minister, while Musharraf would remain President. It is clear that the perceived national security interests of the United States militate the democratic opening of the system and today and genuinely democratic elections would likely bring an Islamic regime to power. Maintaining a pro-US regime in Pakistan, as a nuclear power in the region, is critical from the US national security perspective.

Lebanon. After the assassination of Rafiq al- Hariri on February 14, 2005, the US and Israel demanded that the Syrians be expelled from the country. There was much praise for the emerging democracy, which became known as the "Cedar Revolution." However, democracy in the country had been destroyed in the past, not just by the interference of Syria, but by the invasion of Israel in 1982 that disrupted the country. The difficulty involved the growing power of Hezbollah and the desire of Israel to install a weak puppet government in Beirut. In the summer of 2006, the United States encouraged Israel to wage a major air campaign against Hezbollah in Lebanon as explored in the next chapter. However, the damage to the infrastructure of the country was so widespread and brutal that even many of the Lebanese opposed to Hezbollah were angered by the destruction of the Israelis. The latest Israeli assault on Lebanon destroyed some 20,000 homes and created a million refugees. This attack seems to have backfired and greatly strengthened Hezbollah. By mid-2006, the US and Israel had struck at the two major examples of democracy to have emerged in the Middle East. It seemed at this point that the so called Greater Middle East Initiative was dead, having lost all credibility.

The above examples show that genuine democracy, and the likely results, is unthinkable and unacceptable to the US in most cases in the Middle East. Only a doctrinaire facade of democracy that allows the US to control elections is likely to be acceptable to Washington. On the other hand, in Latin America, and particularly in Venezuela, where genuine democracy has taken place, the US has launched a massive program to destroy this democracy.

The Neoconservatives: Where is the Democracy?

Just how far the US has departed from those who founded the Republic can be seen in a quote from John Quincy Adams. "America is not a nation meant to order others how to live and then push them at bayonet point into that lifestyle. The cost of such a policy would be the loss of America's Soul."[42]

Moreover, recent polls have shown that majorities neither in the US not in the Middle East support the goals of the US spreading democracy to the region. This would question whether the Bush approach, itself, has democratic backing. It simply does not. A poll by the Chicago Council on Foreign Relations and the Program on International Policy Attitudes of the University of Maryland (PIPA), showed that of 808 randomly selected respondents in the US, the following results were obtained. Only 35 percent favored the use of military force to overthrow dictators; 74 percent said that the goal of overthrowing the Baathist Regime and installing democracy was not a good enough reason for war, with 60 percent of Republicans agreeing; 66 percent said that threatening military intervention to bring about democratic change does more harm than good; only 26 percent said that more democracies would make the world safer, only 26 percent believed that Saudi Arabia would be more friendly to the US if it was a democracy; and only 42 percent said democracy, in general would make countries more friendly to the US. While 80 percent said that democracy was the best form of government, only 50 percent believed that it was best for all countries; 33 percent believed that democracy and Islam are incompatible, with 55 percent believing that Islamic countries can be democratic; 54 percent said that the US should not press for democracy if it is likely it would lead to an Islamic fundamentalist government; only 27 percent said that promoting democracy is a very important foreign policy goal, with 49 percent saying it was somewhat important; 75 percent said the US should not spend money to influence elections in its interests (69 percent of Republicans and 83 percent of Democrats); and 68 percent favored working through the UN. When asked how democratic the US is on a scale of 0 to 10, the mean response was 6.2. When asked how much impact the views of the majority have on decisions of elected officials, the mean was only 4.5, but at the same time, the respondents said it should be 8.0.[43]

As another measure of how well democracy is working in the US, 49 out of 57 communities in town meetings in Vermont approved resolutions to withdraw troops from Iraq. Some 53 percent of Americans said the Iraq War was not worth fighting, 57 percent disapproved of Bush's handling of the War, and 70 percent said the US casualties were too high a price to pay. Further, only 8 percent supported a hegemonic role for the US in the world, 70 percent opposed the idea of the US as a world policeman and 57 percent said the US should not have an absolute veto at the UN. Some 60 percent approved of making the UN more powerful. A majority approved of the US joining the International Criminal Court, signing the Kyoto Treaty on Global Warming, ratifying the Nuclear Test Ban Treaty, and ratifying the convention on the ban of land mines.[44] This simply shows that the neoconservative agenda in the US is not supported by a majority.

Moreover, Bush's claim to the legitimacy of spreading democracy is not popular in the Middle East. A recent poll in six Middle East countries showed that 69 percent said that democracy is not the real objective of the US (78 percent on Egypt and 77 percent in Morocco); only 6 percent said that spreading democracy was an important objective and would make a difference; and some 16 percent said that spreading democracy was an important objective but that the US was doing it in the wrong way.[45]

When the 2006 mid-term congressional elections in the United States produced a backlash against the pro-war policies of the Republicans in Congress, George W. Bush reacted by escalating the war under the name "surge." This was hardly a democratic response to the grassroots voice of the people. On the other hand, it did warm the hearts of many CEO's of big American corporations making large profits in Iraq.

Conclusion: Neo-totalitarianism and Global Capitalist Accumulation

The US GMEI for democratization in the Middle East cannot be taken seriously as democracy is incompatible with the central tenets of the ideology of neoliberalism, which is itself essentially a totalitarian system. The neo-conservatives hold that the US must be the global hegemon with no possible rival and that there can be only one possible political and economic system, to which there is no alternative. The recognition of this fact actually means that politics, that is democracy, is actually eliminated for all practical purposes. There can be no democratic struggle over the division of the spoils, as this question has already been settled. If there is no alternative, then there can be no democracy.

Genuinely democratic states of the Middle East, on the other hand, would demand to control their own resources, particularly oil. They would demand autonomy from US and Israeli capital with freedom to run their own economies. In genuinely democratic states, people would be free to oppose political regimes and at the same time, the agendas of Washington, including IMF austerity programs. The United States has shown that it is not comfortable with aspects of democratization in Turkey, or elsewhere, in populations oppose US hegemony.

That the US would tolerate a genuine democracy in the Middle East is actually preposterous and inconceivable. The US neo-conservative agenda is all about controlling global resources and power. Democracy would quite clearly be a threat to this agenda. The GMEI is not about making the

Middle East genuinely democratic, except in rare cases where it serves national security interests. Rather, it is about engineering an alternative to past control through the autocratic ruling elites, which is seen by the US as having outlived their historical usefulness. Therefore we can expect that realism will prevail. Neoliberalism is to be clamped upon the area and the established global institutions brought in to "govern" the region in the interests of the domestic US ruling class. There is nothing the neo-conservatives fear more than genuine democracy.

It is ironic that the neoconservatives have already contributed greatly to the democratization of the Middle East, but in a way that was unintended. By smashing the benign image of the United States which was established after WWII, resistance to Washington has strengthened. The aims of the global superpower have been laid bare as the pursuit of imperialism. This is likely to contribute to the larger movement for democratization around the world today. The Greater Middle East Initiative is not about bringing "democracy" to the Middle East, but precisely the opposite. It is a program to ensure that the only "democracy" to emerge in the region is that which serves the interests of the US domestic ruling class, the corporate or business class.

In a further strike against democracy, US officials schemed with Israeli leaders in 2006 to engineer yet another regime change in the Middle East. First the Israelis would be unleashed to crush Hezbollah in Lebanon. This would be a practice run for the dismantling of Iran and the eventual overthrow of the regime. We not turn our attention to the 2006 Israeli war against Hizbollah in Lebanon.

References

1. Larry Everest, *Oil, Power and Empire: Iraq and the U.S. Global Agenda.* Monroe, Maine: Common Courage Press, 2004.
2. The fascinating past of the CIA is explored in Tim Weiner, *Legacy of Ashes: The History of the CIA.* (New York,

Doubleday, 2007), and Francis Stonor Saunders, *The Cultural Cold War: The CIA and the World of Arts and Letters*. (New York: The New Press, 1999). Chalmers Johnson and Tom Engelhardt, "Agency of Rogues," TomDispatch, July 25, 2007.

3. William Blum, *Killing Hope: U.S. Military and C.I.A. Interventions Since World War II*. Monroe, Maine: Common Courage Press, 2004; William Blum, *Rogue State: A Guide to the World's Only Superpower*. London: Zed Books, 2002; Richard J. Barnet, *Intervention and Revolution: America's Confrontation with Insurgent Movements Around the World*. New York: Meridian Books, 1968. Lawrence S. Wittner has noted how the term "democracy" has been used as a marketing device for policies, such as the Truman Doctrine that would otherwise be difficult to sell to the public. Lawrence S. Wittner, "The Abuse of Democracy," History News Network, Nov. 28, 2005.
4. Eddie J. Girdner, ""The US Neo-Wilsonian Grand Strategy for the Middle East: Subterfuge for Neo-liberal Conquests" *World Affairs*, 10 (3) Autumn 2006, pp. 86-104.
5. Noam Chomsky, *Deterring Democracy*. New York, 1992.
6. Chomsky, *Deterring Democracy;* Blum, *Killing Hope*. See Husam A. Mohamad. "Democracy Promotion in Arab Politics," *Journal of International and Area Studies*, Vol. 14, No. 2, 2007, pp. 103-117.
7. Victor Davis Hanson, "Democracy in the Middle East: It's the hardheaded Solution," *Weekly Standard*, Vol. 8, Issue 6, 21 October 2002.
8. "In Pursuit of Arab Reforms: The Greater Middle East Initiative," Aljazeera-net, 20 May 2004.
9. "Greater Middle East Initiative Working Paper," al-Hayat, 13 Feb. 2004; Tamara Cofman, "The New U.S. Proposal for a Greater Middle East Initiative: An Evaluation," Saban Center Middle East Memo #2, May 10, 2004; Gunduz Aktan, "Latest developments on the Greater Middle East Initiative," *Turkish Daily News,* May 24, 2004; "G-8 Broader Middle East and North Africa Initiative," USINFO, 9 June 2004; Gary C. Gambill, "Jumpstarting Arab Reform: The Bush

Administration's Greater Middle East Initiative," *Middle East Intelligence Bulletin*, Vol. 6, No. 6-7, June/July 2004; "In Pursuit of Arab Reform: The Greater Middle East Initiative," Aljazeera_net, 20 May 2004; Gamal Essam El-Din, "Reformed and Reformulating," *Al-Ahram Weekly*, No. 678, 19-24 Feb. 2004; Robin Wright and Glenn Kessler, "Bush Aims For 'Greater Mideast' Plan," *Washington Post*, Feb. 9, 2004, p. A1; Richard Youngs, "Europe and the Greater Middle East Initiative," *Arab Reform Journal*, April 2004.

10. Nasim Zehra, "The Greater Middle East Initiative," *Media Monitors Network*, March 15, 2004.
11. Richard W. Murphy, "The Greater Middle East Initiative," *Arab Media Internet Network*, April 19, 2004.
12. Pamela and Robert Pelletreau, "Greater Middle East Initiative: A View from Washington," *Arab News,* 29 April 2004.
13. Zeyno Baran, "Getting the Greater Middle East Initiative Right," *The National Interest*, March 3, 2004.
14. *Ibid.*
15. One need but notice how the focus upon Middle East business has become the most prominent thrust in the commercial ads on CNN International television. The image is one of Arabs all over the Middle East dancing to the glories of capital. The lack of social and economic freedom for local populations is, in fact, long forgotten.
16. Gambill, "Jumpstarting Arab Reform."
17. Gamal Essam El-Din, "Reformed and Reformulating."
18. Gambill, "Jumpstarting Arab Reform."
19. "Democratization In The Middle East: Solution or Mirage," *Middle East Review of International Affairs (MERIA)*, Vol. 7, No. 1, March 2003; Richard Youngs, "Europe and the Greater Middle East Initiative," *Arab Reform Journal,* April 2004; Daniel Neep, "Dilemmas of Democratization in the Middle East; The 'Forward Strategy of Freedom,'" *Middle East Policy Council Journal*, 11, (3), Fall 2004. Neep realistically points out that the GMEI provides ideological cover for US "realpolitik" and is about domestic politics, rather than what is good for the region.

20. Hanson, "Democracy in the Middle East." The idea of spreading democracy by the sword, by force and violence, has been challenged by a wide range of comment, including former National Security Advisor Brent Scowcroft. In the words of Michael Scheuer, it is "Pure Wilsonian claptrap." In the case of Bush himself, it appears to be related to his believe that he has been anointed to carry out a divine mission. See Charley Reese, "The Prospect for Democracy in Iraq," Antiwar.com, Dec. 7, 2005; Steve Clemons, "Brent Scowcroft 'Breaks Ranks' with George W. Bush in Major New Yorker Article," October 23, 2005, The Washington Note Archives; Larry Everest, "Lessons of History: Nothing Good Can or Will come from U.S. Occupation," Sept. 21, 2005, ZNET; Michael Scheuer, "Deliberately Desroying America's Soul," April 22, 2005, Antiwar.com.
21. *Ibid.* Juan Cole has pointed out the hypocrisy of Western intellectuals accusing the Middle East of resisting democracy. The West has a history of suppressing democratic urges in the region. Juan Cole, "Bush's War and the Egyptian Elections," Sept. 19, 2005, Salon.com News. Robert Fisk and Justin Podur, "The Great War for Civilization," rabble.ca, Dec. 7, 2005.
22. Philip Agee, "How United States Intervention Against Venezuela Works," *www.zmag.org.*, September 9, 2005.
23. Philip Agee, "The Nature of CIA Intervention in Venezuela," *www.zmag,org*, March 23, 2005.
24. Agee, "How United States Intervention Against Venezuela Works."
25. Agee, "The Nature of CIA Intervention in Venezuela."
26. Philip Agee, "Use of a Private U.S. Corporate Structure to Disguise a Government Program," *www.smag.org*, September 10, 2005.
27. Thomas Patrick Carroll, "Turkey's Justice and Development Party: A Model for Democratic Islam?" *Middle East Intelligence Bulletin*, Vol. 6, No. 6-7, June/July 2004. The notion that the Ak Party could actually want democracy to function is not even taken seriously. For example, allowing the Turkish Parliament to democratically reject the bill for

a US invasion of Iraq from Turkish soil is often explained as due to the "inexperience" of the leaders of the Ak Party. That is seen as a mistake, despite the fact that around 90 percent of the Turkish people opposed the bill. The mainstream US sentiment is that once the leaders get the knack of ruling, the new ruling party will fall into the grove of crushing democracy in the interests of United States. See Alexander Cooley, "Base Politics," *Foreign Affairs*, 84 (6), Nov.-Dec., 2005, p. 84. For Cooley, this democratic decision revealed an "institutional weakness" typical of "young democracies." In this US view, the Turkish Prime Minister was mistaken that it was a 'victory of democracy." Rather, "democracy," in US terms, would have meant going against the will of 90 percent of the Turkish people. It would be difficult to find a better example of how "democracy" for the US is defined as that which serves US national interests.

28. Support in Turkey for joining the European Union was overwhelming in 2002 when the Justice and Development Party came to power. By 2008, the popularity of the European Union had been greatly reduced, with support less than 50 percent, primarily due to the demands made on Turkey on the Cyprus question and the increasing hostility toward Muslims in Europe. Both Angela Merkel and Nicholas Sarkozy were hostile to the idea of seeing a Muslim-majority country in the EU. These hostile attitudes merely served to bolster Turkish nationalism.

29. Samir Amin has noted that Islamist movements have never pursued progressive social reform but rather defend the exploitation by capital. This serves the interests of Western Imperialism. "Political Islam in the Service of Imperialism," *Monthly Review*, 59 (7), December 2007, pp. 1-19. In the case of Turkey, with a low level of education in the country, democratization can most certainly undermine secular institutions, which have been Jacobin rather than popular-democratic.

30. The victory of the Ak Party in the July 2007 elections, in which they increased their vote over 2002, was largely due to the fact that the Party has been successful in stabilizing the economy and has provided some semblance of

government assistance to the poor people in Turkey. For example, the massive construction of housing around the country, and the demolition of shanty towns in the cities, has helped many to get better housing.

31. *Ibid.*
32. George W. Bush has recently called President Hugo Chavez a "threat to Democracy" and a "demagogue." Venezuela has been identified by the Pentagon as a "post-Iraq threat." In November in Brazil, Bush launched an attack on Chavez. Yet, Chavez got 56 percent of the vote in the 1998 elections, some six percent more than Bush in Florida in 2000. Some 56 to 60 percent have supported Chavez in eight elections and referendums, including his reelection. The US recognized the short-lived coup in 2002, headed by Pedro Carmona, head of the Venezuelan Business Association. Chavez, unlike Bush, has used the nation's wealth for social welfare, that is, for the people. Some 1.4 million have learned to read, three million adults have enrolled in schooling projects, thousands of medical clinics have been built, 20,000 doctors have been brought in from Cuba to provide free health care to 70 percent of the population and 60 percent get free food. A chain of 14,000 stores have been created to sell at a 35 percent discount to the poor. This, in US terms, is not democratic and the US is worried that "other leaders like Chavez may emerge." The political parties which boycotted the national assembly election in early December 2005, may have been encouraged by the United States to do so. They were expecting to do poorly at the polls. Roger Burbach, "Bush vs. Chavez," Nov. 11, 2005, ZNET; John Pilger, "The Rise of America's New Enemy," Nov. 10, 2005, ZNET; Elisabeth Bumiller and Larry Rohter, "Bush Targets Venezuela's Chavez in Tough Speech," New York Times, Nov. 6, 2005; Chris Kraul, "Chavez: Ever a Bush Critic, Ever Popular," Los Angeles Times, Nov. 6, 2005; Howard LaFranchi, "Clash of Visions for Latin America," Christian Science Monitor, Nov. 3, 2005; Richard Gott, "Chavez Leads the Way," The Guardian, June 4, 2005; Natalie Obiko Pearson, "U.S. Criticizes Venezuelan Vote," AP, Dec. 6, 2005; Mark Weisbrot and Larry Birns, "Venezuelan Elections," ZNET, Dec. 3, 2005.

33. Chalmers Johnson, *Blowback: The Costs and Consequences of American Empire*. (New York: Metropolitan, 2000).
34. Edward Herman, The Farce of the Bush Pursuit of Democracy Abroad, while undermining it at home," *www.smag.org*, August 26, 2005.
35. Robert Fisk, "How We Denied Democracy to the Middle East," The Independent, 8 November 2003.
36. The Deputy Assistant Secretary of State for the Near East is Elizabeth Cheney, who is Vice President Dick Cheney's Daughter. In a recent trip to Egypt, she stated to Gamal Mubarak (the President's son and leader of the ruling National Democratic Party) that the Bush Administration's commitment to expanding democracy in the Arab world is "Absolute and very firm" and that the US national security is at stake. Now let me get this straight. The son of George Herbert Walker Bush sends the daughter of the US Vice President to talk to the son of Hosni Mubarak about democracy? We can, then, surely all take the proposition that this is about democracy seriously! See Juan Cole, "Bush's War and the Egyptian Elections," Salon.com, Sept. 19, 2005; Nadia Abou El-Magd, "U.S. Official Urges Egypt on Democracy," AP, Sept. 30, 2005; "Egypt's Muslim Brotherhood Seizes increased freedom ahead of polls," The Daily Star, Agence France Presse, Nov. 8, 2005.
37. Stephen Zunes, "The U.S. and Iran: Democracy, Terrorism, and Nuclear Weapons," ZNET, August 31, 2005; Karl Vick, "Political Lines Blurred for Iran Vote," Washington Post, June 16, 2005. Norman Soloman, "From Tehran to Washington, an Axis of Demagogues Just Got More Dangerous," ZNET, Jan. 28, 2005; Nassar Karimi, "Iran's Leader Vows to Aid Iraq Stability," AP, July 17, 2005. Stephen Zunes points out that there are no real competitive elections in Saudi Arabia, Jordan, Egypt, Oman, Kuwait, Bahrain, Qatar, UAE, Pakistan, Uzbekistan, and Azerbaijan. Nevertheless, these regimes have received economic and military support from the US.
38. Michel Warshawski, "The New Israel," *Monthly Review* 56 (7) Dec. 2004, pp. 16-25.

39. Juan Cole, "Thoughts in the Middle East, History and Religion," Informed Consent, Sept. 2, 2005; Dafna Linzer, "U.S. Says it Did Not Carry Out Plans to Back Iraqis in Election," Washington Post, July 18, 2005. Juan Cole points out that the Iraqi Constitution is a serious setback for women and they could yet be subject to Islamic personal law. Linzer reports that Bush authorized covert plans to try to rig the Iraqi elections but that the plans were not carried out. This contradicts the report by Seymour Hersh that the US did carry out a large election operation using retired CIA officers to try to cover their tracks. In any event, the US attempt to get Iyad Allawi elected was a hopeless failure. Perhaps it was a small victory for democracy in the collapse of the US plans.
40. Eddie J. Girdner, "Another Bill of Goods and Democracy," *Turkish Daily News*, Spetember 17, 2007, p. 15.
41. Milan Rai, "Saudi Arabia under the Spotlight," ZNET, Aug. 3, 2005.
42. Michael Scheuer, "Deliberately Destroying America's Soul," April 28, 2005, Antiwar.com.
43. Jim Lobe, "Public Skeptical About Bush's Democracy Crusade," IPS, Sept. 29, 2005.
44. Zia Mian, "American Domination is in Trouble," April 24, 2005, ZNET.
45. "Middle East Not Swayed by Bush's Democracy Pledge," Angus-reid.com, Dec. 7, 2005.

6

The US-Israeli Attack on Lebanon: Imperialism, Zionism and the "New Middle East"

"We will take Lebanon 20 years back."

(Former Israeli Army Chief of Staff, Dan Halutz)

"It is very important to understand that we are not instilling world order."

Israeli Vice Premier Shimon Peres

"One and only one language is spoken by Israel, the language of force." **Gideon Levy**[1]

"...Many would have had the chance of life had Western governments not regarded this dirty war as an 'opportunity' to create a 'new' Middle East by humbling Iran and Syria." **Robert Fisk**[2]

"There will be a new Middle East, but it will be a nastier and messier one."

Aaron David Miller (Former advisor on Middle East to both Democratic and Republican Administrations)

"We would like to return to the old Middle East, because we don't see anything in the new Middle East apart from more problems."

Saud al-Faisel (Saudi Foreign Minister)

Introduction

This chapter will explore the US-Israeli attack upon Lebanon in the summer of 2006 within the context of the ongoing occupation of Palestine by Israel since 1948 and the occupation of the West Bank and Gaza since the 1967 War.[3] The Israeli drive to establish a Jewish religious state, absorb the West Bank into the state of Israel and install a client regime in Lebanon is at the root of the conflict in the summer of 2006.

The exclusivist, racist and confessional state of Israel, based upon the ideology of Zionism, is increasingly bankrupt in the modern world.[4] Such a state is, at root, incapable of being democratic or practicing equality, as it is based upon the "belief that Jews have superior national, human and natural rights in the land."[5] The radical solution to the Israeli Palestinian conflict is the dissolution of Israel as a confessional state and the establishment of a modern secular unitary state in Palestine which would include and grant rights to all individuals to enjoy equal rights and citizenship, including Jews, Moslems, Christians and others, based on their humanity, rather than upon ethnicity or religion. This would enable the Palestinians to claim their just right to return to their homeland from which they were ethnically cleansed by their expulsion and the ongoing Israeli occupation.

However, what needs to be done to address the conflict in terms of a two-state solution is known, and supported by most countries in the world. These remedies include the exchange of prisoners between the Israelis and Arabs, the withdrawal of occupying forces in Palestine, Syria and Lebanon, and the acceptance of the broad international consensus based upon a two-state settlement.[6] The Golan Heights should be returned to Syria and the issue of the Shebaa farms, occupied by Israel, settled. This solution, however, has been unilaterally blocked by the US and Israel for some 30 years.[7] Increasingly, it seems that the situation on the grounds is making a two-state settlement impossible.

The Zionist Movement resulted in the conquest of Palestine in 1948 and 1967 and the dispossession of the

Palestinians of their historic homeland. The ideology of Zionism, however, has changed since the conquest.[8] In the 1948 war, the Israelis took 78 percent of the land of Palestine as it existed under the British Mandate. In the 1967 war, Israel conquered the rest of Palestine. Up until 1967, the settlement of Palestine was based upon the socialist-Zionist vision, while after this the "nationalist-religious camp gained the upper hand. It was "messianic" a "super-nationalist movement" with "fascist fringes." The old socialist camp was "robbed of its vision." With the break down of the kibbutz movement, there was a loss of the original ideology. Many turned to capitalism as the utopian socialist vision weakened. With the take-over of the religious elements, it became "a tribal religion" with the desire to "evict the Palestinian population" and create a "homogeneous Jewish religious state." The right-wing political parties, Likud and Kadima, have come to control everything and the neoconservatives want to jettison all socialist-welfare ideology for a purely neoliberal state.

The present crisis in the state of Israel is between the democratic majority and the settlers, "who represent a theocratic state where rabbis fix the law" very similar to Iran. The religious leadership considers itself above the Parliament and the government. The police and the army tend to support the settlers and will not challenge them. The recent Israeli "withdrawal" from Gaza was intended to gain greater support for the take-over of more of the West Bank.[9] Following the war with Lebanon in 2006, Prime Minister, Ehud Olmert, announced that the "pull-out" from parts of the West Bank had been put on hold and 700 houses would be constructed near Jerusalem.[10] The West Bank is being divided up into Bantustan-like arrangements which could only become a "pseudo-state" dependent upon Israel.[11] Many believe that today Israel lacks the fundamental requirements to be a democratic state, such as equality for all under the law.

Lebanon is one of the most cosmopolitan societies in the Middle East. With such a diversity of people and communities, it has had the possibility of democracy as seen in the "cedar revolution." The population is 35 percent Christian, 35 percent Shiite, 25 percent Sunni and 5 percent Druze. With the recent war in 2006 and the strengthening of Hezbollah, however, religious fundamentalism may strengthen in the society changing the character of the country, largely as a result of US-Israeli policy under the guise of "democratization."

Hezbollah came about as a result of the Israeli invasion of Lebanon in 1982 in order to resist the Israeli invasion. It is also a political party and gets logistical, financial, and military support from Syria and Iran. In its broad social programs, it funds free schools, hospitals, and social programs and is providing up to $12,000 to families who lost their homes in the recent war. With a few thousand fighters, it is the first Arab force which has defeated an Israeli army. Sheikh Hassan Nasrullah assumed the leadership of Hezbollah when the Rabin Government murdered Sheikh Abbas Mussawi and his wife and child with missiles from a US helicopter.[12] It is clear that Israel has long desired to see a client regime installed in Beirut which would serve its purpose of consolidating control of the West Bank in Palestine. It also attempted to ethnically cleanse southern Lebanon by flooding the area with thousands of cluster bombs in the last three days of the 2006 war.

While Israel claims to have ended its occupation of Gaza, this is clearly not the case, as everything continues to be controlled by Israel both in Gaza and the West Bank. A blockade on Gaza was imposed in 2007 after Hamas (Islamic Resistance Movement) under Prime Minister Ismail Haniyeh took over rule.[13] The recent attacks on Gaza by Israel have constituted "collective punishment" which is illegal and the cutting of funds and closures have created a humanitarian crisis among the 1.3 million population.[14] This has been noted by Jan Egelund, Undersecretary General for Humanitarian Affairs at the United Nations. Targeted assassinations continue along with the destruction of the civilian infrastructure. The situation which arose in July 2006 was a political crises linked to the failure of Israeli unilateralism. There is no semblance of treating the 3.9 million Palestinians in "the world's largest prison camps" as a people with human and civil rights under international law.[15] According to the World Court, the Israeli settlements are illegal, as is the separation wall, which Israel continues to build. This is a violation of international humanitarian law. Moreover, Israel continues to pursue a West Bank expansion plan as noted above. Israel controls the water and all critical resources in the West Bank. The destruction of the physical infrastructure of the Palestinian Government and society has been ongoing with practically every building built with European Union funds having been reduced to rubble by the Israeli onslaught. According to Noam Chomsky, the Israelis want to "consummate long-standing plans to eliminate Palestinian national rights for good."[16]

In fact, the US and Israel have proceeded to punish the Palestinians for carrying out the "fairest elections in the Arab world" on January 25, 2006. The results, in which Hamas, the Islamic Resistance Movement won, have been "sabotaged" by Washington. While the US had called for democratic elections, the US and Israel were shocked when Hamas won. Hamas is an offshoot of the Muslim Brotherhood Society in Palestine and was established by Sheikh Ahmad Yasin in 1988. The US State Department has designated both Hamas and Hezbollah as foreign terrorist organizations and is unwilling to recognize a coalition Palestinian government controlled by Hamas.

While it is often stated correctly that Israel "has a right to defend itself," the Palestinians are not perceived by Israel and the United States as having the same right. Lacking any armed forces for self defense, and under siege, the

Palestinians are jailed for simply defending themselves in whatever manner they can. There are thousands of Palestinians in Israeli jails. Meanwhile large expansions of the settlements are ongoing in the West Bank, under the pretext of withdrawal. Israel and the United States have never been willing to address the refugee issue from 1948,[17] when the Palestinians were ethnically cleansed to make way for the Israeli settlers. The struggle to get the truth to the American people has proved to be all but impossible given the existing political situation in the United States.

It is clear that politics in Palestine has been based upon "terrorism" dating from the arrival of the Israeli settlers in 1948 and continuing. The rise of resistance to the settlers led to the founding of the Palestinian Liberation Organization (PLO) and Hamas. That Israel is a state which has used terrorism massively from the beginning is not normally recognized in the international arena. The rise of Hamas as a religious-based organization, using "terrorism" to defend itself, is simply a reaction to massive Israeli state terrorism. Further, the Israelis promoted Hamas in the past to weaken the secular nationalist Palestinian movement, which posed a threat to Zionism and its absolute control over the Palestinians and other Arabs. Thus in many ways, Hamas, in its significant religious obscurantism, is but a reflection of the religious obscurantism of Zionism, the basic religious ideology of the state of Israel. Both are anachronistic but feed upon the American-Israeli imperialist thrust to rule the Middle East. The radical future solution can come about only with the transcendence of both Islamic and Jewish religious obscurantist ideologies based upon progressive humanism.

Ongoing Mayhem in Iraq

In the second half of 2005 and the first half of 2006, the US occupation in Iraq continued to lurch from crises to crises as Iraqi society continued to disintegrate under the presence of the American military, with more than 130,000 troops. While a new constitution was put into place in late 2005, after a referendum on October 15, 2005, the new law tended to be regressive particularly in terms of the rights of women. While the draft constitution was approved by 78.6 percent of the Iraqi population, 97 percent of the population of Sunni Anbar Province voted against the document and 82 percent voted against it in Sunni Salahuddin Province.[18] Parliamentary elections were held on December 15, 2005, but a government could not be formed until May 20, 2006. Nuri al-Maliki, a Shiite, was chosen as Prime Minister after the US put pressure on Iraq not to reelect Ibrahim Jaaferi. Even with a new government in place, however, larger numbers of people continued to die in the widespread violence. The "peace" and "democracy" promised by the American rulers failed to materialize and the country moved toward civil war with increased numbers of sectarian killings.

On February 22, 2006 (Black Wednesday), the Imam Hasan al-Askari shrine in the holy city of Samarra was destroyed by a large bomb. It was one of the holiest Shiite mosques in Iraq, along with Najaf and Karbala, and connected to the "Hidden Imam" or "the Mahdi." Its large dome with 72,000 gold pieces and its light blue tiles were destroyed.[19] Hundreds of Iraqis died as Sunni mosques were attacked around the country in retaliation, even though Shiite cleric Ali al-Sistani called upon the Shiites not to attack Sunnis in revenge. The attack was quickly blamed upon Abu Musab al-Zarqawi by US Ambassador, Zalmay Khalilzad. The Prime Minister Ibrahim al-Jaaferi concurred. Some saw the bombing as a possible "apocalyptic moment" for the Mahdi Army of Shiite cleric Moqtada al-Sadr. At least 29 Sunni Mosques were burned across Iraq.[20] That al-Zarqawi was responsible was not proven, but the attack, perhaps intended to set off religious tension, sparked the onrush of sectarian killings which would only spread in the coming months as the hot summer months approached. The US occupation forces and Iraqi security forces were not able to control the various militias and death squads which operated throughout the country.[21]

The formation of a new Iraqi government some four months after the election, under increased pressure from the US, did little to stem the tide of increasing violence. The Iraqi Interior Ministry was widely believed to be responsible for part of the death squad activity. Nor did the death of al-Qaeda in Iraq leader, Abu Musab al-Zarqawi on June 8, 2006 do anything to stem the mayhem.[22] In fact the US venture in Iraq, it seemed, was turning into the greatest folly and disaster in history, surpassing that of the Vietnam War in the 1960s. Many began to see the Iraq failure as a major blow against US prestige and the US image which would last for at least a decade. The "war on terror" was seen more and more as a shibboleth for imposing US imperialist rule.[23]

Between May and June 2006, some 6000 Iraqis had died in the violence. In Baghdad alone, 1850 people were killed in Baghdad. Across the country, the figure was running to at least 100 a day in the summer of 2006. While the Bush Administration continued to claim that democracy had been brought to the country, more and more people began to make the rather obvious observation that most Iraqis would have been better off under Saddam.[24] A Pentagon study, "Measuring Security and Stability in Iraq," showed that casualties in Iraq had risen 51 percent in recent months. From May 20, 2006, when the new government was formed, up to August 11, 2006, the average number of weekly attacks was 800. This was double the number of attacks in early 2004. By August, 2006, casualties among Iraqi citizens and security forces reached 120 per day up from 30 a day two years ago. But now more of the attacks were against civilians and were sectarian, between Sunnis and Shias. More of the killings were execution style. President Bush tried to present a strong case for progress, but 12,000 additional troops were sent to Baghdad, including 7000 additional American troops. In Anbar Province alone, there were some 30 attacks a day. But many police were simply leaving the job.[25]

By September 2006, the US President was claiming that the decisive ideological battle of the twenty-first century would be decided in the streets of Baghdad and comparing the "terrorists" to Hitler. This grasping at straws reflected the desperation of the Bush Administration. It was not the "insurgency" in Iraq, which was in its "death throes" as Vice-President Dick Cheney would have it. Rather, the Iraq War itself was in its death throes. As is now recognized by the political establishment in Washington the United States has lost the war in Iraq.[26] The only question was how to break the news to the American people. After the Congressional Elections in November 2006, Rumsfeld was fired and a new strategy devised which called for sending more troops to Iraq to get control of the situation in the capital.

Meanwhile, the twin occupations of Iraq by the Americans and Palestine by the US-Israeli combine continued to drive politics in the Middle East. While US intervention had proved a disaster in Iraq and was increasingly failing in Afghanistan, many of the neo-conservatives seemed anxious to move on to yet another war against Iran. President George W. Bush appeared to believe that Iran would be the definitive criteria for the success or failure of his Presidency.

Israel in the United States

Many commentators have noted the "attention deficit" of Americans toward Israel.[27] Rather we must acknowledge the actual situation which prevails in the United States, in which many Americans do not know the real situation in Palestine and in which there are critical and sometimes Christian fundamentalist religious orientations which shape people's thinking. On the one hand there are the Zionists in the Bush Administration and among the Jewish community who believe that it is necessary to go to war against Hezbollah, Hamas, Iran and Syria to eliminate any threat to the ideology of Zionism.[28] On the other hand, are the Christian fundamentalists, who believe that chaos in the Middle East is a "sign" given by God and that it will lead to the rapture by which they will be taken up to heaven.[29] There are a number of clear reasons for this. Early in 2006, a debate raged in the US intellectual establishment over an article on the American-Israeli Political Affairs Committee (AIPAC).[30] The thrust of the article, which really revealed nothing shocking, was documentation about how the Jewish lobby in the United States shapes US foreign policy in the Middle East. But in the United States it is politically taboo to even mention certain facts which everybody knows to be true. The Israeli lobby is so powerful that practically no member of the US Congress dares to vote against its wishes for fear of being targeted and defeated at the polls. AIPAC gives in depth briefings to every candidate running for the US Congress and they are asked to write a position paper. This is generally readily provided by AIPAC. This produces much of the policy that makes up Israel's "lifeline."[31] This helps to account for the Jewish organization's influence over Congress. Anyone, however, who even mentions this fact is targeted and blasted by nasty attacks from the organization and its high profile supporters.[32] Many people have written about this, including Noam Chomsky.[33] Harvard Law Professor, Alan Dershowitz, accused the authors of the article of taking some of their information from neo-Nazi web sites. The article pointed out that since the October war in 1973, US aid to Israel has totaled over $140 billion in 2004 dollars, currently exceeding three billion dollars a year. This amounts to 20 percent of the total US foreign aid budget and $500 for every Israeli citizen.

AIPAC was recently involved in a scheme apparently to spy on the United States, preparing for an attack on Iran by Israel.[34] AIPAC was helping to plan the attack and it was reported by *Haaratz* that an Israeli Embassy official knowledgeable about the affair was sent out of the US to avoid federal prosecutors.

Certain Bush Administration neoconservatives have been arguing for an attack on Iran for some time,[35] a "forward strategy" against Iran. But it appeared that in 2005, the US may have decided against an attack on Iran, at least for the time being, since the Iraq operation was going so badly. Bush indicated that the US would support Israel and the US would not stand in Israel's way if the UN talks became deadlocked.[36] The US has not had diplomatic relations with Iran since 1980. The Administration may have considered going to "Plan B," a proxy attack on Iran by Israel. It had been reported that Ariel Sharon gave an authorization for an attack on Iran in July 2005. It was also reported that Israel practiced in the desert at a mock-up site to destroy the Iranian Natanz Uranium enrichment plant using commando units and air strikes dropping bunker busting bombs.

In this context some classified documents were reportedly leaked to Israel by AIPAC by the deputy of Douglas Feith,[37] Larry Franklin. Franklin worked in the Office of Special Plans (OSP) run by Feith. OSP was actually a "shadow" intelligence service on Iran providing information which would justify the attack. Feith was formerly the Undersecretary of Defense for Policy. Franklin was later indicted on five counts of spying for apparently passing the documents to AIPAC and they were later passed on to Israel. He was arrested in May 2005. Two others from AIPAC were also indicted, including a founder of AIPAC, Steve Rosen, who built the organization into a $40 million organization. Although Rosen resigned, he is considered to be still closely involved with running the organization.[38]

Given this situation, it is difficult to see how US foreign policy in the Middle East could be changed in the short run.

Moreover, the driving force behind US policy in the region is the need to control resources and markets for US and Israeli corporations. While there is wide criticism of public policy in the Israeli press, this is not true in the United States, which largely pays the bill and underwrites Israeli actions on the ground.

Why the Israeli push for war in 2006?

The US-Israeli attack on Lebanon in July 2006 was planned in advance in Israel and Washington. According to Seymour Hersh, the Israelis told Condoleezza Rice in early summer, 2006, that they needed 35 days to crush Hezbollah. Washington was anxious for the Israelis to get the job done and urged that it be carried out quickly as the Bush Administration would have only two more years left to take care of Iran.[39] The strike on Hezbollah installations was apparently seen as a test run for a coming US attack on Iran.

The Israeli occupation of Palestine has long been a part of US hegemony in the Middle East. Today Israel serves essentially as a US military base in the region. The ethnic cleansing of Palestine, known among Palestinians as al-Nakba, the "catastrophe," began in 1948.[40]

After Hamas won the election on January 25, 2006, the US and Israel announced that the Palestinian people would be punished. Funds were cut off from the Palestinian Authority.[41] The US Senate passed a bill which would block aid to the Hamas government. While under justice and international law, the correct approach would have been to recognize the Hamas Government this would not be done under the circumstances.[42] Demands were made on Hamas that it must renounce terror, honor previous accords and recognize Israel as a Jewish state. However, similar demands have never been applied to Israel in relation to the Palestinians. Israel has violated all the requirements of the Oslo Accords of 1993. According to these agreements, a

Palestinian state was supposed to come into existence after five years, but Israel has continued to colonize Palestinian land.

On the part of Hamas, Prime Minister Ismail Haniyeh has said that the Party will not play the same old game of bowing to US and Israeli demands, but rather honor only those accords which serve the interests of the Palestinian people. This seems reasonable enough if equality in principle and practice were to be accorded to both sides. Israel has certainly never recognized the right of the Palestinians to exist and wishes to destroy any organization or state in the region which genuinely represents the Palestinian people. The position of the Israeli government is also not democratic, since some 62 percent of the Israeli people said they favor negotiations with Hamas. The US and the EU seem to be discrediting their advocacy of democracy by not honoring the democratic choice of the people.[43] Attempts to make an agreement between and Fatah leader Mahmoud Abbas (Abu Mazen), President of the Palestinian National Authority, and a member of Fatah, to form a new coalition government failed and could not have been supported by Washington.

The first large scale Israeli invasion of Lebanon was carried out in 1982 for the purpose of installing a puppet government in Beirut. The aim of attacking Hezbollah in 2006 was again to crush Hezbollah and accomplish the goal of establishing a client regime in Beirut. This goal goes back to the effort of David Ben-Gurion in 1955, to install a Christian officer as President, which was not possible at the time.[44] Moreover, the strengthening of Hezbollah represents a threat to Israeli security should the United States or Israel carry out a preemptive strike against Iran. It is clear that the plans for the strategic bombing operation in Lebanon had long been prepared.

In 1982, Secretary of State Alexander Haig, told Ariel Sharon that he needed a "clear provocation" that would be accepted by the world to carry out the attack on Palestinian camps in Lebanon. This was provided by the attack by Abu Nidal in London in an attempt to assassinate the Israeli Ambassador, Shlomo Aragov. In July 2006, the pretext which would trigger the war was the Hezbollah capture of the two Israeli soldiers on July 12, 2006 as ordered by Hassan Nasrallah.[45] In 1982, Sharon succeeded in installing Bashir Gemayel but Gemayel was murdered soon after this. Subsequently, his brother, Amin Gemayel, signed a peace treaty with Israel but was driven out of office. Gemayel again supported the Israeli operation. In 2006, the Israelis believed that the population of Lebanon would be angry with Hezbollah and that Israel could set up a regime favorable to Israeli interests. This is ironic since the Lebanese government at the time had been set up under American pressure after the "Cedar Revolution" in 2005.

Another goal of the operation was to restore the Israeli Army's pride.[46] Ilan Pappe has pointed out that nothing can satisfy the Israeli generals except the total destruction of Lebanon, Syria and Iran. On the other hand, the IDF has detested the Intifadas in 1987 and 2000, because such movements produce "low intensity conflict" which is difficult to deal with and wastes the military's training for large-scale war. Moreover, a war of occupation is not winnable. A real war was needed including "shock and awe" to restore the officers' confidence. Good news came for those who wanted to bomb when the Israeli Foreign Minister, Tzipi Livni, said that the best way to retrieve the two captured soldiers was to destroy the Beirut International Airport and then bomb all the roads and bridges in the country.[47] This, in addition to being a violation of international law, clearly could not succeed.[48]

Beginning of the War

The shelling of Gaza had been going on for quite some time with illegal arrests, which shows that the claim of

Israeli withdrawal was fictitious. Gaza remained under Israeli occupation. By 2006, there had been a ten month siege of Gaza following 39 years of Israeli occupation of the territories since 1967. Up until this time, 176 Palestinians had been killed in 2006, many of them civilians and children. Only 16 Israelis had been killed in the same time period. Some 8300 Israeli shells had been launched into Gaza while the Palestinians had fired 840 home made Qassam rockets toward Israel. While the Palestinians were holding one captured Israeli soldier, Israel was holding 9000 Palestinians in prisons, many civilians with no due process of law and under torture. These procedures are a violation of the Geneva Convention of 1949. Some 64 Hamas leaders, most of them democratically elected had been arrested. Many are Palestinian Authority Ministers and elected members of the Palestinian Legislative Council (PLC). The program of land seizure for settlements on the West Bank continues and is being expanded.[49]

The world had just been shocked by the death of the family of Huda Ghalia, 11, who became a symbol of the Israeli brutality in the Gaza Strip. She had seen seven members of her family killed when an Israeli shell landed[50] on the beach where they had gone for an outing.[51] While this shelling and destruction was going on in Gaza the western press claimed that the "opening event" took place on June 25, 2006. This was the capture of an Israeli soldier, Corporal Gilad Shalit, near the Gaza border. The Palestinians carried out the raid through a tunnel at Karem Shalom, an Army post, killing two Israeli soldiers in a tank and capturing Corporal Shalit. From this army post, the Israelis had fired hundreds of shells into Gaza, killing 30 civilians. The Western press referred to the incident as "a major escalation in cross-border tensions."[52] Nevertheless, the escalation was actually by Israel which reentered the Gaza strip with tanks on June 28, killing 50 Palestinians.[53] There were also bombings in Gaza and the Palestinian Foreign Ministry was bombed a few days later.

Nevertheless, the day before Israeli forces seized two Gaza civilians, a doctor and his brother who were sent to an Israeli prison with no charges. As reported in *The Observer* on June 25, "a team of Israeli commandos entered the Gaza strip to "detain" two Palestinians Israel claims are members of Hamas." They were in fact kidnapped, as Chomsky points out, which is a worse crime than the capture of soldiers. The raid was a violation of Palestinian control of the territory.[54] The major media did not report the event, giving only some short comments.[55] This bias in the press has been noted.[56] Israeli Prime Minister Ehud Olmert said he wanted "no one to be able to sleep in Gaza tonight" due to nocturnal "sound bombs" made by jet fighters breaking the sound barrier. This constitutes "collective punishment" and is a violation of Article 33 of the Fourth Geneva Convention. Again, the leading US newspapers, the *New York Times,* the *Washington Post,* and the *Los Angeles Times*, did not report Olmert's statement but supported "Israel's right to retaliate after the capture of an Israeli soldier."[57] Israel attacked and destroyed Gaza's only electrical power plant, also in violation of international law and left the territory in the dark. This also disabled the water pumping stations. The Palestinian Interior Ministry was bombed along with the Prime Minister's office and a school. Fighter jets were sent over the Presidential Palace in Damascus. The Israeli Defense Forces dropped leaflets from the air warning the civilian population in Gaza to follow their orders. Children were killed by missiles fired into residential areas. Some 4000 homes had been demolished since 2000 in Gaza and the West Bank and hundreds of acres of olives destroyed.[58] Prime Minister Ismail Haniyeh pointed out that the Israeli strategy to turn the infrastructure into rubble was designed to destroy the results of the free and fair elections held in January 2006 and that the capture of Corporal Gilad Shalit was merely a pretext. After 50 years of US support to Israel of some $160 billion, Hamas held the "fairest elections in the Arab world" and these results have met with "sabotage" from the White House. There are some 3.9 million in the territories, which Haniyeh called the "world's largest prison camps." If Israel has a right to defend itself, then the same right should be recognized for the Palestinians.[59]

In fact, it is clear that at this point Israel was looking for a pretext to carry out the long-planned attack upon Lebanon in order to weaken Hezbollah and force the Lebanese Government to do its bidding. It is recognized that the root conflict is the Israel-Palestinian conflict, and the continued battle for the West Bank. It is also clear that the US Government was closely involved in the planning for the attack. President Bush and Vice-President Cheney wanted to go after Hezbollah by bombing the underground missile and command sites and control complexes in Lebanon. There were consultations with the Israelis in the Spring of 2006. The US was interested in knowing how to successfully hit underground facilities, that is "hard targets," in preparation for bombing nuclear installations in Iran. Iranian engineers had advised Hezbollah on the tunnels and underground facilities. The campaign in Lebanon would serve as a demonstration run for the hoped-for attack on Iran.[60] It is ironic that the result of the Lebanon operation was almost the opposite of that which was expected.

The Pretext and War

On July 12, Hezbollah crossed from Lebanon into Israel capturing two Israeli soldiers, Ehud Goldwasser and Eldad Regev, and killing three soldiers.[61] It may have been that the activity by Hezbollah was intended to force Israel to fight on more than one front at once, relieving pressure on the Palestinians. Five more Israeli soldiers were killed in the pursuit into Lebanon. Hezbollah also destroyed an Israeli tank. The raid was called "an act of war" by Prime Minister Ehud Olmert and he warned that Hezbollah would pay a heavy price. It was clear, however, that the incident was nothing more than a pretext which Israel had been anxiously awaiting, similar to the incident that led General Ariel Sharon to invade Lebanon in 1982. For Hezbollah, it was expected that there would be a prisoner swap and Hassan Nasrallah did not expect that the action would trigger a large-scale bombing campaign against Lebanon.[62] Residents of south Beirut fired guns and distributed sweets in celebration of the capture. At the Ein el-Hilweh Palestinian refugee camp in Beirut, fireworks were set off. Israel proceeded to order residents in northern Israel into bomb shelters. Meanwhile, 60 Palestinians had been killed since the capture of Corporal Gilad Shalit in Gaza as Israel continued to attack the territory by night.

Israel commenced a large-scale bombing raid on Lebanon, beginning with bombing bridges on the Litani River and Beirut Airport.[63] The main Lebanese army air base in eastern Lebanon was also bombed along with Rayak Air Base in the eastern Bekaa Valley. Israel also bombed the Hezbollah TV station, al-Manar TV, and a transmission antenna near Baalbek but failed to put the station off the air. The civic center at Baalbek was also bombed. A one-fourth ton bomb was dropped on a house in Gaza killing 7 children and two adults. The Palestinian Foreign Ministry building was also bombed, apparently in an effort to exterminate all Palestinian government institutions.[64] Israel continued to bomb Lebanon from land, sea and air and this would go on for 34 days. Prime Minister Olmert said that he "held the government in Beirut fully responsible" and would not negotiate. The attack on Lebanon was presented to the outside world as an attempt to get the two soldiers back, but this was not taken seriously. It was obviously the launch of the long-planned US-Israeli attack to destroy the infrastructure in Lebanon. It was well known from the beginning that the two Israeli soldiers would be returned only by negotiation and a prisoner swap. Israel also sent tanks short distances into Lebanon, placing soldiers in the range of Hezbollah rockets. Hezbollah fired Katyusha rockets into northern Israel continuously, many reaching Haifa and causing injury and death, but doing very little damage compared to the massive pounding of Lebanon by the Israel Air Force.[65] Egyptian President, Hosni Mubarak, attempted to mediate for Corporate Shalit's release. The efforts came to nothing and were "sabotaged" while Palestinians were demanding the release of 1000 Arab and other prisoners for the captured soldier.[66]

Dan Halutz, Israeli Army Chief of Staff, said that "nothing is safe" in Lebanon and that the road to Damascus would be cut, which indeed happened shortly as oil jumped to around $76 a barrel in international markets.

After a call for a halt to Israeli attacks two days later, US Secretary of State Condoleezza Rice said that a cease fire should be put off until "the conditions are conducive."[67] It was clear that the Bush Administration would stall to allow the Israelis to "finish the job." The Democrats in the US called on the US to "defuse the crisis," but the preset plan was clear. Rice declared, "A cessation of violence is crucial, but if that cessation is hostage to Hezbollah's next decision to launch missiles into Israel or Hamas's next decision to abduct an Israeli citizen, then we will have gotten nowhere."[68]

From the US perspective, Syria and Iran were responsible for the "kidnapping" of the two soldiers captured by Hezbollah. Bush stated: "My attitude is this: There are a group of terrorists who want to stop the advance of peace."[69] This continued to be the US line. A statement from a White House spokesman read: "The United States condemns in the strongest terms this unprovoked act of terrorism, which was timed to exacerbate already-high tensions in the region and sow further violence...We also hold Syria and Iran, which directly support Hezbollah, responsible for this attack and the ensuing violence."[70] Assistant Secretary of State, C. David Welch, said Iran and Syria's hand is in all of these crises, referring to Palestine, Lebanon, Syria and Iraq. Welch accused Hezbollah of planning the crisis to "escalate and widen the battlegrounds."[71] Another hard-core statement was made by Robert Malley, director of the International Crisis Group's Middle East Program. "Here you have actors who are basically pariahs who are trying to find their way back in. They're doing it the way they know best...brinksmanship... The common tactic in each case is daring defiance by Iran... They want to change the rules of the game." The western press continued to serve the US Administration by tying the crisis to Iran[72] as the number of Palestinians killed since the capture of Corporal Gilad Shalit rose to 71.

Refugees began to pour out of Lebanon into Syria, some 15,000 in the first few days after the bombing began, crossing the border to safety. There was no electricity in Lebanon and water and many bridges were out with large numbers of civilians dying from the bombing. Some 100 missiles had been fired into northern Israel so far[73] and the number would rise to almost 4000. Airports, roads, petrol stations, electrical plants, oil storage depots, factories, and light houses were all targets of the bombing. The ports of Beirut, Tripoli, Jounieh and Ansheet were bombed. In Beirut, the nine-story Hezbollah headquarters was destroyed. Some Christian areas were bombed too. A van fleeing from Marwaheen Village was hit by an Israeli bomb, killing 20, and there were many other events of this kind. In the first four days of bombing, some 103 people were killed, all except four being civilians, while only four Israelis were killed.[74] Efforts were being made by some foreign embassies to evacuate tourists but these efforts were hampered by Israel's assault and blockade on air, sea and land transportation.

In for the Long Haul

In the first five days of the war, Hezbollah fired some 400 rockets into Israel as the bombing continued.[75] It became clear early on that Israel was planning several weeks of "precision bombing" a classical strategic bombing campaign to take the infrastructure of Lebanon apart and inflict as much damage as possible on the country. It was calculated that this would make the Lebanese people upset with Hezbollah for triggering the war and result in a more pro-Israel government. These calculations were incorrect and were to badly misfire. In fact, precisely the opposite happened as Israeli planes continued to pound Lebanon day after day.

It also became clear early on that the Bush Administration was set to back Israel all the way, stonewalling on requests from Lebanese Prime Minister Fuad Siniora, the European Union, and other countries for a cease fire. British Prime Minister Tony Blair in England also backed the US and Israel all the way as did Stephen Harper, Prime Minister of Canada.[76] The European Union proved to be relatively irrelevant, as the Europeans called for an immediate halt to the Israeli strikes at the G-8 meeting in St. Petersburg. A statement was issued from the G-8 that said: "These extremist elements and those that support them cannot be allowed to plunge the Middle East into chaos..We call upon Israel to exercise utmost restraint." Dan Bartlett, Counselor to US President Bush, said that "Israel needs to concentrate carefully on targets clearly linked to Hezbollah."[77] Perhaps, but this clearly was not what the Israelis were doing.

Hezbollah was to be eliminated as a "security threat," badly damaged but not completely destroyed. The US-Israeli plan was to "strangle" Syria, Iran, Hezbollah, and Hamas, which were seen to be "trying to change the playing field." That is, they were seen as daring to act in self defense, as is their sovereign right, but a right clearly not recognized by the US-Israel combine and within Zionist ideology. Defense of their own interests was unacceptable. Therefore those who rose to resist Zionism would have to be crushed under the order of US global hegemony.[78] The war in Gaza continued with 103 Palestinians killed since the Israeli invasion on June 28.[79]

After the first week of the war, Israeli Defense Minister Amir Peretz announced that Israel would need two more weeks to finish the war against Hezbollah and suggested that a land offensive might be launched.[80] The Lebanese Army of some 70,000 seemed to be nowhere, the defense of the country being carried out almost entirely by the Hezbollah fighters.

After the first week of war, many began to question the massive bombing and ask whether such a strategy would succeed. As a "classical strategic bombing campaign" some military analysts considered that it might not be possible to succeed without a land offensive.[81] It was pointed out that there were generally no links between the targets being hit and Hezbollah. On the other hand, there were many civilian casualties creating one million Lebanese refugees. All persons in the south were ordered by Israel to get out which was often impossible with the roads destroyed and fleeing vehicles being shelled and bombed. Along with bridges, roads and ports, the Liban Lait milk factory on the road to Baalbek was bombed.[82] Also facilities such as dairies and cold storage depots were pounded with Israeli bombs.

The United States officials apparently continued to believe that they could rely upon their conservative Sunni Arab allies to back them against the "hegemonic Persian threat,"[83] the fear of the increasing power of the Shiites across the Middle East. According to a senior Israeli official, the "cross border raid" by Hezbollah" created a "unique moment" with a "convergence of interests among Israel, some Arab regimes and even those in Lebanon who want to rein in the country's last private army."[84] In the words of Israeli Ambassador, Daniel Ayalon, "We'll have to go for the kill..Hezbollah neutralization."

With Bush in St. Petersburg, Stephen Hadley, the US National Security Advisor, talked about the need to implement UN Security Council Resolution 1559 which called for Hezbollah to be disarmed. A US official talked about a "natural dynamic to these things," as if it was out of the hands of the US government. "They do have space to operate for a period of time. There's a natural dynamic to these things. When the military starts, it may be that it has to run its course."[85] However, there was nothing natural about the destruction of Lebanon. As journalists pointed out, the United States had gone for a "battlefield plan" with "diplomacy redefined by the war on terrorism." In the last Israeli offensive in April 1996, a ceasefire agreement had been reached much earlier after 150 Lebanese had been killed.[86]

One of the worst incidents of the war happened in South Lebanon in the village of Qana, where a massive bomb was dropped on a building from an Israeli aircraft, killing 54 Lebanese civilians, including 37 children.[87] The civilians had taken cover in the basement of the building. It was the same village where Israeli shells killed up to 120 refugees in April 1996.[88] Later a United Nations report concluded that the incident was unlikely to have been the result of an accident as claimed by the Israelis. It appears that many of the civilians did not leave the area due to Israeli bombing and shelling of vehicles on the roads, which was observed by journalist Robert Fisk. Prime Minister Siniora continued to demand an immediate cease fire, but with no results from the Israelis or Americans.

Some observers have concluded that the Israel tactic of flooding southern Lebanon with cluster bombs in the last 72 hours of the war before the ceasefire on August 14 can only be described as a campaign of ethnic cleansing.[89] The United Nations has determined that some 250,000 Lebanese are unable to return to their homes, either due to unexploded cluster bomblets, or because their homes were destroyed. Some 90 percent of the cluster bombs were dropped at the end of the war when it was clear that a cease fire resolution was already in the works. Israel was trying to depopulate the area as much as possible. It was not clear how long such a racist strategy perpetrated by the neo-conservatives in Israel and Washington could prevail. But the Lebanese were determined to resist. This makes it clear why Hezbollah is so popular in Lebanon. At the end of the war, 78.7 percent of Lebanese believed that Nasrallah had made an excellent performance during the war.[90] A large amount of depleted uranium munitions was left behind to pollute the country and Israel refuses to supply the map showing where land mines have been planted. In the end, most Lebanese put the blame not on Hezbollah but on the United States and Israel.[91]

Israel signaled that it was prepared to violate the cease fire in future as it carried out an illegal commando raid, in the village of Boudai, west of Baalbek, apparently in an attempt to kidnap Sheikh Mohammed Yazbek a member of the Shura Council, the highest decision-making body of Hezbollah.[92] Israel claimed that the raid was carried out for the purpose of preventing arms smuggling to Hezbollah,[93] which was not credible. One Israeli officer was killed in the failed raid. The community center in the center of the town had been bombed at the beginning of the war. The local people confronted the Israelis and drove them out. Israeli Defense Minister Amir Peretz said that they were preparing for the "next round."

Approximately 4000 of the 13,000 rockets owned by Hezbollah were fired into Israel during the war. In the West Bank, it was business as usual, as the Palestinian Deputy

Prime Minister, Nasar al-Shaer, was seized at his home and illegally held by the Israelis.[94]

The Aftermath of the War

The cease fire came into effect on 14 August 2006. Robert Fisk wrote that this was when the "real war" would begin.[95] After 34 days of destruction, Lebanon lay in ruins, the longest Israeli war since 1949. More than 1300 Lebanese citizens had been killed and more than a million refugees displaced from their homes. Some 37 Israeli civilians and 117 Israeli soldiers were killed. There were 425 Israeli soldiers wounded.[96] The number of Hezbollah fighters killed has been estimated at around 500, although Hezbollah claimed only about 60 were confirmed killed.[97] Billions of dollars of damage had been done with no hope that Israel and the United States could be held accountable and made to pay reparations to the small poor country, even though the war was a clear violation of international law as stated by the UN humanitarian official, Jan Egelund. This was true, even though the US and the Israelis were morally and politically culpable and clearly guilty of major war crimes against Lebanon. It was estimated that five to ten billion dollars would be needed to rebuild the country. Almost everything built up in the last twenty years was turned to rubble. Fuad Siniora called the war "barbaric." Maronite leader, Emile Lahoud, the President of Lebanon, seen as linked to Syria, believed that Israel wanted a civil war. The south was now called by some as "Hezbollistan."[98]

The UN Security Council passed Resolution 1701 on 11 August 2006 which, among other things, called for a cessation of hostilities by Israel and Hezbollah, the deployment of Lebanese troops and United Nations Interim Force in Lebanon (UNIFIL) forces in Southern Lebanon, the extension of the control of the Lebanese Government over all Lebanese territory, the "disarmament of all armed groups in Lebanon," and the deployment of some 15,000 UNIFIL troops to Lebanon.[99]

The Israelis and the Americans were clearly not happy with the results of the war.[100] Prime Minister, Ehud Olmert, said to be humbled, had promised a "new Middle East."[101] The consensus was that Israeli lost the war.[102] The IDF came in for wide criticism across the board in Israel. The planning of the IDF for the war was a failure. The bombing campaign could not succeed and backfired.[103] The military began to blame the government for stabbing them in the back, while Olmert claimed that the government had approved everything the military had asked for. The lack of planning for what would happen to the fleeing civilians in Lebanon and the defense of Northern Israel was also criticized. The famed Merkava tank was shown to be very vulnerable to Hezbollah rockets.[104] The IDF performance was "primitive, brutal, unsophisticated." By late September 2006, Prime Minister Olmert's popularity rating had dropped to some 22 percent with large-scale demands for his resignation.

To some extent the loss could be attributed to the inflated ego of General Dan Halutz, Israeli Chief of Staff.[105] The positive side of Israel's loss was that it might make the Americans see that there was "no advantage of pushing Israel into military ventures," show that the IDF power is limited, and that a new less violent policy is needed.[106] The IDF had rejected an international force in Lebanon before the war but was now in a position of needing it for protection from Hezbollah. Some commented that Ariel Sharon would not have made the mistake of fighting such a "foolish war."[107]

The White House, however, characteristically claimed victory.[108] The neoconservatives again clamored for a war with Iran saying that whether Iran is defeated will be the crucial "test of the Bush Presidency."[109] Some of those groups lobbying for accelerating a war with Iran attacked the war against Hezbollah as not being pursued with enough force.[110]

Others argued that the real question was not who won, but who lost the most. With the US push for "democratization" essentially dead, Islamist groups had been strengthened.[111] The domestic political repercussions in Israel would deal with the failure of Prime Minister Olmert and Chief of Staff, Halutz. The Kadima Party was badly damaged politically and was expected to fall, although this did not happen. The moral image of Israel had already fallen to, perhaps, its lowest level ever.

With the mission to get rid of Hezbollah now defeated, some suggested that it was possible that the US would change its policy and now talk to Syria.[112] There has been no formal dialogue with Syria since George W. Bush has been in office. This would make possible a deal on the Shebaa Farms issue, which Lebanon claims, and could address the issue of the Israeli occupation of the Golan heights. Essentially no efforts have been made in this regard. However, a delegation from Syria was invited to the Annapolis Conference in the last week of November 2007.[113]

The cease fire also came too late to salvage the image of the United States and Britain in the Arab world after their stonewalling on a cease fire for almost five weeks.[114] In the Arab view, the US and Israel had become one country, a perceptive and fairly accurate observation. Many Arab states had decided that "friendship with the United States is worth little because the United States will back Israel no matter what..."[115] Nor would the US again be trusted as an "honest broker." The Arabs ridiculed the line of US Secretary of State, Condoleezza Rice, that the world was seeing the "birth pangs of a new Middle East" in the war. Further, the war had clearly weakened those states, such as Lebanon and Egypt, which had attempted to accommodate US pressures for democratization. Instead, it was the fundamentalists who benefited. The US and Israel now appeared weak with no chance of disarming Hezbollah, the unlikely prospect of extending Lebanese control to the South, and the lack of incentive for Israelis to negotiate with the Palestinians for peace. And the war had strengthened Iran and "severely impaired the chances of freeing the Middle East of the threat of an Iranian Revolution."[116] Even the states that condemned Hezbollah at the start of the war, Egypt, Saudi Arabia, Jordan, and Bahrain, rallied to Nasrallah's support.[117] King Abdullah of Saudi Arabia remarked: "If the peace option is rejected due to the Israeli arrogance, then only the war option remains, and no one knows the repercussions befalling the region, including wars and conflict that will spare no one, including those whose military power is now tempting them to play with fire."[118]

Nevertheless, it was clear that the aftermath of the war had "enormous political significance to the Middle East."[119] The "unique moment" which was to have restored Israeli invincibility had resulted in exactly the opposite. The weakness of the Israeli army had been exposed in being unable to overcome the few thousand Hezbollah fighters with a massive air assault and more than a month of war while the reputation of Hezbollah soared across the Arab world. In the last days, the Israelis had lost some 40 soldiers in 36 hours. Israeli soldiers became easy targets of Hezbollah fighters and they could not reach the dead crew of a helicopter which had been shot down. Moreover, 33 of the Israeli soldiers died in a foolish and futile attempt to get a picture of the Israelis on the banks of the Litani River, after the war had essentially ended.

In the west, the "root of the problem" was seen to be Hezbollah, as a "terrorist organization," while the 18 year Israeli occupation of South Lebanon and the 39 year occupation of Palestine was forgotten.[120] The Lebanese Government had aligned itself with the US and France before the war in opposing Hezbollah. After the war support for Hezbollah rose to 87 percent in the country. With the brutal pounding of residential areas in Lebanon and with one-third of the victims being children, the targeting of northern Israel with Katyusha rockets came to be seen as justified. With the bitter anger against the US and the UK, the Lebanese Government would not be able to act against Hezbollah. The war crushed any chance that the US would be perceived as interested in promoting democracy in the Arab world.[121] The US and Israel had pursued a racist approach that assumed that Arabs only understood force and such blanket support for Israel proved to be a disaster.[122]

Robert Fisk reported the story from Southern Lebanon the day after the fighting stopped. As the Lebanese began to dig their dead out of the rubble of the villages, the vulnerability of the Israelis on the ground was exposed. In the village of Srifa, which had been reduced to rubble, some 26 trapped corpses were found. Nevertheless, Hezbollah was seen as victorious. The village Mukhtar, Hussein Kamel el-Din and the local people, saw the Hezbollah fighters as heroes[123] and proud that Hezbollah fought Israel to a draw.[124] The Israeli Army had retreated from the area unable to penetrate the smashed town of Khiam where the village Mukhtar was found dead in the ruins of his home. In Roueiss 13 bodies of civilians were found, including seven children and a pregnant woman. Fisk saw only one tank outside Bint Jbeil, the area empty of armor, with the Israel Army retreating even from the safe Christian town of Marjayoun. Bint Jbeil had been taken three times as the Israelis failed to drive out the Hezbollah fighters. Fisk believed there were no more than 1000 Israeli soldiers left in all of Southern Lebanon and the 30,000 Israeli army, spoken of in the press, had never existed. It proved a mistake for Israel to send troops, some 10,000, in on the ground where the Hezbollah fighters were waiting hidden in caves, basements and tunnels. In three hours, 20 Israeli soldiers were killed making the Israeli Army appear impotent. At one village there was a poster of Nasrallah and Iranian President Ali Khamenei at the village entrance.[125] The massive exodus from Beirut began, people returning to their villages, carrying Hezbollah flags and pictures of Sayed Hassan Nasrallah. Songs were being composed in his honor all around the Arab world.

The task of digging corpses out of the rubble began in South Beirut and all across the south. Lebanese soldiers, Hezbollah and local people joined in where dead families were trapped, with the Lebanese Red Cross on the scene and civil defense personnel trying to save lives. In South Beirut, local people said they could still hear the screams of neighbors trapped beneath the rubble. Some people tried to retrieve personal items such as photo albums. Hezbollah attached banners to the rubble reading "Made in USA." One resident stated that he could live without walls but he must first have his freedom. Freedom, in this case, meant freedom from the destruction of his country by the US and Israel.

Disarmament of Hezbollah

Clearly, Hezbollah would not submit to disarmament, nor was it reasonable to do so, given the regional and global dimensions of the problem.[126] An internal Lebanese Army statement called for Lebanese troops to stand with Hezbollah. The Army has seen Hezbollah as a "legitimate national defense force" since 1996. Also the Lebanese share military intelligence with Hezbollah. In the words of Rami G. Khouri, "Hezbollah's arms should be assessed in the wider domestic, regional and international context in which they exist and operate."[127] As for the Cedar Revolution, it may have been killed as the war has greatly weakened Lebanese Prime Minister Siniora.

On the other hand, Hassan Nasrallah gained new stature and began to sound more like a prime minister after the war. Practically the whole country was crazed in his support when the Israelis failed to overcome the guerrillas. Disarming could not be a viable question with Hezbollah having the "multiple roles" of resistance movement, Islamic movement and political party and also being an integral part of Lebanese society. Hezbollah won two seats in the cabinet and held 14 seats in the Parliament in the last election. This strength could easily increase now that Nasrallah is by far the most popular politician in the country. The Arabs across the Middle East are no longer willing to suffer defeat as they have for decades at the hands of the Israelis backed by the billions of dollars and weapons from the United States.[128] In Lebanon, those who did not want to live under Hezbollah lost, realizing that the Israeli way of dealing with the fundamentalist group had badly backfired.

Later in a statement, Nasrallah said that he would not have ordered the capture of the two Israeli soldiers if he had known that it would lead to a devastating war.[129] By the end of August, 2006, negotiations were under way for the exchange of prisoners to resolve this part of the issue. The war in Gaza continued. The population was under siege from Israel and hardly able to find enough to eat.[130]

Conclusion

The US-Israeli attack on Lebanon was an attempt by Israel to implement the neo-conservative strategy laid out in 1996 to bring about a "new Middle East" with a strengthened Zionist Israel. It was also an attempt to carry out a practice run for the coming attack upon nuclear facilities in Iran desired by US President George W. Bush and the neo-conservatives in Washington. In a larger sense, the attack was a further attempt to ethnically cleanse the area of all those who would dare to defend themselves from Israeli Zionist hegemony and US imperialism. The United States and Great Britain shamefully demonstrated to the world how little it honors the values of democracy, equality, human rights and civil rights which it continues to preach. The trust of the United States in the Arab world sank even lower, alienating the government of Lebanon and other governments in the region. US foreign policy and the Israeli Zionist ideology were shown to be bankrupt. Some considered the possibility of the disintegration of Israeli society under the conflict between those who valued democracy and a nationalist religious and belligerent right.

At the same time, the mighty Israeli military, bloated by tens of billions of dollars funneled into the country from US taxpayers, mostly from the working classes of America, was humbled by a few thousands courageous Arab fighters who claimed the right to defend themselves. All of the goals of the neoconservatives in Israel and Washington failed. The two captured soldiers will be returned only through negotiations and a prisoner swap, as was well understood before the war. Hezbollah was not defeated, but emerged in a stronger position. The UNIFIL forces in Lebanon, unwanted by Israel, would now restrict Israel's ability to unilaterally carry out strikes against Lebanon. The bankrupt ideology of Zionism, it its angry and futile fury, was exposed to the world as a brutal and bullying force which hates democracy, equality, fairness and the rights of Palestinians and other Arabs.

It is not yet clear at this time if the neo-conservatives in the Bush Administration will learn the lesson and decline to attack Iran after the failure of the Israeli military to reduce Lebanon to a subservient client state. The neoconservatives in the United States were already barking up a different tree, arguing that the Israel-launched war failed not because of Israel's hubris but because of its timidity, that is the failure to push the attack hard enough.[131] Part of their argument was that Israel risked losing its relationship with the United States if it failed to eliminate Hezbollah as a threat to Zionism. Charles Krauthammer, a leading neoconservative, argued that Hezbollah is the "leading edge of an aggressive nuclear-hungry Iran." Johan Goldberg of the National Review argued for a large ground campaign into Lebanon. Max Boot, at the Council on Foreign Relations, who previously praised the United States for exceeding Hitler's war prowess in the push to Baghdad in 2003, argued that Israel needed to destroy

Syria and to secure its borders. Meyrev Wurmser, another prominent neoconservative, argued in the National Review online that Israel should hit both Syria and Iran. Meyrev Wurmser is the director of the neoconservative Hudson Institute Center for Middle East Policy and is married to David Wurmser, who is a top advisor to US Vice-President Dick Cheney.

The US-Israeli war on Lebanon raised tensions in the Middle East and made the world a more dangerous place. The "war on terrorism" yet again was setting the stage for more terrorism as the neoconservatives recklessly pursued global hegemony through imperial wars.

An important aspect of US imperialism in the Middle East and elsewhere was the environmental dimension, particularly, the polluting of countries with the scourge of depleted uranium from the type of weapons which have come to be used by military forces around the world. It is will be useful to understand this as a genuine, but largely ignored, weapon of mass destruction in its own right which the US has used more massively than any other country, killing unknown hundreds of victims. Iraq is the foremost example of such destruction which will persist for thousands of years. These developments are explored in Chapter Seven.

References

1. Gideon Levy, "Operation Peace for the IDF," *Haaretz*, July 17, 2006.
2. Robert Fisk, "Lebanon's pain grows by the hour as death toll hits 1300," *The Independent*, 17 Aug. 2006.
3. The literature on the Israeli-Palestinian question is vast. Useful background can be found in Maxime Rodinson, *Israel and the Arabs*, Middlesex, Penguin, 1968. Noam Chomsky, *Fateful Triangle: The United States, Israel and the Palestinians*. Cambridge, Ma., South End Press, 1999. Edward W. Said, *The Politics of Dispossession: The Struggle for Palestinian Self-Determination 1969-1994*. New York, Pantheon Books, 1994.

4. Kathleen Christison, "The Moral Bankruptcy of Israel's Founding Idea: The Coming Collapse of Zionism," *Counterpunch*, Sept. 12, 2006. A confessional state is a state based upon a religious ideology, such as Israel and Iran.
5. Christison, "The Moral Bankruptcy of Israel's Founding Idea." It is interesting that the practice in Israel is to deny essential civil rights based upon religion, which would be outlawed in the United States. On the other hand, the US is the primary sponsor of the state of Israel which perpetrates such discrimination. However, this is not widely understood in the United States, especially among the Christian supporters of Israel.
6. Noam Chomsky and Kaveh Afrasiabi, "On Israel, Lebanon and Palestine," August 12, 2006.
7. Chomsky and Afrasiabi, "On Israeli, Lebanon and Palestine."
8. Martin Buber, *Paths In Utopia*. Boston: Beacon Press, 1958. The last chapter, "Epilogue: An Experiment That Did Not Fail" explains the utopian socialist vision for the communal Kibbutzim movement.
9. Uri Avnery and Tikkun, "Interview" *Tikkun*, Sept. 11, 2005. Avishai Ehrlich, "Israel's Religious Right and the Failure of the Peace Process," *Monthly Review* 53 (5), October 2001, pp. 16-30.
10. Amy Teibel, "Olmert backs of from West bank pull-out with settlement plan," *The Independent*, Sept. 5, 2006. Such settlement is a violation of international law. There are 240,000 settlers on the West Bank and 2.4 million Palestinians.
11. John J. Simon, "Palestinian Geography and the Peace Process," *Monthly Review* 53 (5), October 2001, pp. 30-34.
12. Chomsky and Afrasiabi.
13. The leader of Hamas, Khaled Mashal is living in exile in Damascus.
14. Patrick Cockburn, "Gaza is a Jail. Nobody is allowed to leave. We are all starving now," *The Independent Online*, 9 Sept. 2006. Meron Rapoport, "When rockets and phosphorus

cluster," *Haaretz,* Sept. 14, 2006. On January 23, 2008, Hamas blew down the border between Gaza and Egypt at the Rafah crossing (with bombs) allowing Palestinians to flood into Egypt to buy food, medicine, fuel and other necessities. In a week, they had brought back some 150 million dollars worth of goods. The situation illustrated the real extent to which the territory really is a prison for the million and a half occupants with the Israeli-US blockade. However, the US was conspicuously silent, only demanding, along with Israel, that the Egyptians close the border. The border with Egypt was closed on February 3, 2008, after 11 days, with Hamas demanding closer links with Egypt for fuel and electricity. The US and Israel reject control of the border by Hamas since it would imply recognition of Hamas rule in Gaza.

15. Phyllis Bennis, "The Gaza/Lebanon Crisis: Escalating Occupation and Danger of New Border Fighting," Institute for Policy Studies, July 17, 2006. Ismael Haniyeh, "Aggression Under False Pretenses," *Washington Post*, July 11, 2006.
16. Chomsky and Afrasiabi.
17. Haniyeh, "Aggression Under False Pretenses."
18. Kenneth Katzman, "Iraq: Elections, Government, and Constitution," CRS Report for Congress, Congressional Research Service, June 15, 2006.
19. Sam Knight, "Al-Askariya shrine not just a major cathedral," *World Times Online*, Feb. 22, 2006.
20. Dam Murphy, "Attack deepens Iraq's divide," *Christian Science Monitor*, Feb. 23, 2006.
21. Sami Moubayed, "Payback time in Iraq," *Asia Times Online*, Feb. 25, 2006.
22. Patrick Quinn, "Reports: Iraq's al-Qaida chief dead," *Associated Press*, June 8, 2006.
23. Andrew Greeley, "Arrogance, ignorance, invite disaster," *Digital Chicago, Inc.*, Aug. 11, 2006. It has been widely acknowledge that the so-called US "war on terrorism" is actually responsible for breeding terrorists.

24. David Corn, "Better Saddam Than Dead," *TomPaine.com,* Aug. 16, 2006.
25. Michael R. Gordon, "Iraq Casualties Have Risen 51 %, U.S. Study Finds," *New York Times*, Sept. 2, 2006.
26. Robert Dreyfuss, "Iraq's Reality Sinks In," *TomPaine.com*, September 8, 2006. A fact that this author has been arguing since November 2004.
27. Paul Craig Roberts, "Attention Deficit Americans Are Being Misled to War," *Antiwar.com*, July 15, 2006.
28. Stephen Zunes, "The United States, Israel, and the Possible Attack on Iran," Foreign Policy in Focus, *www.zmag.org*, May 2, 2006. While the national intelligence estimate is that it would take Iran at least 10 years to develop a usable nuclear weapon, and Iran has no capacity to deliver a delivery system in the near future, the Bush Administration argues that it is justified in striking Iran under the doctrine of pre-emptive war, by which they actually invoke the principle of preventive war. It is alarming that it appears that George W. Bush believes that Iran must be dealt with before the end of his presidency in January 2009. The line being taken by most of the Democrats is equally threatening and hostile to a diplomatic approach. It is seldom mentioned that the under the Shah, Iran had a program to develop nuclear weapons actively supported by the United States. Similar to Iraq, the dangerous consensus emerging in Washington is that the only answer to the problem is "regime change."
29. Roberts, "Attention Deficit."
30. John Mearsheimer and Stephen Walt, "The Israel Lobby," *London Review of Books*, vol. 28, No. 6, 23 March 2006. John Mearsheimer and Stephen Walt "Is It Possible to Have a Civilized Discussion About the Role of Israel in American Foreign Policy?" *Counterpunch.org*, May 5, 2006. John J. Mearsheimer and Stephen Walt, *The Israel Lobby and U.S. Foreign Policy* (Farrar, Straus and Giroux, 2007). Michael Massing, "The Storm Over the Israeli Lobby," *The New York Review of Books*, Vol. 53, No. 10, June 8, 2006. Grant F. Smith, "Where Did AIPAC Come From?" Antiwar.com,

October 9, 2007. This battle continued to rage through 2007 with at least one prominent academic, Norman Finkelstein, having been denied tenure at Depaul University for discussing the issue of human rights violations in Israel and the blocking of diplomacy in Israel, in his book: *Beyond Chutzpah: On The Misuse of Anti-Semitism and the Abuse of History* (Univ. of California, 2007). Harvard Law professor, Alan Dershwoitz, tried to stop the publication of the book, threatening a libel suit and writing to the Governor of California. The absurdity is profound, no doubt, but indicates the level of paranoia in the US and the fragility of the situation, should the truth spread widely to the American public.

31. John Walsh, "Look What You've Done: AIPAC Congratulates Itself on the Slaughter in Lebanon." Aug. 16, 2006. In a letter to friends and supporters, AIPAC declared: "Only one nation in the world came out and flatly declared: Let Israel finish the job. That nation is the United States of America and the reason it had such a clear, unambiguous view of the situation is you and the rest of American Jewry."
32. Rosa Brooks, "Criticize Israel? You're an Anti-Semite," *Los Angeles Times*, Sept. 1, 2006.
33. Noam Chomsky, "Comments on Dershowitz," *www.zmag.org*, Sept. 6, 2006.
34. Doug Ireland, "The Real AIPAC Spy Ring Story...it Was All About Iran," August 7, 2005.
35. Richard Perle, et.al., "A Clean Break: A New Strategy for Securing the Realm," *http://www.israeleconomy.org/strat1.htm*, June 1, 1996. This Israeli strategy paper proposed a "new Middle East," possibly the source of the phrase as it is used by the Bush Administrations like Condoleezza Rice in which Israel would increase its hegemony. The recommended strategy would be for Israel to scuttle the "Peace Process," overthrow Saddam Hussein, get Turkey and Jordan to help curb Syria, launch pre-emptive strikes against Syria, Iran and Hezbollah in Lebanon, stress greater independence from US policy, engage in "hot pursuit" of Palestinians, and curry greater favor with the US Congress.

36. On the George W. Bush Administration's policies toward Israel, see Husam A, Mohamad, "The Bush Administration and the two-state solution," in Jamil Hilal (ed.),*Where Now for Palestine: The Demise of the Two-State Solution* (Zed Books, 2007).
37. A prominent neo-conservative in the Bush Administration.
38. Ireland, "The Real AIPAC Spy Ring Story"
39. Seymour M. Hersh, "Washington's interest in Israel's War," *The New Yorker*, Aug. 21, 2006. While the Mearsheimer Walt article was weak in its analysis of the political economy of oil and power, arguing that the support of Israel was a liability for the United States, the article was courageous in broaching a practically taboo subject in American politics and academia. Stephen Zunes, "How Washington Goaded Israel," ZNET, August 25, 2006.
40. See Noam Chomsky, *Fateful Triangle*. Sandy Tolan, "The Palestinian Catastrophe, Then and Now," *Tom Dispatch*, July 10, 2006.
41. Aaron D. Pina, "Palestinian Elections," Congressional Research Service, The Library of Congress, February 9, 2006. Out of the 132 seats in the Palestinian Legislative Council, Change and Reform (Hamas) won 74 seats. Fatah Party won only 45. Khaled Meshaal, the head of Hamas is living in Damascus. A Hamas Government was formed in March 2006, but lost funding. If a Hamas-Fatah government comes about, it is not clear if it would be recognized by Israel and the United States. Rory McCarthy, "Palestinian PM says talks close to conclusion," *The Guardian*, Sept. 5, 2006.
42. Tanya Reinhart, "The Hamas Government Should Be Recognized," *Yediot Aharonot*, June 1, 2006. Even Jimmy Carter said the elections were honest and fair.
43. Reinhart, "The Hamas Government Should Be Recognized."
44. Uri Avnery, "The Real Aim."
45. Uri Avnery, "The Real Aim," Gush Shalom, July 17, 2006. Ilan Pappe, "What Does Israel Want?" *Electronic Intefada*, July 17, 2006.
46. Avnery, Pappe

47. Pappe, "What does Israel Want."
48. Interview with Wolf Blitzer, Late Edition, Sept. 17, 2006. Livni claimed that Israel was only trying to get at the infrastructure which served Hezbollah. But the bombing was so massive and wide ranging that much of what was destroyed could not be construed to be related to Hezbollah. Rather, the infrastructure of the entire country was being taken apart.
49. Patrick O'Connor, "Crisis in US Media Coverage of Gaza," July 5, 2006, www.zmag.org.
50. Jonathan Cook, "Kidnapped By Israel: The British Media And The Invasion of Gaza," *Media Lens*, July 7, 2006. Critics of the press noted that the language used by the Western press was the same as that used by Israel. The British media took the view that the occupation is finished, but everything is under Israeli control. The Israelis were said to "detain" Palestinians while the soldiers were "kidnapped," not captured. The seizure of Palestinian officials is referred to as "arrest' or "detention," while the Israelis have to legal jurisdiction over Gaza. Clearly they were taken as bargaining chips. Israel was also said to "round up" Hamas politicians, as if they were cattle.
51. Stephen Farrell, "Girl who saw family die on beach becomes icon and media celebrity," *The Times*, June 13, 2006.
52. BBC, June 25, 2006.
53. "50,000 Turks Protest Israeli Invasion," *Zaman.com*, July 9, 2006. The demonstration was organized by the Fazilet Party (Happiness Party), an Islamic political party in Turkey.
54. Cook, "Kidnapped by Israel."
55. Chomsky and Afrasiabi
56. Patrick O'Connor, "Crisis in US Media Coverage of Gaza," July 5, 2006, www.zmag.org
57. *Ibid.*
58. Sandy Tolan, "The Palestinian Catastrophe, Then and Now," *Tom Dispatch,* July 10, 2006. Ismail Haniyeh, "Aggression Under False Pretenses," *Washington Post*, July 11, 2006.

59. Haniyeh, "Aggression Under False Pretenses."
60. Hersh, "Washington's Interest in Israel's War."
61. Noam Chomsky, "Noam Chomsky: U.S. Backed Israeli Policies Pursuing End of Palestine; Hezbollah Capture of Israeli Soldiers 'Very Irresponsible Act' that could lead to Extreme Disaster," *Pacifica Radio*, July 14, 2006.
62. "Hezbollah leader says he wouldn't have ordered the capture of two Israeli soldiers knowing it would lead to such a war," *BostonHerald.com,* August 27, 2006. Prisoner swaps took place in 1985 and 2004. In 1985, 35 Israeli soldiers were traded for 1150 Lebanese and Palestinian prisoners. In 2004, 436 Arab prisoners and the bodies of 59 Lebanese fighters were traded for an Israel civilian and the bodies of four Israeli soldiers.
63. Sam F. Ghattas, "Israeli Warplanes attack Beirut airport," *Associated Press*, July 13, 2006.
64. Amos Harel, "IAF planes bomb PA foreign ministry building in Gaza City," *Haaretz*, 13 July, 2006.
65. Scott Wilson, "Frustration in Northern Israel," *Washington Post*, July 13, 2006.
66. "Israel bombards Lebanon after Hezbollah seizes two soldiers," *Agence France Presse*, July 12, 2006.
67. Hersh,
68. Bruce Knowlton, "Rice Says Israel May Need to Prolong Offensive." *International Herald Tribune*, July 16, 2006.
69. Sam F. Ghattas, "Israeli Warplanes attack Beirut airport." Bush apparently does not realize that this statement could just as well apply to groups other than those he had in mind.
70. Rex Nutting, *MarketWatch, Inc.*, July 12, 2006.
71. In fact, the war came as a surprise to Hezbollah, while it was Israel and the US which had planned to widen the battlefield.
72. Steven Erlanger, "Sign That Crisis is Regional, Not Just Israel vs. Palestinians," *New York Times,* July 13, 2006. Robin Wright, "Options for U.S. Limited As Mideast Crises Spread," Washington Post, July 13, 2006. This article noted

that of the three regional crises: Hamas-Hezbollah, Iran and the Iraq civil war, "a common thread in the three crises is Iran." It was not mentioned that another common thread was the U.S. The US press was filled with such propaganda statements apparently taken as objective. Another charge was that Hezbollah was "provoking a military confrontation with Israel to show that without Syria Lebanon will retreat to anarchy." Iran was accused of trying to divert attention from its nuclear program. Richard Beeston, "Hezbollah Supports Watch from the Wings", *The Times*, July 13, 2006.

73. Dahr Jamail, "Lebanon Refugees Speak of Catastrophic Bombing," *Inter Press Service*, July 15, 2006.
74. Laila Bassam, "Israel kills 34 civilians in strikes," *Reuters*, July 15, 2006. David Hirst, "Israel's monstrous legacy brings tumult a step closer," *The Guardian*, July 14, 2006.
75. Dahr Jamail, "Fleeing Lebanese Speak of Indiscriminate Bombing," *Inter Press Service*, July 17, 2006.
76. Greg Albo, "The Israeli Military Assaults, The Crisis in Lebanon and Canada," *The Bullet,* July 17, 2006.
77. Brian Knowlton, "Rice Says Israel May Need to Prolong Offensive."
78. Robin Wright, "Strikes Are Called Part of Broad Strategy: U.S., Israel Aim to Weaken Hezbollah Regime's Militants," *Washington Post*, July 16, 2006. Pepe Escobar, "Leviathan run amok," *Asia Times* Online, July 19, 2006.
79. Craig S. Smith, "Israeli Tanks in Central Gaza; Fighting Is Fierce," *New York Times,* July 19, 2006.
80. Amos Harel and Ari Issacharoff, :IDF: We need two weeks to end Lebanon operation," *Haaretz,* July 20, 2006.
81. Jim Krane, "Military analysts question Israeli bombing," *Associated Press*, July 20, 2006.
82. Pepe Escobar, "Lebanon left for dead," *Asia Times Online*, July 21, 2006. Sam F. Ghattas, "Israel tightens noose around Lebanon," *Associated Press*, July 17, 2006.
83. Jim Wright, "Military Analysts Question."
84. Jim Wright, "Military Analysts Question."

85. Jim Wright, "Military Analysts Question."
86. Jim Wright, "Military Analysts Question."
87. "Israeli raid in Lebanon kills 54," *Reuters*, July 30, 2006. Martin Asser, "Qana makes grim history again," *BBC News*, 31 July 2006.
88. Robert Fisk, "Massacre in Sanctuary: Eyewitness," *The Independent*, April 19, 1996.
89. Kathleen Christisen, "The Moral Bankruptcy of Israel's Founding Idea."
90. "Most Lebanese hail Hezbollah chief for war conduct," *Agence France Presse*, Sep. 7, 2006.
91. Emile Lahoud, President of Lebanon, United Nations, General Assembly, Sept. 21, 2006.
92. Lauren Frayer "Lebanese town full of Hezbollah fighters," *Associated Press*, Aug. 20, 2006. Nadim Ladki, Israel Strikes Hizbollah Stronghold," Aug. 19, 2006.
93. "Israel defiant on Lebanon raid, prepares for 'next round'", *Agence France Presse*, Aug. 20, 2006.
94. Nadim Ladki, "Israel Strikes Hizbollah Stronghold."
95. Robert Fisk, "As the 6am ceasefire takes effect..the real war begins," *The Independent*, 14 Aug. 2006.
96. Robert Fisk, "Lebanon's pain grows by the hour as death toll hits 1300," *The Independent*, 17 August 2006.
97. Joshua Brilliant, "Hezbollah's Recovery Timetable," *The Washington Times*. Sept. 7, 2006.
98. Jon Lee Anderson, "Has Israel's assault weakened Hezbollah or made it stronger," *The New Yorker,* Aug. 7, 2006.
99. United Nations, Security Council Resolution 1701 (2006), S/RES/1701 (2006).
100. Robert Fisk, "Desert of trapped corpses testifies to Israel's failure," *The Independent*, 15 August, 2006. Patrick J. Buchanan, "Olmert's War, and the Next one," Antiwar,com, Aug. 15, 2006. John Walsh, "Look What You've Done: AIPAC Congratulates Itself on the Slaughter in Lebanon," Aug. 16, 2006. Anne Gearan, "Analysis: Pact Won't improve U.S.

image," *Associated Press*, Aug. 12, 2006. Robert Fisk, "Lebanon's pain grows by the hour as death toll hits 1300," *The Independent,* 17 Aug. 2006.

101. Uri Avnery, "From Mania to Depression," Antiwar.com, Aug, 18, 2006,
102. Justin Raimondo, "Israel Defeated," Antiwar.com, Aug. 14, 2006. Dan Rabinowitz, "The pitfalls of machismo," *Haaretz*, Aug. 17, 2006.
103. Uri Avnery, "The Buck Stops Where?" Antiwar.com. Aug. 12, 2004.
104. Uri Avnery, "What Has Happened to the Israeli Army?" Antiwar.com, Aug. 14, 2006.
105. Avnery, "What has Happened."
106. Gideon Levy, "To Failure's Credit," *Haaretz*, Aug. 14, 2006.
107. Avnery, "The Buck Stops Where."
108. That it was not a victory for Israel was confirmed by the Winograd Commission Report in January of 2008. Among other things, the report stated: "Overall, we regard the 2nd Lebanon War as a serious missed opportunity. Israel initiated a long war, which ended without its clear military victory. A semi-military organization of a few thousand men resisted, for a few weeks, the strongest army in the Middle East, which enjoyed full air superiority and size and technology advantages." "English Summary of the Winograd Commission Report," *New York Times*, Jan. 30, 2008. This report, in fact, largely concealed the real disaster that the war represented.
109. Buchanan, 'Olmert's War"
110. John Walsh, "Look What You've Done: AIPAC Congratulates Itself on The Slaughter in Lebanon," Aug. 16, 2006.
111. Leon Hadar, "And the Loser Is..Everyone," *TheGlobalit.com*, Aug. 24, 2006.
112. David Nason, "US changed tack on Syria," *The Australian*, Aug. 14, 2006.
113. The one-day Annapolis Conference held on November 27, 2007, was largely window dressing, designed to give the

appearance that the Bush Administration would broker a peace settlement between the Palestinians and Israel before Bush leaves office. Syria asked that the return of the Golan Heights be put on the agenda. However, Israel had said that they would not discuss this issue. Hamas, which took over the Administration of Gaza from Fateh in Mid-June 2007, and is classified as a "terrorist organization" by Israel and the United States was, of course, not invited. No serious analyst expected the Bush Administration to make significant progress on a settlement and Israel forged ahead with new construction of illegal housing projects on the West Bank even as the conference was held. Scott Wilson, "Syria Is to Attend Talks in Annapolis," *Washington Post,* Nov. 26, 2007.

114. Anne Gearan, "Analysis: Pact won't improve U.S. image," *Associated Press*, Aug. 12, 2006.

115. Gearan, "Analysis: Pact won't improve U.S. image,"

116. Dan Rabinowitz, "The pitfalls of machismo,"

117. Patrick J. Buchanan, "Olmert's War and the Next One," Antiwar.com, Aug, 15, 2006.

118. Chomsky and Afrasiabi, "On Israel, Lebanon and Palestine."

119. Robert Fisk, "Desert of trapped corpses testifies to Israel's failure." *The Independent,* 15 August, 2006.

120. Rashid Khalidi, "Hezbollah gaining strength where democracy once dwelt," *Chicago Tribune,* Aug. 13, 2006.

121. Glen Kessler, "Push for Democracy Loses Some Energy," *Washington Post*, Feb. 25, 2006. The US had no interest in promoting the type democracy which would bring Hamas to power in Palestine or the Muslim Brotherhood to rule in Egypt, as can be well understood. Democracy must be understood to mean that which serves the US interests, primarily capitalist accumulation for American corporations.

122. Khalidi, "Hezbollah gaining strength."

123. Fisk, "Desert of trapped corpses."

124. Rami G. Khouri, "Beirut's future: Paris or Mogadishu," *Daily Star*, Aug. 28, 2006.

125. Fisk, "Desert of trapped corpses" and "As the 6 am ceasefire takes effect."
126. Clancy Chassay, "Stand alongside Hizbullah, Lebanon's army tells troops," *The Guardian*, Aug. 19, 2006.
127. Rami G. Khouri, "A foretaste of larger furies to come," *Daily Star*, Aug. 16, 2006.
128. Khouri, "A foretaste of larger furies."
129. "Hezbollah leader says he wouldn't have ordered the capture of two Israeli soldiers knowing it would lead to such a war," *Associated Press,* Aug. 27. 2006.
130. Patrick Cockburn, "Gaza is a jail."
131. Jim Lobe, "Hard-Line Neocons Assail Israel for Timidity," Antiwar.com, Aug. 12, 2006.

7

Waste, War and Toxic Imperialism: The Political Economy of Depleted Uranium

"The United States took its nuclear waste and threw it at Iraq." **Doug Rokke (Former US Army)**

"The US used us as laboratory rats, and the whole country as a dump to throw their nuclear waste in!"

Marko Brezancic (Belgrade)

"I spent thirty-three years [in the Marines]... I was a racketeer, a gangster for capitalism."

General Smedley Butler (US Marine Corps, retired, 1935)

"Because we're Americans...why should we have to pick up our mess [in Iraq]? **Michael Moore**

War in the Middle East has proved to be a disaster for the environment. Depleted uranium(DU) munitions are increasingly being adopted by countries around the world for use on battlefields. The United States left at least 320 tons of DU behind in Iraq after the 1991 Gulf War. Some 1000 to 2000 tons of DU was expended by the US in the 2003 invasion of Iraq, mostly in urban areas, including downtown Baghdad. By 2006, more than 1000 tons of depleted Uranium had been used in Afghanistan and more than 3000 tons in Iraq.[1] It has been suggested that DU has the potential to destroy the genetic future of Iraq. Information about the resulting environmental pollution and effects on exposed populations is systematically suppressed as the US and Great Britain scramble to conceal relevant knowledge from their publics. They fear a popular outcry that will lead to the demand that depleted uranium munitions, which are de facto weapons of mass destruction (WMD), be banned from use. After locating the problem of depleted uranium within the logic of capitalist and imperialist accumulation of capital, this chapter will review the relevant facts about the origins and uses of depleted uranium and its most serious known effects on the environment and human health. Finally, the chapter will argue for the urgent necessity of totally banning depleted uranium from use in war.

There is a large amount of information on depleted uranium weapons which can be found on the Internet and in some recent publications.[2] Here, we will only attempt to summarize some basic facts and information which can be used as a starting point for increasing one's knowledge about the emerging crisis.

Capitalism, Imperialism, and Environmental Destruction: The Iron Logic

It has been suggested that a useful framework in which to think about environmental degradation and conflict is that of imperialism. The "history of colonialism and imperialism" is the "geography of the domination of nature."[3] The roots of capitalist and imperialist expansion can be traced to the enclosure movement in sixteenth century England as a basis for appropriation of natural resources, including labor, from the displaced populations for the purpose of profits and capitalist accumulation. The history of capitalism has shown that it must necessarily strip peoples and countries of their resources and access to the means of production, as it renders them dependent upon capital controlled by national and imperialist ruling classes.

Capitalism is essentially and necessarily a system of environmental destruction. The assault upon nature is an integral part of the logic of capitalist accumulation.[4] The capitalist logic of expansion necessarily becomes imperialistic in seeking to command and expropriate the resources of nature on a global scale, including human resources, which are also a part of nature. It is therefore part of the logic of capitalism that any technological innovation, such as DU, once invented, will be employed for the extension of national and corporate control over nature, regardless of its destructive effect upon the earth, living individuals and communities. That is, the logic of profits trumps any concern with "environmental protection" or so-called "sustainable development," regardless of much deceptive rhetoric about "conservation," "sustainable development," "intergenerational equity," and so on. These terms, in practice, generally become shibboleths, in practice, serving as fig leaves to conceal the ongoing agenda of the wholesale rape of the earth by local and transnational corporations. The driving force behind capitalist and imperialist neoliberal "globalization" at the beginning of the twenty-first century is the logic of capitalist accumulation. By the same logic, democracy and scientific truth must be swept out of the way and become victims of this inexorable logic of power-domination over the earth and other peoples, when they become threats to the rate of accumulation of capital. Increasingly, in the age of neoliberal mass consumption, environmentalists are coming to realize that there can be no compromise with capitalism if the earth and, indeed, the human species, is to be saved from destruction. This truth, while denied by the apologists of capitalism and globalization, is becoming ever more obvious in the rapid melting of the polar ice caps and disappearance of glaciers.

In the case of depleted uranium, there are a number of significant aspects of the problem. It becomes immediately clear that the use of DU is a part of the imperialist-capitalist expansion of the Unites States after World War II in its quest for the position of unchallenged global hegemon. This continues today. First, DU is a further extension of military production and the system of military Keynesianism, which was at the root of US political economy after WW II, by which the US triumphed as the unchallenged global hegemonic empire. Second, the use of DU is a part of the US military industrial complex (MIC), which has been the basis for the institutionalization of the US as a war economy and emerging militaristic state.[5] Third, the increasing use of DU is an extension of the "toxics political economy" in the US, which emerged primarily as a result of the war technologies, including nuclear and chemical, that were developed during WW II. DU is a toxic waste and its use in marketable products, including war materiel, is a form of sham recycling and de facto toxic imperialism in which toxic and radioactive waste is dumped in the open primarily on another country.[6] Fourth, the use of DU weapons is an integral part of the extension of American-Western neoimperialism after WW II and the extension of global control by US capital and transnational corporations. Fifth, the use of depleted uranium is an extension of the triumph of the anti-people, anti-welfare, neoliberal political economy, which has been consolidated after the victory of right-wing supply-side economics during the 1980s under Margaret Thatcher in Great Britain and Ronald Reagan in the US, and the resurgence of right-wing economic ideologies, such as that of F. A. Hayek. Sixth, at the beginning of the twenty-first century the thrust of US foreign policy has gone beyond neoimperialism and capitalist globalization to a full fledged ideology of global control and a new era of overt imperialism, based in part on the fact that the US now spends more on its military budget than the rest of the world put together. This is not a defense budget, but an offense budget, with the rest of the world on the defensive from the one superpower.[7]

Seventh, the use of DU is related to conditions within the political economy of the United States which have led to a primarily mercenary US military.[8] The inability of neoliberal capitalism, under trade pacts such as the North American Free Trade Agreement (NAFTA), to provide an adequate number of living-wage jobs has led to the treating of foreigners as scapegoats, Mexicans, and other foreign immigrants who come to the US and take jobs that are not desired by most Americans.[9] Foreigners are blamed when the real cause is neoliberalism, free trade pacts, and the export of jobs to lower-wage countries. This has exacerbated the upsurge in racism in the US toward foreign peoples, particularly Arabs in the Middle East, following the twin-tower attacks on September11, 2001. Overt racism toward blacks among the white working classes has partially been suppressed since the Civil Rights Movement in the 1960s. Consequently, US workers are increasingly forced into the US military, as a mercenary force, just to make a living and in the process are poisoned and irradiated, along with their offspring, by the use of DU on the battlefield. The working class is encouraged to "kick ass," around the world, especially among Arabs and other "people of color." The working class is led to believe that it will benefit from cheap oil, even if its members do not have an adequate income.[10]

Eighth, the toxics political economy in the US is built around a monopoly waste industry which has systematically and secretly "recycled" the resulting toxic waste into a myriad of products, such as fertilizers, structural building materials, cement, asphalt, and so on, causing a large number of cancers, toxic buildings, toxic towns, toxic work places, toxic waste sites, and so on in a systematic way.[11] The monopoly toxic waste industry has become highly profitable and serves to manage the defecation of capitalism in such a manner as to maximize capitalist accumulation, regardless of the negative effects upon the environment. This is now being extended on a global scale. The use of DU in the production of weapons of war is a form of sham recycling of low-level hazardous nuclear waste into various products, such as munitions, tank shielding, counterweights for missiles and planes, and so on.

Capitalist profit and accumulation is based upon exchange value, rather than use value. The use-value of DU waste, for people in general, is negative, given its debilitative health effects. As a waste, DU also has a negative exchange value for industries which own it, as it is expensive to store and dispose of legally. However, when "recycled" into marketable products, this negative exchange value is magically transformed into positive exchange value in the form of marketable products. This is alchemy, as once practiced in ancient Mesopotamia, come true, as the DU is transformed into gold for the defense companies producing the weapons. Capitalist accumulation is consequently accelerated, even as the use of DU clandestinely causes cancers, kills people, and pollutes entire countries for generations to come. To the extent that the political system is democratic, knowledge of these effects must be suppressed from the people so that capital can continue to realize the exchange value and capitalist accumulation. These factors show that the production and use of DU, and the suppression of knowledge about its effects on people and countries, is deeply enmeshed in the process of capitalist accumulation on a global scale.

Within the US toxics political economy, once a toxic waste has been found to be useful as a substance which has exchange value, standard operating procedure is to simply declare the substance to be non-toxic (in the legal sense). This is systemic in the US Environmental Protection Agency (EPA). Once a substance is no longer treated legally as a toxic waste, the way is clear for free dumping into the environment, after the exchange value has been realized and it has contributed to capitalist profit and accumulation. This essentially gets around all existing or potential environmental regulation and legislation, as the capitalist class has become the ruling class under neoliberal capitalism. With local and global control superseded, the way is clear to pollute whole regions of the earth, as sacrifice zones, and people, as sacrifice populations, particularly sections of the working classes, Native Americans, and foreign populations. This strips populations of environmental justice and demonstrates an acute degree of racism, sexism and imperialism. A colonialist mentally comes into play here as indigenous populations, Indians, third world peoples, Arabs, those people who Americans and Europeans have come to hate and scapegoat after 9/11, are sacrificed to the imperialist quest, under the pretexts of "national security," "homeland security," "keeping America safe," and so on. This mentality can also be rationalized under the logic of Samuel Huntington's communalist "clash of civilizations" racist and fictitious construction. As noted above, the US military is increasingly a mercenary army. At the same time, more military operations are being privatized, so that there is little accountability for the actions of private firms under international law. This was seen in the Abu Gharib Prison scandal in Iraq.[12] As neoliberal economics has continued to swell the ranks of the reserve army of the unemployed around the world, there are plenty of helping hands, who must work to live, for this extension of imperialism. But many of these workers also become victims of the debilitative health effects of DU.

The implications for the peoples of the world and at home are so horrendous and at the same time so sharply in contradiction to the professed values of the society, such as democracy, justice, equality, freedom, the "good life," and so on, that the ruling class is compelled to engage in a massive campaign of propaganda and deception in order to protect and further the "national security" of the empire. This typically takes the form of statements about priorities of "national security," "homeland security," the "war on terrorism," "bringing democracy and freedom to people who have lived under tyranny," and so on. In the same way, the truth about capitalism, imperialism and the de facto empire must be suppressed at home. Or as Michael Moore says in his film, Fahrenheit 9/11, 9/11 is the temperature at which truth melts.[13] The media participates in the repression of information about environmental degradation in the interests of capitalist accumulation. A useful model of understanding this is the Chomsky-Herman propaganda model of the US media.[14]

The result, in the case of DU, is an epidemic, the poisoning of the population, veterans and their families at home, and the indigenous population in the target country. The soldiers are a sacrifice population, as are the Iraqis, Bosnians and so on. The use of DU on the battle field is a form of toxic imperialism, nuclear waste dumped on the enemy, but which is also a form of "friendly fire" in that it results in poisoning its own troops. It is also a case of "collateral damage" in which those who survive the quick death by bombs are made to suffer the slow death of toxic and radiological poisoning. In that sense it is also a form of class warfare. The troops most likely to suffer are the lower ranks made up of working class, a mercenary proletariat. The populations most likely to suffer are those who inhabit poor and weak nations on the global periphery. The utility of DU is as a tool in the capitalist-imperialist domination of nature and geography to enhance capitalist accumulation on a global scale. We should not forget that former US Defense Secretary, Donald Rumsfeld, spoke of a list of some sixty countries which are potential targets of the US in the 'war on terrorism."

What is Depleted Uranium?

Depleted uranium (primarily U-238) is the waste product which is left over in the process of enriching natural uranium for use in nuclear reactors or nuclear weapons. This article will necessarily give a simplified explanation. More technical explanations can be found elsewhere.[15] Enrichment is the process of raising the amount of fissile uranium (such as U-

234 and U-235) in natural uranium. Natural uranium, which is derived from soil containing one to three parts per million of uranium, consists of 99.27 percent by weight of the U-238 isotope, 0.72 percent of the U-235 isotope, and 0.0055 percent of the U-234 isotope. The proportion of U-235 must be raised to 3.2 percent (for boiling water reactors) or 3.6 percent (for pressure water reactors). This can be done through two processes: the gaseous diffusion process or the centrifuge process. After enrichment, the depleted uranium waste stream (U-238 and small amounts of other isotopes) is about seven times larger than the enriched uranium product stream. About one-third of the U-235 isotopes remain in the waste stream tailings of the DU, which consists of 99.75 percent U-238, 0.25 percent U-235, and a smaller amount of U-234. Some portion of these contaminants (such as U-235 and other isotopes) remains in the DU when it is used as munitions and tank shielding. So the term "depleted uranium" is a misnomer in that it is still very dangerous in terms of its chemical toxicity and radioactivity. DU is "depleted" in the sense that it is sixty percent less radioactive than natural uranium because two-thirds of the U-235 has been removed. DU has a half life of about 4.5 billion years and decays totally in 25 billion years.

It is possible to reprocess (strip) the DU waste to retrieve more of the fissile U-235. This, in fact, is regularly done. It is not economically feasible, as such, but considering the costs of storing and disposing of the waste, then it becomes profitable to do so. A practice in Europe is to ship DU waste to Russia after a second processing, to avoid the costs of storage and disposal. It appears that the Russians are reprocessing (stripping) the waste a third time to obtain the available fissile U-235. Bessines, France is an area where some 200,000 metric tons of DU waste is stored. However, legally, DU is not considered a waste in Europe, due to the technicality that it can be used for other things. As noted, shipping the waste avoids the cost of storing or disposal of the waste. Similarly, in the United States, the Nuclear Regulatory Commission classifies DU as a "resource material" governed by licensing requirements.

Given the large number of nuclear reactors and nuclear weapons currently existing, an enormous amount of waste DU has been produced. For example, the US has about 728,000 metric tons of DU, in the form of uranium fluoride. This material is a solid at room temperature and can be stored in large cylinders. It is chemically toxic and an emitter of alpha radiation. Technically, it is low-level nuclear waste.

Of course, a major problem within a modern toxics political economy, which capitalism attempts to saddle upon the entire world, is how to get rid of the waste. This has been an enormous problem since W.W. II. As noted above, the path most frequently taken, if politically possible, is to secretly "recycle" the waste material into a product which has exchange value. A notable example is the systematic dumping of toxic wastes into fertilizers. The beauty of this, for capitalist profits, is that practically nobody knows anything about it.[16] Several such uses have been found for DU waste. It is a steel-alloying constituent; it is used as a chemical catalyst; it is used as counter weights in aircraft and flywheels; it can be used as radiation shielding from gamma radiation; and it can be used in building materials for roads, and no one knows what else, further down the road. It is likely to be secret. But by far the most popular use for DU has been in war, for munitions and protective armor for tanks.

After World War II, the US Department of Defense discovered that DU had a number of useful properties which would make it extremely useful for munitions and tank armor.[17] Some of these same properties, however, would make it extremely hazardous for soldiers and indigenous populations. Therefore it would have to be used within a context of building up its positive properties and playing down or not mentioning its negative properties. This was known as a "policy of "proponency," which would guarantee the military the unrestricted use of DU on the battlefield. In actuality, this phenomenon is not uncommon in dealing with wastes. As noted above, the Environmental Protection Agency (EPA) in the United States regularly "delists" de facto toxic wastes from the toxics list, for political, rather than objective scientific reasons, when dealing with them as toxic wastes would be unacceptably costly to industry.

DU and the US Military

So why did the US military fall so madly in love with this "wonder metal?" It is cheap (free), plentiful (a glut), and works like a charm (melts its way right through tanks). DU makes the perfect bullets for penetrating tanks. DU is pyrophoric, that is, it catches fire, oxidizing at room temperature. When fired, it begins to burn even before it hits its target. It has a high density of 19 grams per cubic centimeter, 67 percent heavier than lead, so it can easily penetrate conventional tank armor. It is made into "kinetic energy penetrators" which are almost entirely U-238. There is a wide range of munitions manufactured from DU from 7.62 mm to 120 mm rounds. It is also used in large multi-ton "bunker-buster" bombs. Munitions include 7.62 mm; 50 cal.; 20 mm (180 gms); 25 mm (200 gms); 30 mm (280 gms); 105 mm (3500 gms); and 120 mm (4500 gms). For use it is allied with molybdenum, titanium, zirconium, or niobium, or a combination of these metals and covered with aluminum as a protective coating.

However, there are alternatives to DU. Among these are lead alloy, hardened steel alloy, and tungsten alloy. But DU is free and not only plentiful but a liability when simply stored. Use helps to get rid of it. However, DU weapons will not solve very much of this disposal problem; there is simply too much of it. Other uses must be found. It seems that largely, this sort of sham recycling has become widely systemic in the American toxic economy and as long as industries can get by with it, they will engage in the practice and even expand it. For example, there are plans to use DU in buildings and roads. These secret ways of "disposing" of toxic waste is as American as cherry pie, part of the system, and indeed a part of global capitalist accumulation today.

DU munitions are now used in tanks such as the M1A1 Abrams Main Battle Tanks and M1A2 Abrams Tanks. Some 1900 M1A1 Abrams tanks were used in the 1991 Gulf War, firing 120 mm rounds which contained 10.7 pounds of DU each. Also several hundred M1 and M60 tanks were used, firing 105 mm rounds, each containing 8.5 pounds of DU. At least 14,000 tank rounds were expended, some 3000 rounds being lost in fires or accidents. The British Challenger Tanks also use DU munitions, but are said to have fired only 100 rounds in the Gulf War.[18] Bradley Fighting Vehicles also use DU munitions. The US Air Force A-10 Thunderbolt II plane (Warthog or tank killer) won, hands down, in the DU contamination race, however, defecating some 940,000, 30 mm, rounds in combat, with each bullet contributing 272 grams, for a grand total of 564,000 pounds of DU. The GBU-28 and GBU-31 "Bunker Buster" bombs, used in Afghanistan, Yugoslavia, and Iraq contain 1.5 tons of DU, which burns on impact. Some of these bombs contain up to seven tons of DU, such as the one dropped on the restaurant in Baghdad in 2003, where Saddam was falsely said to be eating. Such bombs are designed to destroy command and communications centers, but one was dropped on the Amiria bomb shelter in Baghdad, in the Gulf War, killing 800 people, women and children.[19] British Harriers, US F-16's, US Apache Helicopters, and the US Navy Phalanx Close-In Missile (for missile defense or from enemy planes) all got in on the act. DU was also used as balance weights in Tomahawk Cruise Missiles and is used on a number of civilian aircraft.[20] The M-6 rifle also fires DU munitions.

When the bullet hits the target, some 40 to 70 percent of the DU burns, producing uranium oxide, while the rest of the kinetic penetrator is simply left lying, appearing in the shape of a cigar.

Where has DU been used and who used it?

Many sources claim that DU munitions were first used on the battlefield in the first Gulf War. But it appears that DU was also used in the Arab-Israeli War (1973), by Israel in Lebanon, and by British Naval boats in the Falkland Islands (1982).[21] DU has been tested on many firing ranges in the US, Okinawa, South Korea, Solway Firth in Scotland and elsewhere including Vieques Island in Puerto Rico, resulting in the permanent pollution of these areas.[22] Some 11 tons of DU munitions were used in Bosnia (1995), and in Serbia and Kosovo (1999). The Israelis have used DU munitions in Palestine, and of course it has been used twice in the Gulf, in Kuwait and Iraq in 1991, and in the 2003 US invasion of Iraq. In Jefferson County, Indiana, a 200 acre DU test range has been so badly contaminated that it would cost $7.8 billion dollars to clean up the DU. It seems destined for a "national sacrifice zone" after it was offered to the "National Park Service" for a "nature preserve" and turned down.[23] At a plant in Paducah, Kentucky, where missiles containing DU are produced, some 1000 people have been contaminated.

Not surprisingly, these munitions were effective against the Iraqis, who did not have DU munitions and used Russian T-72 tanks, that were easily knocked out from ranges up to and beyond 3500 meters (2 miles).[24]

The Health Effects of DU

It is standard industry operating procedure to claim that various toxic wastes are "safe enough to eat" when attempting to site toxic waste storage dumps. Sure enough, a US Army briefer has been reported as informing reporters that DU was "safe enough to eat."[25]

The following is primarily a summary of the information provided by Asaf Durakovic.[26] Primarily, three isotopes of DU have medical effects: U-238 (half life of 4.5 billion years), U-235 (half life of 710 million years), and U-234 (half life of 250,000 years). These isotopes are alpha, beta and gamma emitters. It is generally well known that these isotopes of uranium cause health damage starting from the mining of uranium, and through all other processes, including the use of uranium products. These materials are both toxic and radiological.

Some of these forms of uranium are soluble and some are not. For the soluble ones, (uranyl U-VI compounds), they cause chemical damage when they enter the body, primarily in the tubules of the kidneys. The less soluble, (uranous U-IV compounds), are retained in the lungs when inhaled, or in the "bone mineral phase." Both chemical and radiation damage occurs to "target organs," such as the bronchoalveolar tree, the kidneys and bone. These compounds can cause somatic effects (affecting the body) and genetic alterations. According to Durakovic, "uranium compounds retained in the bone may cause malignant changes in the cells of the skeletal tissue and in the stem cells, while DU retained in the respiratory tree may result in the induction of lung cancer."[27]

Since most of the U-235 and U-234 isotopes have been removed, depleted uranium is 60 percent less radioactive than natural uranium, as noted above. Nevertheless DU emits alpha particles (fast helium atoms with their two electrons removed), beta particles (high speed electrons), and gamma rays (high energy electromagnetic radiation emitted by radioactive decay). From an external DU penetrator, alpha radiation is not a significant danger. Beta particles can be dangerous, even externally however, since they have a range of several centimeters in human tissue. Danger from gamma rays is similar to that of natural uranium.

Internally, DU is both a chemical and radiation hazard. It can enter the body through the skin (dermal), the mouth (oral), or lungs (pulmonary portal), or through wounds or burns, such as shrapnel wounds. Experiments done on animals showed that when DU pellets were implanted, uranium isotopes in body fluids increased within six months. Durakovic points out that DU can also be absorbed into the body through intact skin from soluble uranium compounds and can cause severe poisoning and death. During and after wars, DU primarily enters people's bodies through breathing the fine particles left behind from the oxidizing DU in munitions and armor. How much of the DU in munitions becomes "airborne" varies greatly from about one percent to 70 percent, depending upon the penetrator size, velocity, target material and so on. For example, a 150 mm DU penetrator releases about 2.45 kg. of airborne DU, with about half in the respirable range of from 1 to10 microns in diameter. But the percentage of respirable particles may be up to 70 percent. The generally accepted model predicts that of the DU particles breathed in, about 25 percent are immediately exhaled, 50 percent are "translocated to the nasopharynx," to be exhaled or swollen, while the other 25 percent are deposited in the bronchoalveolar tree. Most of these are also expelled, with some 10 percent, which are soluble, reaching "systemic circulation," while a portion of the others that are not soluble are retained in the respiratory system. The particles retained in the lungs may cause radiation, while those absorbed in the blood stream are "deposited in the target organs."[28]

In the case of soluble DU, there is quick access to the blood stream, causing toxic effects on the kidneys and bones. About 60 percent of the soluble DU is retained in the kidneys and bones, with about 40 percent excreted in urine. Up to half may be excreted in the urine in from 7 to 100 hours, but not much research has been done in this area. Increased uranium isotopes have been found in the urine of 1991 Gulf

War soldiers up to nine years after the war. The insoluble particles can be retained in the lungs for years. Resulting lung cancer from this cause has been confirmed. The beta and gamma radiation (high speed electrons and high-energy electromagnetic waves) derives from the nuclear decay activity in DU and can cause genetic damage in the nuclei of cells, including sperm cells. This may account for the observed birth defects in children of veterans with "Gulf War Syndrome."[29]

A US Army Medical Command team sent to the Gulf to take charge of the cleanup, consisting of 100 members, all became sick and thirty of them eventually died from their exposure to DU. Verified adverse health effects from DU include chronic fatigue, loss of endurance, frequent infections, sore throat, coughing, skin rashes, night sweats, nausea and vomiting, diarrhea, dizziness, headaches, memory loss, confusion, muscle spasms and cramps, joint pain and loss of mobility, swollen glands, dental problems, reactive airway disease, neurological abnormalities, kidney stones, chronic kidney pain, vision degradation, night vision losses, lymphoma, various forms of skin and organ cancer, neuropsychological disorders, uranium in semen, sexual dysfunction, birth defects in offspring and other effects.[30] According to Guenther, some 50,000-80,000 Gulf War veterans have Gulf War Syndrome (GWS), and 2900-5,000 have died. In Britain at least 3500 are suffering from GWS.[31]

In the Persian Gulf area, including Iraq, there are several important environmental conditions related to DU use. After DU has been oxidized and spread around as fine particles, upon impact, the uranium oxide particles can easily be inhaled. In the fine desert sand, the uranium micro-particles attach themselves to the sand because they are electronically charged. This means that they can remain suspended in the air for long periods and therefore transferred to neighboring countries, such as Saudi Arabia and the United Arab Emirates. A massive increase in cancer rates in Saudi Arabia and Bahrain has been observed. In Basra, it has been estimated that the cancer rate for local people might be as high as 20 percent, just from the effects of the 1991 war. This contamination can cause damage for tens of years or more; nobody knows how long. It is claimed that there has been a six-fold rise in cancers, in southern Iraq, especially leukemia and lymphomas, along with a large number of birth defects. Iraqi health officials claimed a 200 percent rise in cancer, including leukemia after the 1991 Gulf War and the appearance of rare forms of leukemia.

Estimates are that about 320 tons of DU was left behind after the 1991 Gulf War and from 1000 to 2000 tons in the 2003 invasion of Iraq. The 320 metric tons from the first war would create from 3,000 to 6,000 kg of DU aerosols.[32]

When these fine particles enter the lungs, the uranium and "daughter products" of radioactive decay radiate the lung, killing and mutating adjacent cells. Some of the particles enter the bloodstream and are then carried to all parts of the body. Research at Johns Hopkins University showed that radioactive dust has entered the food chain in Iraq through the water table and soil. This contributes to the incidence of genetic defects in babies.[33]

There is much evidence from on the ground on DU effects in Iraq, and a few stories have made it into the mainstream press.[34] Around burned out armored vehicles in Iraq, levels of background radiation have been measured up to 1300 times normal, with no notification for the general public to avoid such sites. One reporter measured a DU tank round in Saudi Arabia in 1991 emitting 270 millirads of radiation per hour. The current safe limit is only 100 millirads exposure per year. Children have been observed picking up and playing with fragments of DU penetrators. Burned out vehicles are widely scattered in Iraq where children play and people pass by them close enough to get radiated daily. The radioactivity was found to remain even after 12 years. Ground water pollution was found to be up to 100 times the normal level of radioactivity.[35] At lease 16 contaminated US vehicles left behind in the 1991 Gulf War were brought back to South Carolina and dumped in a low-level radioactive waste dump. The US army claims that about 30 such vehicles were contaminated. In one area of Southern Iraq, the following statistics on cancer were recorded. In 1988, 34 died of cancer; in 1998, 450 died of cancer; in 2001, 603 died of cancer.[36]

Birth Defects as caused by DU

By all indications, the number of babies born with birth defects has greatly increased in Iraq. In 1989, there were eleven babies with birth defects per 100,000 births. In 2001, there were 116 birth defects per 100,000. Doctors have compared the birth defects to those after the Hiroshima and Nagasaki nuclear bombings. In Basra, after the Gulf War, babies were born without eyes and without brains; one was just a head with legs. There were babies without genetalia, a girl born with her brains outside her skull, and one was just a pair of buttocks with a face and two amphibious arms.[37] In the period, 1991-94 in Basra, there were only 11 congenital anomolies recorded. In 2000, there were 221. Given that DU has an incubation period in humans of about five years one may expect a much more serious upsurge in cases in the years after the 2003 Iraq War.

In 1993, 15 children developed leukemia; in 2000, it was 60. Jawal al-Ali, director of oncology at Basra Teaching Hospital, noted that the numbers of cancers were doubling every year.[38] But when the BBC reported from Basra in 2002 that Iraqi doctors reported a 20-fold increase in cancers after the 1991 Gulf War, the BBC was attacked for giving pro-Saddam propaganda.[39]

In hospitals in Iraq, many children with leukemia could not be saved due to the effects of the sanctions. By 2001, some 2000 children a month were dying from a lack of drugs. What could be bought was decided secretly by a committee of the UN Security council, called the 661 Committee. Many basic needs were rejected on the basis of "dual use." For example, beef extract and broth, and pencils, because they contain graphite. Also deep x-ray equipment, blood component separators, and needles for biopsies were rejected. The US/UN sanctions left an estimated 1.6 million children dead and more stunted.[40]

In February, 2003, it was reported that the World Health Organization had kept secret a report on the effects of DU on the people of Iraq.[41] Dr. Keith Baverstock, a top expert on radiation and health at the WHO for eleven years, claimed that a report was deliberately kept secret. It was suggested that the report may have been suppressed following pressure from the International Atomic Energy Agency (IAEA), which promotes nuclear power. The report said that the breathing of DU dust is likely to cause growth of malignant tumors and pointed out that the DU is contaminated with plutonium (U-239). The report also pointed out the danger that contaminated metal could be recycled into kitchen utensils, such as forks and knives.

Soldiers and Gulf War Syndrome

The "legacy of lies, secrecy, and treating soldiers as guinea pigs"[42] goes back beyond World War II to experiments carried out by the US not only on soldiers but on civilians too. Soldiers were subjected to radiation from atomic blasts in the United States and sprayed with Agent Orange in Vietnam. The US carried out experiments on syphilis using black men in Tuskegee, Alabama. Disease causing germs were secretly released in the metro systems of major US cities and dropped from air over cities to study the result of such contamination.

A controversy exists as to whether Gulf War Syndrome is caused by or related to the use of DU munitions in the

1991 Gulf War. The statements put out by the US Government are contradictory in the extreme. For example, the Presidential Advisory Committee of Gulf War Veterans Illnesses stated in 1996 that "The committee concludes that it is unlikely that health-effects reports by Gulf War veterans today are the result of exposure to depleted uranium during the Gulf War." However, this contradicts several government documents. From the Army Environmental Policy Institute (AEPI) in 1995 comes the statement that "If DU enters the body, it has the potential to generate significant medical consequences. The risks associated with DU in the body are both chemical and radiological." Another line from the report states that "Personnel inside or near vehicles struck by DU penetrators could receive significant internal exposures." Another government document states that "Short-term effects of high doses can result in death, while long-term effects of low doses have been implicated in cancer." The same document states that "Aerosol DU exposures to soldiers on the battlefield could be significant with potential radiological toxicological effects." And from the Government Accounting Office came the statement, "Inhaled insoluble oxides stay in the lungs longer and pose a potential cancer risk due to radiation. Ingested DU dust can pose both a radioactive and toxicity risk."[43]

A report in July 1990 on a study done by Science Applications International Corporation (SAIC), a defense contractor, states that the Pentagon knew DU was harmful before 1991, but sent troops to be exposed anyway. The SAIC report states that "a low level alpha radiation emitter" could be "linked to cancer when exposures are internal." Of course, it is well known that DU emits beta and gamma radiation as well as alpha. The SAIC report goes on to state: "DU exposures to soldiers on the battlefield could be significant, with potential radiological and toxicological effects. Short-term effects of high doses [of DU] can result in death, while long-term effects of low doses have been implicated in cancer." The report also notes that "widespread knowledge of depleted uranium's harmful properties could lead to public outrage about the acceptability of the continued use of DU kinetic energy penetrators for military applications."[44] Indeed, it is the last point that the Pentagon seems to be most concerned about.

An objective review of the literature is likely to convince one that the US military knew the dangers, but intentionally withheld information from troops until it was too late. Malcolm Hooper, Emeritus Professor of Medical Chemistry at the University of Sutherland, and Chief Scientific Advisor to the UK Gulf Veterans Association, states that "the inhalation of these fine dust particles represents a health hazard that was known to the military as long ago as 1974."[45] There was massive exposure to the troops in the 1991 Gulf War, such as on the "highway of death" where Saddam Hussein's troops were bombed and strafed while retreating from Kuwait. In spite of this, warnings were not issued to troops before they went into battle. Several months after the war, soldiers were told: "precautions must be taken to avoid inhaling or ingesting DU particles." When entering a burned out vehicle "respirator or protective mask should be worn along with gloves." They were told that protective clothing should be worn and then discarded.[46] A US Army fact sheet also warned: "When a DU penetrator impacts a target surface, a large portion of the kinetic energy is dissipated as heat. The heat of the impact causes the DU to oxidize or burn momentarily. This results in smoke which contains a high concentration of DU particles. These uranium particles can be ingested or inhaled and are toxic."[47] Even when driving a tank, the driver is radiated by 0.13 mrem per hour from the overhead DU armor. This means that a tank crew's exposure will exceed the maximum standard given by the Nuclear Regulatory Commission in only 32 days. The US military, on the other hand, argues that the minimum standard would never be exceeded no matter how long the soldiers remained inside the tanks.

A law passed in 1997 in the US which requires pre and post deployment medical screening of troops was not being followed in 2003. It was only on April 29, 2003, however, after a campaign launched by the National Gulf War Resources Center that the Pentagon announced it would start screening veterans.

As part of the apparent cover up, Dr. Asaf Durakovic, who was Clinical Chief of the Department of Nuclear Medicine of the US Veterans Administration was fired because he diagnosed DU contamination in some US soldiers after the Gulf War in 1991, who became ill. Two of those soldiers later died of unknown causes. The Uranium Medical Research Center in the US found that 14 of 27 veterans still had DU in their urine after nine years.[48] Another doctor who has done research on DU at the University of Waterloo, Ontario, Dr. Hari Sharma, found DU contamination in the urine of veterans eight years after the Gulf War, even though the Department of Defense in the US says it passes through the body quickly.[49] One notable example is Carol H. Picou, who was a nurse in the Persian Gulf War and became an activist opposed to DU. She compares the struggle of the Gulf War Syndrome victims to get their medical problems recognized and treated to the struggle of the veterans who suffered from the effects of Agent Orange in the Vietnam War. It took 22 years for the US Veterans Administration to recognize the medical problem caused by dioxin poisoning. Picou, who was exposed on the "highway of death" and did not know of the danger of being around the burned out tanks and trucks, lists her resulting medical problems. These include short-term memory deficit (toxic encephalopathy), thyroid deterioration, squamous cancerous cells of the uterus, deteriorating muscles, loss of control over bowels and bladder, and having her tubes tied due to fear of having children with birth defects.[50]

It has been estimated that some six to ten percent or 36,000 of the 600,000 Gulf War veterans exposed to DU in the 1992 Gulf War will develop fatal cancers. By May 2002, almost 207,000 Gulf War Veterans had applied for medical benefits while 159,238 had been awarded service connected disability by the Veterans Administration.[51]

Children of Gulf War veterans have been born without arms. It has been reported that among one community of veterans' families in Mississippi, USA, some 67 percent of children were born without eyes, ears, brain, and thyroid. There were other organ malformations, a condition similar to that observed in Bosnia after the war, where DU was used. Also observed is "an aids-like syndrome," which causes weakened immunity.[52]

Iraq Cleanup

Experts have pointed out that the sites must be cleaned up, but in terms of Iraq, this is a task that is beyond comprehension. It would take massive war reparations against the US and Britain to even scratch the surface of the problem. The British Ministry of Defense has talked of giving money to Iraq to help clean up DU, but the real cost, of course, would seem to be prohibitive. On the other hand, surely the US should be required to pay for the removal of the burned out vehicles and clean up the worst of the damages they have left behind. But even a superficial cleanup is not likely to happen without an international outcry and perhaps the bringing of the perpetrators of the war on Iraq to dock in an international court.

The Global Scourge

DU munitions are openly available on the global arms market today, manufactured by the major US and other arms makers. It is known that they have already been acquired by the militaries of a long list of countries. Wherever they are used, even for training, this is a sort of "new kind of nuclear war,"[53] although technically, DU weapons cannot be called "nuclear weapons." Surely what is needed is not more "nuclear weapons" but more "new clear thinking" about what is going to happen to the human species with the global radiation and mutation of the human genome. DU weapons, as WMD, are truly a threat to the human species with a fearsome potential for use as weapons of imperialist and racist genocide against nations deemed to have sinned against the global powers that be. Such populations as the people of Iraq, and other mostly non-western 'third world" peoples, considered "lesser peoples, may become targets in future.

For the US and British militaries, the threat is not dying Iraqis, US and British veterans, nor a polluted and dead environment. The real threat, it seems, is an "informed public." Many officials are doing all they can to prevent "public knowledge" of the problem from getting out because this could lead to efforts to ban these weapons. One may observe that the issue is seldom, if ever, mentioned on the major international TV cable networks and very rarely in the mainstream press. As noted above, when BBC broadcast a report by Rageh Omaar,[54] which claimed that DU shells caused cancer in Iraqi children, the Telegraph newspaper accused the BBC of "peddling propaganda on behalf of Saddam Hussein" and claimed that a huge body of scientific evidence discredited links between DU and cancer. Then the British establishment circled their wagons and claimed that the increase in cancer rates was caused by Saddam's chemical weapons. This episode probably indicates the extent to which the establishments in both Britain and the US are concerned with preventing the truth from getting out about DU. Goeff Hoon, the former British Defense Secretary, told the British Parliament that there is "not the slightest scientific evidence" to suggest that depleted uranium left a poisonous residue."[55] Official lying seems to be more advanced in certain quarters. Similarly, NATO, UN and European Union officials have all lined up in broadcasting the official denial that DU weapons present any health risks.

Col. James Naughton, US Army, at a Pentagon briefing, March 14, 2003, just a week before the invasion of Iraq was launched, charged that opposition to DU is a "product of Saddam's Propaganda." A White House report, "Apparatus of Lies: Saddam's Disinformation and Propaganda 1990-2003," addressed the "Depleted Uranium Scare" in a section of the report charging that the "Iraqi claims" that DU has caused cancer and birth defects is part of a Saddam "disinformation campaign."[56]

International Legal Aspects of DU

The "humanitarian laws of warfare" have been established based upon The Hague Conventions (1899-1907), the Geneva Conventions (1925-49), and the Nuremberg Charter (1945). These laws embody five principles which ban (1) the use of weapons or tactics which cause unnecessary or aggravated devastation or suffering, (2) the use of weapons or tactics which cause indiscriminate harm to noncombatants, (3) the use of weapons or tactics which violate the neutral jurisdiction of nonparticipating states, (4) the use of asphyxiating, poisonous or other gas, and all analogous substances including bacteriological methods of war, and (5) the use of weapons or tactics which cause widespread long-term and severe damage to the environment. On the face of the evidence, DU munitions would seem to violate all of these five principles. They can also be held to apply to DU weapons by virtue of the Martens Clause, which established that a weapon could be banned even though it is not specifically mentioned in international law.

The difficulty is in getting courts to interpret these laws broadly enough to cover DU weapons. The argument against the first principle is that there are "situations where no alternatives to DU exist" if the military objective is to be achieved. The second principle on the prohibition of "indiscriminate harm" is also legally weak in light of court rulings. This is because it must be shown that there is "disproportionate damage to civilians in relation to the military purpose." The third prohibition, concerning neutral states, is also problematical, since the International Court of Justice (ICJ) has refused to rule that even the use of nuclear weapons is illegal in every case. DU weapons might be ruled illegal in certain cases of contaminating other countries. The fourth prohibition, against the use of poisonous substances, is also unlikely to stand up in court due to the fact that the ICJ interpreted this principle to cover "weapons whose prime, or even exclusive, effect is to poison or asphyxiate." In terms of the fifth principle, DU is most certainly devastating to the environment, but the ICJ has said that "military necessity and proportionality" must be considered, in the case of nuclear weapons, and so just proof of destroying the environment does not necessarily condemn the weapon in the eyes of the Court. It seems there is always a loophole for the generals. Short of a global outcry of massive proportion against the DU weapons, or more courageous and enlightened judges, there is probably not much chance of getting DU weapons banned under international law any time soon. This may, however, depend upon much wider public knowledge and activism against the use of the weapons.[57]

In August 1996, a resolution calling for the ban of DU weapons was passed by the UN Sub-Commission on Prevention of Discrimination and Protection of Minorities. Relevant bases for the resolution are the principles of the UN Charter, the Universal Declaration of Human Rights, the International Covenants on Human Rights, and the Geneva Conventions. The US attempted to block this resolution.[58] Iraq made similar arguments in the UN in May 1996, charging that DU weapons are internationally prohibited weapons of mass destruction (WMD).[59]

In October 2001, an effort was launched in the US Congress to have DU weapons banned. The bill was introduced in the US House of Representatives calling for the suspension of the use, sale, development, production, testing and export of DU munitions, pending the outcome of studies of the health effects of the weapons and the effort joined by a number of Democrats. Only some eight members of Congress, however, seemed interested in the issue and, not surprisingly, nothing came of the effort.

Conclusion:

From the above information and considerations, it is possible to see pretty clearly what is going on with the issue of DU weapons. The US military has acquired weapons which will give it an advantage in maintaining and extending its global empire for some time to come and wishes to ensure that the weapon is not lost due to public knowledge and the possible consequence of an upsurge in democratic demands that the weapon be banned. The US Government considers this a much higher priority than the environmental and health consequences of the use of DU. This "policy of proponency," which also involves covering up the negative health and environmental effects of DU weapons, will surprise no one familiar with the practice of the US Government and capitalist industry in the US. It is simply a part of standard operating procedure in the interests of continued capitalist accumulation and global empire. With the capitalist-owned media largely serving the interests of the state and big corporations, and given the "national security argument," irrational fear of "terrorism," and so on, it is an uphill struggle to even get the truth out, much less make significant inroads toward banning DU weapons. The use of DU weapons can likely be stopped only with a massive amount of democratic activism on an international scale. The US military realizes this potential, if the truth were to get out. Meanwhile, future wars, and even small scale skirmishes, are going to necessarily contaminate areas and even entire nations to the point of destroying a livable environment. The use of depleted uranium weapons is a crime against humanity and nature. The use of DU is a depleted policy from morally depleted minds, in the interests of a capitalist economic system which is increasingly depleted of justice for the vast majority. The destruction of the environment of countries with DU pollution is a manifest lesson in how the emerging technology of war along with the ideology of neoliberalism, increasingly threaten the very survival of the human species itself. With the pursuit of an imperialistic agenda by the West being couched in the guise of a noble war against "terrorism" and "Islamic fascism" following the 9/11, 2001, attacks on New York and Washington, the struggle for global justice and the environment is an even more difficult struggle.

Not unlike in the Middle East, while the Bush Administration continued to tout democracy, the threat of democratic activism in the United States raised its head and began to threaten more acutely the neoconservatives occupation of Iraq by 2006. The Bush White House was forced to scramble to overcome the democratic backlash in the 2006 mid-term elections, doing the opposite of what the American people demanded. More troops were sent to Iraq. It was a demonstration and instructive to the entire world as to how willing the political right was to tolerate democracy in their own country. By late 2007, President George W. Bush's domestic approval rating had fallen to only 24 percent, and White House foreign policy was at only 18 percent, while the White House seemed unconcerned with these figures.[60] The eyes of the neoconservatives were fixed firmly on the prize: oil and empire, based upon the continuing occupation of Iraq and the wider Middle East.

References

1. Irving Wesley Hall, "Depleted Uranium for Dunmies: The Most Toxic Battle In Western Military History," *www.globalresearch.ca*, April 17, 2006.

2. See John Catalinotto and Sara Flounders (eds.), *Metal of Dishonor: Depleted Uranium, How the Pentagon Radiates Soldiers and Civilians with DU Weapons*. New York: International Action Center, 1999. *http://www.iacenter.org/* There are many other useful sites on the Internet, such as Laka Foundation and the Campaign Against Depleted Uranium (CADU).
3. Simon Dalby, "Ecological Politics, Violence, and the Theme of Empire," *Global Environmental Politics* 4 (2), May 2004, p. 5.
4. Eddie J. Girdner and Jack Smith, *Killing Me Softly: Toxic Waste, Corporate Profit and the Struggle for Environmental Justice*. New York: Monthly Review Press, 2002.
5. See Chalmers Johnson's trilogy: *Blowback: The Costs and Consequences of American Empire*. New York: Metropolitan Books, 2000; *The Sorrows of Empire: Militarism, Secrecy and the End of the Republic*. New York: Metropolitan Books, 2004 and *Nemesis: The Last Days of the American Republic*. New York: Metropolitan, 2006.
6. Girdner and Smith, *Killing Me Softly*.
7. "National Security Document," September 2002. This document can be found on the White House website. See also, Chalmers Johnson, *Sorrows of Empire*.
8. Indeed, the privatization of the military and many former CIA operations have proceeded apace in the Bush Administration.
9. Eddie J. Girdner, "Struck by Congress: Social Welfare in the United States." www.transform.or.at/images/struckbycongress.pdf. (2007)
10. See the analysis in *Monthly Review*, 55 (11), April 2004, special issue on the "Jobs Crunch" in the US.
11. Girdner and Smith, *Killing Me Softly*. Duff Wilson, *Fateful Harvest: The True Story of a Small Town, a Global Industry and a Toxic Secret*. New York: HarperCollins, 2001. Eddie J. Girdner, "Poisoning Our Food," *Monthly Review*, 55 (7), December 2003, pp. 41-46.
12. In 2007, the number of US troops in Iraq had been escalated ("surged") to 160,000 while the number of mercenaries

working for private firms was about 180,000. The private "security" firm, Blackwater USA, contracted to the US State Department, regularly murdered Iraqis on the streets of Iraq accountable neither to US civilian or Iraqi law or US military law. The most notable example was the incident in September 2007, in which shootings by Blackwater security guards killed some 17 people at a traffic circle in Baghdad.

13. Larissa MacFarquhar, "The Populist," *The New Yorker*, February 16, 2004. http:/www.newyorker.com
14. See Edward S. Herman and Noam Chomsky, *Manufacturing Consent*. Pantheon Books, 2002.
15. See Peter Diehl, "Depleted Uranium: a by product of the Nuclear Chain." in *Depleted Uranium: A Post-War Disaster For Environment and Health*. Laka Foundation, Amsterdam, Netherlands. See the website of Laka Foundation.
16. Duff Wilson, *Fateful Harvest*.
17. Don Fahey, "Depleted Uranium Weapons: Lessons from the 1991 Gulf War" in *Depleted Uranium: A Post-War Disaster.*
18. *Ibid.*
19. Lenora Foerstel, "Military and Media Collaborate in the cover up of DU," in *Metal of Dishonor*, pp. 61-76.
20. Daniel Robichaeu, Desert Concerns. The importance of use in civilian aircraft is seen in the Oct. 4, 1992 crash of an El Al Boeing 747 in Amsterdam. A portion of the 282 kilograms of DU in the plane's tail wings burned, causing contamination in the populated area. Henk Van der Keur, "Uranium Pollution from the Amsterdam 1992 Plane Crash," Laka Foundation.
21. Jack Cohen-Jappa, CADU Conference Feedback. CADU News 6: Winter 2000/2001.
22. "DU shell tests to resume," BBC News, Jan. 31, 2003.
23. Robert Jones Parsons, "America's Big Dirty Secret," *Le Monde Diplomatique,* March 2002.
24. Dan Fahey, "Collateral Damage: How U.S. Troops Were Exposed To Depleted Uranium During the Persian Gulf War," in *Metal of Dishonor*, pp. 25-42.

25. Doug Rokke, "Depleted Uranium: Uses and Hazards," Paper presented in the British House of Commons, Dec., 16, 1999.
26. Asaf Durakovic, "Medical Consequences of Internal Contamination with Depleted Uranium," in *Metal of Dishonor*, pp. S 9-S 16.
27. *Ibid.*, p. S 10.
28. *Ibid.*, pp. S 10- S 12.
29. Leonard A. Dietz, "DU Spread and Contamination of Gulf War Veterans and Others," in *Metal of Dishonor,* pp. 134-149.
30. Larry Johnson, "Iraqi Concerns, birth defects blamed on U.S. depleted uranium," *Seattle Post-Intelligencer*, Nov. 12, 2002.
31. Siegwart-Horst Guenther, "How DU Shell Residues Poison Iraq, Kuwait and Saudi Arabia," *Metal of Dishonor*, pp. 167-170.
32. Dietz, "DU Spread and Contamination of Gulf War Veterans and Others, p. 145. Of course the fighting from 2003 to 2007 has greatly increased the amounts of DU dispersed.
33. Felecity Arbuthnot, "The Health of the Iraqi People." Laka Foundation, Documentation and research center on nuclear energy.
34. Eric Hoskins, "Depleted Uranium Shells make the Desert Glow," *New York Times*, January 21, 1993. This is said to be the first article about DU in the mainstream press. Also, Scott Peterson, "Remains of Toxic Bullets Litter Iraq," *Christian Science Monitor,* May 15, 2003; Christian Fraser, "Uranium 'Killing Italian Troops'", BBC News, Jan. 10, 2007, on use in Yugoslavia. Articles appearing in other publications include: Dennis Kyne, "Depleted Uranium: What happened to the Test-Tube Paradigm," *San Francisco Bayview*, Feb. 23, 2005; Juan Gonzalez, "Vet's Ills Mounting Fast," *New York Daily News*, Feb.7, 2006; Kevin Zeese, "Depleted Uranium: States Take Action to Protect Their Soldiers and Veterans," *Counterpunch*, July 12, 2005; David Rose, "Weapons of Self-Destruction," *Vanity Fair*, Nov. 15, 2004.
35. Slobodan Lekic, "Iraqi Doctors Worry About Use of Uranium," May 24, 2003, AP. Larry Johnson, "Iraqi Cancers, birth defects, blamed on US depleted uranium."

36. Larry Johnson, "Iraqi Cancers."
37. Larry Johnson, "Iraqi Cancers." Andy Kershaw, "A chamber of horrors so close to the 'Garden of Eden" In Foreign Parts in Basra, Southern Iraq," *http://www.cadu.org.uk/info/iraq/9_1.htm*
38. Andy Kershaw, "A Chamber of Horrors."
39. "BBC Slammed for Speaking the truth," CADU News: Summer 2002. http://www.cadu.org.uk/info/iraq/11_1.htm
40. Samia Nakhoul, "Parents of Dying Iraqi Children Vent Fury at Bush," Reuters/Alternet, (ZNET), October 25, 2002. For information on the effects of the sanctions and their injustice see Geoff Simons, *Targeting Iraq: Sanctions and Bombing in US Policy.* London: Saqi Books, 2002.
41. Rob Edwards, "WHO 'Suppressed' Scientific Study into depleted Uranium Cancer fears in Iraq," *Sunday Herald* (Scotland), 22 February, 2004.
42. Frida Berrigan, "Weapons of Mass Deception," *In These Times*, June 27, 2003.
43. *Metal of Dishonor*, Quotes noted in the front of the book.
44. Berrigan, "Weapons of Mass Deception."
45. Alex Kirby, "UK to aid Iraq DU removal," BBC News, April 23, 2003.
46. Fahey, "Collateral Damage: How US Troops Were Exposed...", p. 32.
47. *Ibid.*, p. 28.
48. Johnson, "Iraqi Cancers."
49. Daniel Robicheau, "The next testing site for Depleted Uranium Weaponry," Laka Foundation.
50. Carol H. Picou, "Living With Gulf War Syndrome," in *Metal of Dishonor*, pp. 43-49.
51. Robicheau. Johnson, "Iraqi Concerns."
52. Robicheau.
53. Helen Caldicott, "A New Kind of Nuclear War," in *Metal of Dishonor*, pp. 18-20.
54. Omaar moved up from BBC to produce excellent documentary reports for al-Jazeera on many contemporary

problems around the world. For example, the series "Witness."

55. "BBC Slammed for speaking the truth."
56. Berrigan.
57. Alyn Ware, "Depleted Uranium Weapons and International Law," in *Metal of Dishonor,* pp. 195-203.
58. Philippa Winkler, "UN Sub-Commission on Human Rights Votes Ban of DU," in *Metal of Dishonor,* pp. 191-94.
59. "Note from the permanent Mission of Iraq to the UN Center for Human Rights, May 1996," in *Metal of Dishonor*, pp. 171-76.
60. "Voters unhappy with Bush and Congress," Reuters, October 17, 2007.

8

War on My Mind: Iraq at the Center of the American Empire

"I'm a war President. I make decisions here in the Oval Office...with war on my mind."

(George W. Bush)

"He acts like his head was only made to hold his ears apart." **(Hank Williams)**[1]

"We don't negotiate with evil; We defeat it."

(Dick Cheney)

"If we were to withdraw before the job was done, this enemy would follow us home."

(George W. Bush, Aug. 23, 2007)

"Who cares if Saddam was involved. [Saddam] has already earned himself a death sentence a thousand times over." **(Max Boot, The Weekly Standard)**

"We do not need a trial, we need a hanging."

(The last Judge at Saddam's trial)

It became clear early on that the US occupation of Iraq would fail, by any reasonable standard, although by 2007, the end game was not yet clear. The US would not be leaving Iraq, as in Vietnam. The stakes were clearly higher. Iraq was the basis for global empire. At least twelve extensive and likely permanent military bases were being constructed by the US in the country. US officials continued to stress a long-term presence, modeled, it was argued, on the German, Japanese or Korean model.[2] More appropriately, as noted earlier, the Japanese occupation of Manchuria was probably a closer analogy. Further, it was clear that private security firms, mercenary forces, would be needed to carry out US policy. Just how the occupation would unfold, was still unclear, however, given the extensive disruption of Iraqi society by the war, the ongoing civil war and sectarian cleansing, the possibility of the country breaking up in separate entities, and the operation of the Shia and Sunni militias.

In the north, the Kurdish Regional Government had already taken steps to establish a good deal of autonomy from the central government in Baghdad. If light was not yet clear at the end of the tunnel, for a realistic assessment it was necessary to understand that the US would pull out all stops to find a way to stay, after the inordinate investment which was approaching $800 billion toward the end of George W. Bush's Presidency. Nearly 4000 American soldiers were dead with upwards of 35,000 casualties. The support of the American people was limited, however, but this had not yet proved to be a formidable constraint by any means. The United States is an inordinately militaristic country by international standards and has a very high tolerance for war deaths and casualties. The high degree of depoliticization of American society may partly account for this.

A realistic assessment would also acknowledge that by mid-2004, the war was essentially lost. On the other hand, this fact was largely irrelevant in the event. The bottom line was that the US was now firmly entrenched in the country as a colonialist and imperial power, and while the American military was under great stress, the US could not be easily dislodged from Iraq. It controlled the lion's share of the oil and gas resources in Iraq and indeed the larger region. While Iran had been strengthened considerably by the war and the US would have to deal with this problem in future, the occupation, while chaotic and confused remained in place. And indeed, contingency plans were well underway to reign in the rulers in Tehran. Stiff sanctions against the Iranian Government were passed in October 2007. The Quds Force in Iran was named as a terrorist group by the US.

Many apologists for US interests, like former Secretary of State, Madeleine Albright and others, argued that the war had been "mismanaged." Indeed, it could not be doubted that if the war and occupation had gone smoothly, the architects of the war would have been hailed as great heroes. In truth, it was an imperialist and colonial war to occupy Iraq and strengthen the US global empire. Given the historic failed imperialist mission of the British in the twentieth century and the rise of Iraqi nationalism under the Baathist regime this was a mission impossible. The pretexts of ridding the country of weapons of mass destruction and bringing democracy were bogus to the core. There was no way to properly manage a colonialist invasion and occupation of a country in the twenty-first century, even had Madeleine Albright been in the saddle. The question of "good management" badly missed the point.

Nevertheless, the colonial occupation had been consolidated. The US fully intended to exploit the golden opportunity as ruthlessly as need be, to control the vast prize of oil as a basis for future empire. The US set about to put in place the infrastructure to ensure this imperialistic objective. The US government would maintain a puppet government in Baghdad, with democratic window-dressing, to the extent that it was possible.

The neoconservatives, as noted before, had little use for a historical view, seeking rather to view the conquest of Iraq in the post-World War II perspective, the establishing of Japan and Korea as US satellites in East Asia.[3] Their rejection of the post World War II institutions of world order, based upon international law, was designed from the beginning to push the Middle East into chaos, a sort of political creative destruction. To the "war crazies" who now ran Washington, the facts were irrelevant. It was immaterial that Saddam had no link with al-Qaeda and nothing to do with the 9/11 attacks in New York and Washington. They were the new storm troopers. They were revolutionaries in a hurry, forging their way to a war which was designed to go for broke, make or break America for the next "American Century." The American people had been forewarned when they sent their troops with boots on the ground to Florida in November 2000, in a putsch to install George W. Bush in the White House. The hell with the votes or who won the election. The hell with international law. The hell with anyone or any country that got in their way. They were out for power. Their propaganda instruments were The *New Standard* newspaper, Fox TV and the American Enterprise institute.[4]

By 2004, the "insurgency" both in American and in Iraq was clearly in place. As noted previously, the Orwellian term is a curious reversal of the truth. Those whom the Western press established the convention of referring to as "insurgents" in Iraq, were actually those who resisted the de facto insurgency unleashed against the legitimate government of Iraq. The de facto insurgency in Iraq was led by George W. Bush himself in the overthrow of the legal government of Saddam Hussein.

By mid 2003, early on, the US was warned by the Israelis that the situation was in danger of spiraling out of control. The increasing mayhem in the streets derailed the reconstruction programs and US officials and employees of private companies working in Iraq were able to move about outside their secure compounds only by bringing in private security firms with hired mercenaries. These private security firms, such as Blackwater USA, Dyncorp, and Triple Canopy, with their highly paid "contractors" operated with the unbridled liberty to shoot and kill at will in the ensuing paranoia subject to neither American nor Iraqi law. With these cowboy corps ripping up and down Iraq, and raising hell with the local civilians, it was only a matter of time before the "shit would hit the fan."

Attempts by the occupying power to ensure that the puppet regime was loyal to the US fell substantially short. The favored Iraqi political parties could not be readily installed, even with the secret efforts by the US CIA using behind the scenes machinations, through two elections in January 2005 and December 2005 and the installation of a new constitution, which in many ways was regressive in terms of women's rights and a secular state.[5] Following the December 2005 election, a government could not be formed until May 20, 2006.

The US party line consisted of a distorted illogic that things continued to get better and that victory was just around the corner, even as the country crumbled.[6] But the view on the ground was different. In mid 2005, large bombs continued to be exploded in Baghdad and around the country. The elections had done nothing to slow down the carnage. With 1750 American soldiers dead, support for Bush had fallen to 39 percent in the US. On June 27, Iraqis staged a riot over the lack of jobs, unemployment running at between 30 and 40 percent, and on July 2, 2005, an aid to Ayatollah Ali al-Sistani was murdered. On July 7, the Egyptian Ambassador was killed in Baghdad, as four Britons, of Pakistani nationality, blew up a bus and the London metro killing 52. Insurgent attacks were running at between 300 and 400 incidents a week and nearly 100 civilians a day were being killed by bombs and bullets.

"Operation Lightening" to stop the Baghdad bombing turned into a failure. CNN reported the bleak conditions in the city, although the reporting was poor.[7] For many, there was no water, no electricity and no propane. People were under the fear of what would happen if Americans left and were afraid to send their children to school. Big battles were being carried out by US forces in Anbar province, with 500 pound bombs being dropped near the Syrian border and many villagers being killed in "Operation Steel Curtain." The Americans claimed that "foreign fighters" were coming into Iraq from Syria.[8] There were some 2500 attacks in September 2005 shortly before the US announced that the new constitution had passed by a large margin.

Democratization, to the extent that it happened, militated against the wishes of the US authorities who had hoped to postpone elections for a number of years, and worked against the goals of the occupation. Power in the hands of the Shiite establishment fed the Sunni insurgency in Anbar Province. The situation would eventually reach the point that the US would fall back onto paying the Sunni tribes large bribes to put pressure on the Shias, as they manipulated the locals in a colonial fashion of divide and rule tactics.

In November 2005, reports emerged that the US was maintaining secret CIA prisons in some 20 countries and flying captives around the world in this secret network to the outpoints of the gulag. Several hundred flights had passed through Europe with the local authorities and European Union officials turning a blind eye. By December 2005, increasing numbers of American soldiers were being killed in Iraq, most often by roadside bombs. On December 8, a suicide bomber blew up the police academy killing 47. The trial of Saddam Hussein, which began on October 19, 2005 continued in a state of chaos. Saddam refused to come to the trial on 13 February 2006, but was forced. After the government became disappointed with the direction of the trial, the judge was removed and a judge appointed from Halibja, the scene of where Chemical Ali had killed thousands of Kurds with poison gas.

On 22 February, 2006, the al-Askariya Shrine in Samarra north of Baghdad was blown up. One of the most holy Shia mosques, its gold dome was destroyed in the blast.[9] Three days of mourning was declared by the government. There were protests in Najaf as well as other cities.[10] The Shrine was attacked by four men in police uniforms who arrived early in the mornings, tied up the guards and planted explosives. This meant that it was going to be impossible to form a “national unity government” and the formation of a workable agreement to rule the country would be delayed. Shiites wanted to take the security into their own hands and expected a backlash against the Sunnis.

The President, Jalal Talabani, spoke of civil war and Shia militant, Muqtada al Sadr, said that it was “time for revénge.” Sunni mosques were attacked across Iraq, some 90 coming under attack on February 22 with at least six Sunni imams killed. By the next day, some 100 mosques across the country had been damaged. Large protests were held with Shia protesters in Najaf shouting: “Rise up Shia! Take Revenge!” Shia protesters set fire to a Sunni Shrine on the outskirts of Basra, which contains the tomb of Talha bin-Obeid-Allah, a companion of the Prophet Mohammed. Cars and buses were stopped and some people shot. Anti-American Slogans were shouted by young men marching in Sadr City in Baghdad. Four provinces, including Baghdad, were put under curfew. Grand Ayatollah Ali al-Sistani called for a week of mourning and forbade attacks on Sunni mosques. The Islamic Dawa Party headquarters office in Basra was attacked and protests held in Najaf, Karbala, and Basra.

In Iran, President Mahmoud Ahmadinejad blamed the US and Israel for the attack. George W. Bush pledged that the US would provide aid to help restore the mosque. The US and the Sunnis feared that Shia militias would now get more power as they were linked to the government though the Interior Ministry. The Interior Minister, who controlled the Security Forces was a member of SCIRI, headed by Abdul-Aziz al-Hakim. Al-Hakim had accused the American Ambassador, Zalmay Khalilzad, of sharing the blame for the attack because a few days earlier, Khalilzad had criticized the institutions in the Iraqi Government linked to armed militias, like the Mahdi Army of Muqtada al-Sadr. According to al-Hakim, "These statements gave green lights to terrorist groups. And, therefore, he shares in part of the responsibility."

The US pinned the attacks on al-Qaeda, and suggested that Abu Musab al-Zarqawi may have been involved, although the White House could offer no evidence. It just "fit the pattern." The Sunnis had boycotted the process of forming a new government and by February 28, six days after the bombing, 1300 had died in the ensuing violence.

On March 16, 2006, the US began a large military operation in Samarra, with 1500 soldiers and 50 planes, but this appeared to be largely a publicity operation, as it was not so different from many other operations which were going on simultaneously.

Given this dynamic, it is not surprising that the civil war in Iraq would emerge with a vengeance with widespread sectarian cleansing of neighborhoods. Indeed, it would take sectarian cleansing to begin to "pacify" the areas of Baghdad as tensions between the communities mounted. Hundreds of thousands of Iraqis perished in the chaos the occupying American forces unleashed upon the country, estimates of the number dead ranged up to 655,000 or more.

This estimate was according to a report in the respected medical journal, *The Lancet*, on October 11, 2006.[11] The study found that the extra number dying since the war was more than 500 per day. Some 2.5 percent of the population had died above what would have occurred without the conflict, the researchers found. Further, the number dying had risen each year since the invasion. On the other hand, President George W. Bush rejected the number, claiming that only about 30,000 had died. Professionals, however, said that the methodology of the study was sound. In three months, 3800 persons had been killed in Baghdad alone. The number of US soldiers killed in Iraq was also rising primarily due to urban sweeps in Baghdad.[12]

Some prominent neoconservatives had begun to jump ship, from supporting the war, such as Francis Fukuyama, Richard Pearle, and William Buckley. A cartoon appeared in the Turkish press, depicting the chaos and captioned: "What a democracy we had today."

In January 2007, the National Intelligence Estimate[13] presented a bleak assessment of the situation in Iraq. "Iraqi society's growing polarization, the persistent weakness of the security forces and the state in general, and all sides' ready recourse to violence are collectively driving an increase in communal and insurgent violence and extremism." The report stressed that efforts must be made to reverse these trends during the next 12 to 18 months or otherwise the security situation would continue to deteriorate at a similar rate to that during the second part of 2006. The report does not go quite so far as calling the situation a "civil war" but says that the term "civil war" "accurately describes key elements of the Iraqi conflict.." This is particularly true of the wide-scale ethnic cleansing. "A number of identifiable security and political triggering events, including sustained sectarian killings, assassination of major religious and political leaders, and a complete Sunni defection from the government have the potential to convulse severely Iraq's security environment."

Things were probably worse than the national intelligence estimate reflected. By February 2007, in the last four months alone, the number of American troop deaths had risen to 334.[14] Six American helicopters had been downed in three weeks. There was continuous urban warfare and the scourge of IEDs continued. Iraqi forces were only 55 to 65 percent of their potential strength because the Kurds and Shiites did not want to patrol outside of their areas. Even though the US had spent $15.4 billion on "standing up" Iraqi troops, they were militia infiltrated, incompetent, and riddled with corruption. Senior American diplomats were resisting taking posts in Iraq.[15] At least one out of every seven Iraqis was a refugee with at least 40,000 persons being displaced every month.[16] Over 100 lecturers had been murdered at Baghdad University. A third of the professionals, including doctors and engineers, had fled the country. Women could not go out alone or without veils. Twelve people had been massacred at a TV station in Baghdad. Some two thousand people a day were crossing the border to Syria. Simply, Iraq was no longer a functioning state.

Iraqi police and military officers were selling the new uniforms meant for their troops, abusing prisoners, and taking bribes to free prisoners. In Baghdad, some areas were being turned into ghost areas. In both Sunni and Shia areas of Baghdad, defenses had been prepared for the "surge." The Shia areas were better off than the Sunni areas. The "surge" was starting to depopulate areas. It seems that the insurgent members of militias knew that the Americans were coming and many had left. The new operations being carried out were creating destruction and greater sectarian violence.[17]

Another battle had just taken place south of Baghdad outside of Najaf where some 200 members of the al-Hawatim and al-Khalzali tribes were killed by American and Iraqi forces. The tribes were anti-US and anti-Iraqi Government waging a guerrilla war in the south.

The account of Haifa Street in Baghdad shows in some detail how the civil war was playing out on the ground in the city. The US "surge strategy" was called the "clear, hold, and build strategy." US officials identified the "greatest security threat in Iraq" as the Sadrist Mahdi Army, even though it was linked to the al-Maliki Government.[18] One of the major areas of conflict in Baghdad was Haifa Street, known as "death street." In March 2007, the Haifa Street offensive had been going on for a month. This is a two-mile stretch just outside the Green Zone, a Sunni area which is moderately prosperous. Observers claimed that it was largely quiet, except when American troops attempt to pacify the area. Consequently, anti-American forces, mainly Sunni militias, became the military and political leadership in the area following the invasion. US forces dismantled the old Iraqi military and political leadership, allowing insurgents to become the local government. But these insurgents did not expel the Shias.[19]

When the Americans came, there were snipers, exploding IED's, and gun battles and the area became a "no-go area." The US launched a six-month offensive to take control of the area with sweeps and rooftop snipers. This went on from January to June 2005, when at the end the operation was declared a success. In fact, the insurgents had just melted into the population as the Americans conducted their patrols. There was high unemployment and no public services.

By February 2006, the Americans left without securing the area, allowing the insurgents to return and expel the Iraqi Army. Things returned to calm, with the Sunni insurgents protecting the neighborhood. But the Americans suspected that the area was being used as a base of operations against the Shiites. So the Americans reentered Haifa Street with security forces, some of them Shiites, and again upset the peace. Shia residents were told that they would be killed if they did not get out. On January 9, 2007, there were huge battles. Americans and Iraqis attacked in force with helicopters and F-15 jets. The attacks started before dawn around Tallil Square. When the sun came up, the insurgents began shooting from rooftops and US soldiers used 50 caliber machine guns mounted on Stryker armored vehicles. The Americans used Tow missiles and Mark 19 grenade launchers. Apache helicopters fired Hellfire missiles creating eleven hours of death and destruction.[20]

US forces then began house to house searches with 1000 American and Iraqi troops. They killed and arrested suspected insurgents. One week later, the first result of the new strategy was seen. There was massive destruction, police-state conditions, widespread suffering, and on-going fighting. Now the Shiite Iraqi Army was doing sectarian cleansing, expelling and sometimes killing the Sunni majority. In one block alone, about 60 Sunni families had been expelled.

A curfew was clamped, with no vehicles allowed to drive in the area. There was no electricity, no kerosene, and no running water. Snipers had taken positions on rooftops shooting women trying to get food, but there was no way for them to get to the hospital when hit. There was demolished buildings, deserted neighbors, and the results of sectarian torture on both sides. It was as if the battle of Fallujah had been brought to Baghdad. People collected some belongings in small bags and moved out. It was said of Bush's new "surge strategy" that "[t]he new security plan has given militias permission to go into our houses and apartments and kill people...This plan targets Sunnis and forces them to leave their homes. And they are." But the battle continued, with more American air strikes, residents fleeing, fire-fights between American soldiers and insurgents, and death threats from both Sunnis and Shias. American soldier, Sgt. First Class, Marc Biletski, remarked, "[t]his place is a failure..Every time we come here, we have to come back."[21]

A resident remarked: "They told us they would bring democracy. They promised life would get better than it was under Saddam. But they brought us nothing but death and killing. They brought mass destruction to Baghdad." The comment from the US Ambassador, Zalmay Khalilzad, however, was quite different. "I am encouraged by what I have seen," he reportedly said.

From the Sunni perspective, it was American sponsorship of sectarian cleansing. Harith al-Dari, leader of the Association of Muslim Scholars (AMS), a Sunni resistance group, said it was "a bloody sectarian massacre." A spokesman for the groups read the names of twelve men killed on al-Jazeera TV and said; "[a]ll of their guilt was that they defended their neighborhood...The American President said in 2003, 'mission accomplished.' Now in 2007, he used jet fighters a few meters from the Green Zone."[22]

The Iraqi military and police were accused of assassinating people. "The Americans are doing nothing as if they are backing the militias. This military siege is killing us...if this plan continues for one more week I don't think you will find one family left on Haifa Street." It turned the area into an "unlivable graveyard.

This was the way the new "security strategy" was working with greater use of air power, bombing runs, and assaults with high caliber weapons from helicopter gun ships. It had greatly increased the violence. That some Iraqi police forces were operating as death squads became clear.[23] In October, 2006, the Iraqi Interior Ministry suspended an entire police brigade for participating in death squad killings in Baghdad. The American military admitted that the main cause of Iraqi civilian deaths was the death squads. Falcon, the 8th Brigade, Second Division of the Iraqi National Police (800 special police commandos) were thought to have killed 26 workers in a food factory in the Amel neighborhood. Both Sunni and Shiite death squads continued to operate as part of the Iraqi Government even under warnings from the American Government.[24]

In the Shiite area of Sadr City, the Mahdi Army patrolled the area and this seemed to work. But in January 2007, Bush's new strategy was being put into place as US soldiers began attacking both Shia and Sunni militias. The US arrested a senior member of the Mahdi Army, the local commander in that post. This disrupted the patrols and made the area subject to attack by Sunnis. The Sunni insurgents singled out Shiites to kill. On January 26, 2007,

27 bodies were found dumped in the area as sectarian cleansing was being carried out. Ali al-Dabaggh, spokesman for Prime Minister Nouri al-Malaki, said: "This area must be cleansed."[25] Again in February, much of East Baghdad was subjected to sweeps by security forces to curb the civil war, searching "areas considered sanctuaries for insurgents and militants."[26]

Tal Afar, a city of 300,000 near the Syrian border, was an example of the new US strategy. Here, the whole population was moved for pacification with a great deal of death and destruction.

In fact, no place in Iraq was safe.[27] This was made clear after a suicide bomber penetrated eight rings of security and blew himself up in the Green Zone while Iraqi MPs were eating lunch. The bomber, possibly the body-guard of a Sunni member of Parliament, was wearing a vest with explosives. Three MPs died. About the same time, the al Sarafiya Bridge, a main bridge over the Tigris River, which linked east and west Baghdad, was blown up. It was reported that 20 cars fell into the river as the bridge built by the British 75 years before was destroyed.

By 2007, at least four million, more than one in ten, Iraqis were homeless or displaced. Some two million had fled the country while two million had been forced to abandon their homes inside the country. The occupying Americans were totally helpless in their foundering, as life deteriorated throughout the country. The country lacked electricity, water, fuel, medicines and medical services. People died just struggling to live and the American version of "democracy" became a nightmare. And sometimes this democracy was a joke, not only in Iraq, but around the world.

Yet, the end of the "insurgency" was said to be just around the corner. The Vice-President, Dick Cheney, claimed that the uprising was in its death throes, but it was no more than deception or wishful thinking. This lie was no longer plausible and there were very few who found what Cheney said believable, anyway. American apologists for the war, from the neoconservatives to Iraqi officials, began to sound more and more like "Baghdad Bob,"[28] the Iraqi spokesman for the Saddam regime, in their implausible statements about the war. At the end of 2006, the farcical trial of former President Saddam Hussein came to an end[29] and Saddam was hanged on December 30, 2006.[30]

This event was billed as yet another turning point, similar to the killing of Abu Musab al-Zarqawi on June 8, 2006, which was supposed to finally put an end to Iraqi strife, kill Baathist nationalism, end the insurgency and finally usher in the "new Iraq."[31] The US fired a missile at a house where al-Zarqawi was staying near Baghdad. Again, there was to be no such development as the emergence of peace and tranquility. Al-Zarqawi, of little importance anyway, was quickly replaced and, if anything, things only continued to deteriorate further.

On June 21, 2006, the third and main lawyer in Saddam Hussein's trial had been killed, murdered in Baghdad. About this time, the US began a campaign of blaming Iran for many of the weapons said to be coming into Iraq. General George Casey, the leading Commander in Iraq, appearing on American TV,[32] said that Iran was providing weapons and training terrorist groups to operate in Iraq. The oil industry had still not recovered to produce at the level reached before Saddam was overthrown, exporting at the level of 2.1 billion barrels per day while the previous level was 2.5 billion barrels per day. The aim was to get this up figure up to 6 bbl. per day.

In August of 2006, the war in Lebanon was started by Israel, having been planned for some months, as explored in Chapter Six. By July 2007, some 3438 US troops had been killed in Iraq up from 2600 in May 2006. This was the most violent month yet in Iraq. On August 30, the Hilla Army recruiting station was bombed with 50 recruits killed.

When Democrats in the US called for the war to be halted and the US to bring the troops home, they were labeled the "party of cut and run."[33] Defense Secretary, Donald Rumsfeld, stated that the US was "appeasing" the rise of a new type of fascism, "Islamic fascism." This was clearly an attempt to tie the insurgency to the Nazis, a neoconservative theme which began to emerge.

On November, 2006, there was another bizarre development in Saddam's trial. The judge was changed when he stated in the courtroom that Saddam was not a dictator. The death sentence was handed down to Saddam on November 5, 2006, two days before the US mid-term election on November 7.

Toward the end of 2006, in November, the American grass-roots had a chance to make their voice heard in the mid-term congressional elections. In fact, the message which the people sent was loud and clear. Across the board, the American electorate wanted the US troops home, they wanted the funding for the war cut, they wanted more social spending, and they wanted less money spent for the war. The only disagreement was how soon the troops should be brought back.[34]

After the election, Bush admitted that "we took a thumpin" with both the House of Representatives and the Senate going to the Republicans. Immediately after the election, Defense Secretary Donald Rumsfeld was fired.[35] Robert Gates was chosen to replace him, winning quick approval from Congress. In fact, however, the response of the Bush Administration was to do just the opposite of what the majority of the American people demanded. Gates would be an improvement over Rumsfeld only in the sense that Gates did not tend to antagonize the press and give the appearance of being an inorganic robot, with short circuitry, at press conferences. In terms of the war, it was, in the words of Dick Cheney, "full speed ahead" and Gates would be on board, carrying out the same basic policies as Rumsfeld had done.

By November 23, 2006, some 100,000 Iraqis were leaving the country every month. Zbigniew Brzezinski, former National Security Council advisor for President Jimmy Carter, argued that Iraq was a colonial war and a failure of leadership.[36] Some 2876 American troops were now dead in Iraq.

The long-awaited Baker-Hamilton report of the Iraq Study Group was not to be released until after the election although leaked reports indicated its basic recommendations by the end of October 2006. The Iraq study group, led by Baker and Hamilton, was a bipartisan effort, a congressionally appointed Iraq Study Group, to give policy recommendations to Congress. Baker was White House chief of staff and Treasury Secretary under former President Ronald Reagan. Later he had served as the Bush family lawyer, since the 1970s. He headed the legal team that defeated the Democratic challenges to Bush's victory in Florida in 2000. In 2003-2004 he negotiated substantial reductions in Iraq's foreign debt on behalf of the White House, as well as defending Bush-family connected defense corporations and helping to funnel the vast millions of dollars that poured into the Bush financial empire from the Saudi Royal family.

The Baker report, released on December 6, 2006, called for a significantly different approach to the Iraq War from that being followed by the Bush Administration.[37] The goal of "victory" in Iraq should be abandoned, the report said, along with the goal of "democracy," concentrating rather on "stability." Democracy might, at most, be a long-term goal. The government in Iraq might be made "representative, but not "democratic." The restoration of political stability could be presented as "success." There should be no effort to "stay the course," as Bush and Cheney insisted upon. Talk should be about "success" not victory.[38] There should be no increase in numbers of US troops. Rather, the US troops should be redeployed to nearby areas. There should be a call for a phased withdrawal of the soldiers. Regional powers should be engaged in a diplomatic offensive and talks held particularly with Syria and Iran. Help should also be solicited from the United Nations and the European Union. The primary focus should be upon al-Qaeda. The first task was to concentrate upon stabilizing Baghdad. There should be no dividing up of Iraq. There could be no quick removal of troops, but most combat troops should be out of Iraq by 2008. The US must state clearly that it does not want to control the oil in Iraq.

The Baker report opened up the possibility of falling back upon a pro-US strong man, like Saddam, in order to gain political stability. The new approach should be implemented with urgency, the Study Group urged.[39] The British Chief of Staff, General Sir Richard Dannatt, also rejected "staying the course," out of hand, avoiding the intellectual bankruptcy typical of Washington. The United Kingdom should "get ourselves out sometime soon because our presence exacerbates the security problems. We are in a Muslim country and Muslims' views of foreigners in their country are quite clear," he argued.[40] In the United States, just before the election, only 37 percent had approved of Bush's handling of Iraq and the figures had fallen from 41 percent a month before. Insurgent attacks were up by 22 percent in Baghdad and at this point, in November, 2006, 2786 Americans had died in the war.

Many hoped that Baker had the stature to rescue the White House from the debacle in Iraq and he was seen as a sort of "messiah" and, as a realist, an antidote to the "grim Manichaeism of Vice-president Dick Cheney.[41] But the report, being realistic, was sure to stick in the craw of Bush and Cheney.[42] Especially Cheney which was what really mattered. It seems that Cheney won this round over the challenge, the same way he had tended to win the upper hand over the more moderate approach of Condoleezza Rice.

As Barbara Tuchman had written about leaders in history, like Bush and Cheney, who refused to face reality, "Wooden-headedness...plays a remarkably large role in government. It consists in assessing a situation in terms of preconceived notions while ignoring or rejecting any contrary signs. It is acting according to wish while not allowing oneself to be deflected by facts.[43]

Cheney and Bush, of course, would have none of it. The report was to be almost completely ignored.[44] Once again, the neoconservatives had little use for a well researched and well reasoned report by thoughtful and realistic persons, falling back upon the full-steam-ahead approach of the Vice President. Bush was again acting the part of the local bully, who Hank Williams sang about back in 1951. "He acts like his head was only made to hold his ears apart." Bush's actions, on the other hand, were global.

On December 10, 2006, George W. Bush announced a "change of course" in the war, without giving details. On December 18, Robert Gates was named as the new Secretary of Defense. On the December 20, Bush stated that the number of troops in Iraq would be increased by some 20,500, calling the approach a "surge" rather than the more accurate term, "escalation." The actual number, in fact, was larger than that claimed by Bush.

On December 27, 2006, the Iraqi appeals court in Baghdad upheld the death sentence of Saddam Hussein. The sentence of death by hanging had been announced on November 5, 2006 and appeared in the US morning papers on Monday, the day before the mid-term elections to be held the next day, November 7.[45] The trial had lasted about nine months and the execution was to be carried out within 30 days, but an appeal was filed. The White House calculated that the announcement would help Republican candidates and denied that there was any connection between the conviction date and the US elections, although the timing was curious. When questioned by a reporter regarding this, White House Spokesman, former Fox News anchor, Tony Snow, asked "Are you smoking rope?" Earlier in the bungled trial, two defense attorneys had been murdered. Attorney Sadoon Janabi was kidnapped and shot in the head on October 20, 2005. He was Awad Hamad al-Bandar's Attorney, being tried with Saddam. Al-Bandar was the Former Chief Justice of the Revolutionary Court. On November 8, 2005, Attorney Adil Muhammed al-Subaidi, counsel for the former Vice-President, Taha Yassin Ramadan, was attacked and killed. The judge in the trial was changed more than once.[46] Ramadan was sentenced to life in prison.

Saddam's lawyers, based in Amman Jordan, appealed to Arab government and the United Nations to stop the execution. Many in the country also thought a delay would be a good idea, but many Shiites took to the streets to celebrate. Saddam was being tried at the same time for a much larger crime, the killing of some 180,000 Kurds during the 1987-88 al-Anfal Campaign[47] crackdown. The Dujail killings, for which Saddam had been sentenced, were over a plot to assassinate Saddam. Saddam was being held by the Americans in an American military prison at Camp Cropper close to the Baghdad airport.[48]

Much of the Iraq was put in lockdown. The Shiites marched to celebrate the verdict with round the clock curfews in Baghdad and the two Sunni Provinces of Anbar and Salaheddin. Some 400 protesters marched in Samarra and there were protests in Tikrit, Saddam's home town.[49]

On Dec. 27, 2006, the appeals court upheld the conviction of Saddam on "crimes against humanity" and Saddam was executed early in the morning on the 30 of December at five in the morning. This was the first day of Eid ul-Adha or feast of the sacrifice. Large car bombs went off and killed 31 or more Shiites, after the event at Kufa, and reportedly injured

58. Ramsey Clark, former Attorney General of the United States for President Lyndon Johnson, acting as one of Saddam's lawyers, remarking on the trial, said that it was an "assault on truth and justice and on international law. He said they threw the judges out in the middle of the trial because they did not like the way the trial was going and the last judge had said, "We do not need a trial, we need a hanging." Near the end of the trial, the Judge removed Ramsey Clark from the trial with the words "Get him out! He's coming from America to insult the Iraqi people and the court." This followed the submission by Clark of a court filing which criticized the procedure of the court. It was said that when the verdict was read, Saddam refused to stand and was pulled to his feet by the guards. Saddam reportedly shouted to the judge, "You are servants of the occupiers and lackeys!" Later the Prime Minister, Nuri al-Maliki, went on TV to praise the verdict and compared Saddam to Hitler. It was expected that the sentencing would heighten sectarian tensions.[50] Saddam was secretly buried in Takrit in the night.

The official reaction of the Bush Administration to the Baker Report was not long in coming. In short, the decision was to replace the military command leadership in Iraq[51] and escalate the war, reminiscent of Lyndon Johnson in the Vietnam era as the situation grew more bleak. General John P. Abizaid, the top US commander in the Middle East, was to be replaced by Admiral William Fallon. General George Casey, the top commander in Iraq, was to be replaced with Lt. General David Petraeus. The "surge" was announced on January 10, 2007.[52] More troops, up to 20,500 were to be sent in an effort to secure Baghdad, at the minimum, although the actual increase in troops would exceed 30,000.[53]

But in fact, it seems that the administration was playing with smoke and mirrors. A more careful scrutiny of US military plans revealed that there was a sort of double surge planned, in which the number of combat troops in Iraq would nearly double by the end of the year. This would be done by sending more combat brigades and extending 12 month tours of duty to 15 months. In early January 2007, combat troops in Iraq numbered about 52,500. By the end of the year, they could reach 98,000, increasing the total number of troops from 162,000 to 200,000. The initial surge would add five combat brigades to the 15 already there. But additional combat brigades were on the way that could increase the number of combat brigades up to 28 by Christmas 2007.

It was hard to find anyone with long experience with the war who believed such a strategy could succeed. The polls showed that only 11 percent of the American public approved of sending more troops to Iraq. This was increasingly true of retired military generals whose criticism of the Bush Administration increased. Some prominent neoconservatives had also started to run from Bush's policies.[54] These included Kenneth Adelman who said that Powell, Cheney, Rumsfeld and Rice were incompetent. Richard Pearle said that he held Bush responsible for the war debacle. Frank Gaffney began to charge that the war had been sabotaged by the people around Bush. David Frum, a former presidential speech writer, thought that Bush had either not understood the mission in Iraq or was intellectually deficient. James Woolsey noted that there had been profound American errors. Certainly, those who had been responsible for conducting the war on the ground in Iraq, Generals Casey and Abizaid, seemed to have little faith that the surge strategy of Bush and Cheney could succeed. However, in mid-January, Casey said he believed the surge strategy could work. Zalmay Khalilzad, who was still US Ambassador in Iraq, along with Casey, claimed that the surge strategy had been conceived by both the Iraqis and the Americans. However, it was clear that al-Maliki did not want more American troops in Iraq. According to the plan, "American soldiers will establish a much greater physical presence in neighborhoods across Baghdad, operating hand-in-hand with the army and police at newly created joint security sites." This was part of the administration's effort to build up the anticipation that things would continue to get better through the summer and fall, 2007.[55] The command was being purged of the worn-out leaders and a new commander put in place. General Petraeus was a person willing to salute the President and back the party line. Indeed, it seemed that much of the strategy was dubbed a surge, apparently to avoid using the term escalation, which was too closely associated with the war in Vietnam.[56] Avoiding this conflation, the term "surge" was coined, presumably in the spirit of "Honest Abe" and bringing in the Orwellian language so typical of Bush and Cheney. The White House spin-doctors had indeed become masters of Orwellian language.

On January 15, two more hangings were carried out in Baghdad. These were former officials who had been tried with Saddam Hussein in the Dujail trial. Barzan Ibrahim al-Tikriti, Saddam's half brother, was a leader of Mukhabarat, the Iraqi Intelligence Service. Awad Hamed al-Bandar was the former Chief Justice of the Revolutionary Court and a former intelligence chief. The hangings were bungled with al-Takriti being decapitated when he fell. These events continued to fuel the civil war.

Again, by almost all accounts, the surge was a futile effort. The violence and bombs continued, the IED attacks escalating to more powerful explosively formed projectiles (EFPs), which again were said to be coming from Iran. On January 16, 2007 there were huge bombs in Baghdad. In the last year, at least 34,000 civilians had been killed and deaths were running at some 100 a day. Iraqi and American troops continued to die. The Bush spin-doctors attempted to paint a bright picture, but now fewer and fewer people were buying the optimism. The routine was being repeated again and again, from one six month period to the next. Just wait another six months, seemed to be the idea, and things would begin to turn the corner and right themselves back to normal people were being told. It was the old "light at the end of tunnel" routine reminiscent of the Vietnam era. In fact, most believed that the situation had gone far beyond any possibility that the Americans would bring peace, with the country now destroyed.

On January 28, 2007, at least 250 members of a Shiite sect died in a 15 hour battle near Najaf. Many others died in attacks around Iraq on the same day, 17 in Kirkuk, 55 in Baghdad, and a number of other bombings.[57] The battle happened near the villave of Zarqaa where up to 600 fighters from a Shiite sect, the Mehwadiya, had gathered. This group was reportedly created by Saddam Hussein to confront the influence of Ayatollah Ali al-Sistani. They planned to attack Shiite religious convoys on the way to Karbala to celebrate Ashura, the Shiite religious holiday which began the next day.[58] The Iraqi forces were backed up by American helicopters and tanks. Two American soldiers died when one of the helicopters crashed.

By 2007, it could not be doubted that Iraq had become an endless quagmire in which the Americans were trapped and the comparison with Vietnam could no longer be avoided. The lesson of Vietnam for most was that the US had stayed too long or should never have invaded the country in the first place. For Bush and the neoconservatives, the lesson was that the Americans had not stayed long enough and a premature pull-out had cost American a victory in the war.

Increasingly, a deceptive rhetoric was abroad in the American political arena. The debate about when the troops would come home was out of step with the reality on the ground and the logic of the occupation in the global context. Behind the scenes, the political class, both Democrats and Republicans knew that the real agenda was something of a different stripe altogether. Rather, the real question was how the now permanent empire in Iraq was going to be maintained. What would it take for this, and how much of the disaster, in the public mind, could be saved? The US was not leaving Iraq. The US had never intended to leave, from the first day of the invasion. There was no "exit strategy" because there was to be no exit. Indeed, Iraq was to be a satellite, a rich oil-prize, in the US Empire for the "new American century." This, after all, was the "project" which Cheney and his neoconservatives had launched in the mid-1990s.

Indeed, was it really plausible that the US could leave, as in Vietnam in the early 1970s? In relation to Cindy Sheheen's anti-war activism, and other anti-war movements, like Code Pink in the US, it was never very realistically considered that indeed the US had already "bought" Iraq, spending upwards of $750 million dollars a day in an estimated $2 trillion war and possibly up to $2.4 trillion war.[59] Indeed, it was difficult to get an accurate estimate of the costs of the war. By the end of 2007, some $604 billion already spent for Iraq and Afghanistan, was billed as "supplementary appropriations."[60] This was about $450 billion for the Iraq War and $130 billion for the Afghanistan War. In comparison, the Vietnam War cost $518 billion for the first ten years, but $660 billion by 1975. The Korean War cost $456 billion and the Gulf War cost $88 billion, all figures in constant dollars. The cost of the wars in Afghanistan and Iraq would reach $800 billion by the end of George W. Bush's Presidency. In October, 2007 Bush had asked for another $200 billion. These figures pertain only to Iraq and Afghanistan. The overall "defense budget" for 2008 was some $686 billion.[61] Additional funding was being asked for the production of mine-resistant, ambush-protected vehicles (MRAPS). They cost one million dollars each and would seem to indicate that the locals, where the US military would be operating, were not expected to be particularly friendly. It quickly emerged that part of the extra funding was for the purpose of upgrading air fields in Diego Garcia and modifying the B-1 Stealth bombers to carry huge bunker-busting bombs which might be used to bomb Iran. All of this spending was said to be relatively small, however, in relation to the relatively large US gross domestic product (GDP), only consuming 4.2 percent. One is tempted to say, with the late Edward Abbey, that the US has a gross, very gross, gross domestic product.[62]

Additionally, 12 to 14 major military bases were now in place in Iraq,[63] along with the largest US embassy in the world, costing more than $750 million and rising on the banks of the Euphrates in Baghdad.[64] Nearly 4000 US soldiers were now dead and the US was edging toward the control and exploitation of the oil of the region in perpetuity. The Congressional Budget Office had projected the cost of the Iraq war at $845 billion, if the troop level was reduced to 75,000 within five years. Given these calculations based upon the long-term deployment of troops, there could be little doubt that the US occupation was to be permanent in some form.[65] The American bases in Iraq were becoming little American ghettos with fast food, movies, and all the amenities.

Indeed, for the neoconservatives, the reason the US could not leave was clearly, in one word, Empire. Baghdad was the other eye of the Pentagon, the world-centered eyes of the US Empire. This agenda could not be explicitly spelled out openly. It could only be suggested with fudge terms such as "regional security," "standing by our friends in the region," "our national security interests," "promoting democracy," and comically, "preventing them from following us home." These were the pretexts used to cover up the real US imperialist agenda.

The world held its breath in 2007, hoping that the Administration in Washington would not hit Iran until cooler heads prevailed. But the signs were all there that Washington was focused on Iran and people feared the neoconservatives might bomb Iran before Bush left office. Bush and the neoconservatives had barely more than another year in office and the government in Baghdad was seen as increasingly dysfunctional. The world had tired of fearing, not al-Qaeda and terrorism, but what the White House would do next.

At the end of May, 2007, at least 1000 US soldiers had been killed in Iraq in the previous year. Some 586 bodies of civilians had been found in Baghdad in May alone. The charges against Iran that the country was sending weapons and training insurgents increased from the White House and the US commanders in Iraq. In Washington's sights was the Revolutionary Guards, the Quds Force in Iran, who were said to be supplying weapons to the Mahdi Army of Muqtada al-Sadr. But some 80 percent of Iraqis wanted the US forces to leave Iraq and the same percentage of US troops wanted to be sent out of Iraq. In Najaf, in April 2007, hundreds of thousands of Shias protested the US occupation as Muqtada al-Sadr called America "the great evil." The protest was held on the anniversary of Saddam's overthrow with the chant: "No, no to the occupier. Yes, Yes to Iraq." American flags were burned. The US could not translate military victory into political victory.[66]

On 24 June, 2007, Chemical Ali (Ali Hassan al-Majid) was sentenced to hang in Baghdad for crimes in Halabja, the gassing of some 180,000 thousands Kurds in the Anfal Campaign.

In mid-2007, the Americans switched tactics and begun a campaign to arm and subsidize the Sunni tribes in the Anbar and Diyala Provinces in order to wean them away from cooperation with elements of al-Qaeda.[67] This outright bribing of the local sheikhs seemed to be a very risky strategy, which had failed at least once in Falluja. This led to the killing of a prominent sheikh, Abdul-Sattar Abu Risha, who was working with the U.S. forces in Anbar on September 13, 2007. Abu Risha, was the leader of the Anbar Salvation Council, also known as the Anbar Awakening, an alliance of tribes that backed the US Government. Abu Risha, who had met President Bush at al-Asad air Base on September 3, was the most prominent person in the Sunni Sheikh opposition to al-Qaeda in Iraq.[68]

The payments from`the Americns, while not widely reported, were extensive. South of Baghdad, one Sheikh was given $38,000 and promised another $189,000 over three months in cash to drive the al-Qaeda fighters from a local camp.[69]

As the summer wore on, the anticipation was building as to the expected outcome of the Petraeus Report which was scheduled to be delivered in Washington in September. In the focus also were the so-called "benchmarks," which the Iraqis were supposed to meet as a measure of their dealing with the needs of moving forward. Among these were passing the hydrocarbons law, as to how the oil profits would be divided up among the regions of the country, amending the Constitution, which continued to be delayed, and the review of the de-Bathification Law.

But on July 30, there was more bleak news as a report from Oxfam, which had left Iraq in 2003, on Iraq was released.[70] The report was another window from outside into the state of collapse and degradation the county had fallen under given the long period of sanctions in the 1990s and the American occupation since the US invasion. The report showed, among other things, that one third of Iraqis, at least eight million, needed emergency aid, some 70 percent lacked an adequate water supply, 28 percent of children were malnourished, there was lack of sanitation, there was widespread horrifying violence, lack of human rights, a humanitarian crisis, four million needed food aid, and four million had fled their homes, including professionals, medical doctors, and academics. Two million refugees were living outside the country and two million were displaced within the country, the fastest growing refugee crises in the world. Widows were getting only $100 a month from the Ministry of Labor and Social Affairs. Oxfam recommended that the Public Distribution System (PDS) should issue ID cards so that displaced persons could get rations. This had been the case earlier under Saddam Hussein. The NGO Coordination Committee in Iraq (NCCI) said the Government could do more. It was also stressed that the Multinational Forces in Iraq (MFN) should "respect their moral and legal obligation not to harm civilians or their property, or the essential infrastructure."

The US press was also starting to become sharply critical of the war. On July 8, the *New York Times* called for US troops to leave Iraq, arguing that Bush's plan to stabilize the country through military means and "stay the course" is a lost cause. "Continuing to sacrifice the lives and limbs of American soldiers is wrong The war is sapping the strength of the nation's alliances and its military forces..It is a betrayal of a world that needs the wise application of American power and principles." The editorial concluded, "This country faces a choice. We can go on allowing Mr. Bush to drag out this war without end or purpose. Or we can insist that American troops are withdrawn as quickly and safely as we can manage...with as much effort as possible to stop the chaos from spreading.[71]

After the summer of 2007, the Bush-Cheney war occupation mounted the latest six-month effort to convince the American people that things were going well in Iraq and that victory was again just around the corner.[72] Indeed, the country was being prepared for the spectacle that was to take place in Washington in mid-September designed for this purpose.

In July, the Defense Department sponsored a trip to Iraq by Michael E. O'Hanlon and Kenneth M. Pollack.[73] Pollack was a former CIA analyst who urged that the US invasion and occupation of Iraq should be carried out. Upon return, the analysts published a piece in the New York Times.[74] It appears that the O'Hanlon and Pollack were sent to bring back good news in anticipation of General Petraeus's report which was coming up in September. The authors noted the widespread criticism of the war in the US press and asserted that Bush's critics are "unaware of the significant changes taking place." What the authors claimed to find was that "we are finally getting somewhere in Iraq, at least in military terms." They said they were "surprised by the gains" they saw, claiming that they had been harsh critics of the Bush Administration war in the past. They found a "potential" for "sustainable stability" if not victory. They argued that troop morale is high, that General Petraeus is a "superb Commander," that they could "see real results, that civilian fatality rates were down and that local Sunni sheikhs in Ramadi were competing for US military friendship. Visiting Tal Afar and Mosul in the north, they found the situation to be improving and prosperous. They argued that there was a "popular animus against al-Qaeda" and that the Sunni sheikhs in Anbar Province were "close to crippling al-Qaeda." They found that the new Embedded Provincial Reconstruction Teams were working. They then strongly urged that "Congress should sustain the effort at least into 2008."

It is clear that the article was arranged and deliberately planted in the top US newspaper to influence Congress and the American people in advance of the Petreaus hearings. The same day, the piece was picked up and trumpeted by Fox TV and Dick Cheney.[75] While the authors cleverly claimed that they had been war critics, the record showed that they had always been supporters of the war in their writings.[76] In Iraq they had spoken mostly to American officials and their trip was paid for by the Defense Department. There was little doubt that the Petraeus hearing was staged to lobby for the continued deployment of the troops in Iraq for the next six month interval till March 2008. The tactic was clear from press reports.[77]

While General Petaeus and US Ambassador Ryan Crocker painted a bright picture of progress in Iraq, 70 percent of Iraqis believed that security had deteriorated since the surge began and 60 percent believed that attacks on US forces were justified. In the Sunni community, 93 percent wanted to see Americans in Iraq killed. Only 29 percent of Iraqis thought the situation would get better.[78]

It has surely been a measure of the failure of the occupation that the US State Department has been forced to rely upon private security firms to protect US government and corporate officials in Iraq. The contract for protecting US officials in Baghdad was awarded to the firm of Blackwater USA by the US State Department. On September 16, the killing of 17 civilians in an incident in Baghdad led to the demand by the Iraqi Government that the firm be expelled from the country. However, it was not expected that any employees of the firm, which had received at least $1.2 billion in contracts from the US Government would have to answer for killing Iraqis in cold blood in the streets of Baghdad.[79]

The reputation of America, and its foreign policy, had hit rock bottom. The occupation of Iraq was wearing increasingly threadbare not only in the US but around the world. Even the Vietnam debacle had not risen to such levels of incompetence. The mercenary armies of the private security firms, particularly Blackwater USA, murdering Iraqis in cold blood became a prominent issue in late 2007. With the Iraqi Government demanding that the company be expelled from the country, the US scrambled to put some other arrangements in place. It was clear, however, that the fiction that the US had won control in the streets of Iraq was exposed as a lie. It was not yet safe in Iraq which was still under US control. And the Iraqi Government, indeed, enjoyed very little sovereignty from the US Government. The country, essentially, remained under colonial occupation.

In a larger sense, the war was over, even though the occupation was not and would continue to take its toll in American and Iraqi lives and possibly result in the breakup of the country.[80] In late 2007, the Kurdish Workers Party (PKK) in the area controlled by the Kurdish Regional Government (KRG) began to carry out raids into Turkey. Turkey responded by deploying some 100,000 troops on its southeastern border. These clashes began to kill Turkish soldiers and Kurdish rebels as the two-decades old conflict flared up again. It was also reported that Turkey had fired into villages in northern Iraq and dropped bombs on PKK positions. The Turkish Parliament voted in October 2007 to authorize a Turkish incursion along the border into northern Iraq and the Turkish military began bombing PKK camps along the border in Northern Iraq a few weeks later.

It was noted, early on that the immediate beneficiary of the US invasion and occupation of Iraq was Iran.[81] Indeed, US policies had strengthened Shiites all across the Middle East, bringing unease among Sunnis in the region.[82] Early in 2007, Retired Lt. General William E. Odam pointed out that neoconservative policies in Iraq were based upon myths and that they must abandon the goal of "winning." The Baker-Hamilton report had already made this clear, of course. The first myth was that there was a right way to invade and transform Iraq. He argued that it was never a possibility that the US could invade and create a liberal constitutional democracy in Iraq. The second myth was that further war could contain and curb Iranian influence in Iraq. The war had brought pro-Iranian parties to power and to attack Iran would only make the situation worse for the Americans. A third myth was that continuation of the war was necessary to deny al-Qaeda a haven in Iraq. In fact, al-Qaeda was depending upon the presence of the Americans to further their support among the local people. Fourth, it was a myth that support for the war was support for the American troops. The troops had never been asked what they wanted and even veterans' groups were asking that the troops be brought home. As the Baker Report had emphasized, the US needed to redeploy the troops, create new strategic options, and realize that the US could not stabilize the Middle East without the help of the countries in the region. The US should aim for a "stable Iraq," not 'a democratic Iraq," as continued wars were destabilizing the region.[83]

That the US policy was producing more terrorism was emphasized in a National Intelligence Estimate released in July 2007. This report on Washington's "counterterrorism strategy," concluded that al-Qaeda "has protected or regenerated key elements of its homeland attack capability," by establishing a haven in Pakistan and reconstituting its top leadership. Al-Qaeda has "recruited and indoctrinated operatives"...by "associating itself with an Iraqi subsidiary." The report said that bin-Laden's organization will use the contacts of al-Qaeda in Iraq in trying to "attack the homeland." Bush and the Republicans used the report to argue that it showed that the US must remain and fight al-Qaeda in Iraq, while the democrats used the report to argue that the US must pull US troops out. Bush's Homeland Security Advisor, Francis Townsend, said that the US was "harassing al-Qaeda." But a former CIA analyst, Paul R. Pillar commented that the "US presence in Iraq was only fueling the terrorist's cause." Al-Qaeda in Iraq did not exist until the US invaded.[84]

It was clear by 2007 that the goal of "democracy" in Iraq was merely a faint memory.[85] In fact, as predicted by more sober analysts, democracy, where it had happened in the Middle East, presented a serious problem for US foreign policy. The Hamas victory in Palestine in December 2005 was a "dangerous trend." In Egypt, there had been gains for the Muslim Brotherhood. The major democratic thrust in Lebanon was driving the popularity of Hezbollah. US Secretary of State, Condoleezza Rice, backed down on her earlier criticism of President Hosni Mubarak in Egypt.[86] So the hypocrisy of the US had been exposed. It was a similar story in Afghanistan, where the Taliban continued to strengthen. The Taliban was also making a return to democracy in Pakistan highly problematical. So whatever the new Middle East was to be about, it was not likely to be democracy.

The situation in Iraq had become a huge historical catastrophe by any reasonable measure. The reputation of the US around the world had fallen to historical lows. The US Empire must go on, but in what form, was the historical question.

That the occupation of Iraq would not end was being made quite explicitly clear by US officials.[87] This seemed to be producing a rather sharp contradiction between this reality and the thrust of the anti-war movement toward the end of 2007 and as the US presidential campaign began to gear up for the election primaries in 2008. Navy Admiral Michael Mullen, Chief of Naval Operations, who was chosen to replace General Peter Pace as Chairman of the Joint Chiefs of Staff, said "the US will be in Iraq for years." It was projected to take three to four years to redeploy one-half of the 160,000 troops in Iraq. The party line in Washington had become that the surge is working, but the Iraqi Government has not made very much political progress and national reconciliation. Iraqi Prime Minister Nuri al-Maliki was being criticized more by the Americans, seemingly in a shifting of the blame for the occupation failure. In July, General David Petraeus, now the top commander in Iraq, said that it would take until 2009, six years from the invasion, to achieve "sustainable security."[88]

As the fifth year of the US occupation of Iraq ebbed away, however, the farce on the ground deepened. A crisis, indeed, but more than a crisis: the number of US military troops killed approached nearly 4000 and some 30,000 wounded; tens of thousands of Iraqi civilians were dead, some four million displaced, with two million in exile abroad; there was mass ethnic cleansing of neighborhoods; lack of water and electricity; the country on the verge of splitting apart along sectarian lines; the US military bribed Sunni Sheikhs in Anbar Province in an effort to stabilize the situation in a small part of the country, window dressing for the September 2007 report in the US Congress by General David Petraeus. Iraq was a country destroyed. But America was not leaving the prize in which they had invested so much. The goal was to gradually remove some troops and pull the rest back to secure US military bases.

The point had been made over and over. The tragedy of this war. The folly of the American rulers, certainly, but on the other hand, the hard and infallible logic of the neo-conservatives in Washington, understanding clearly that the conquest of Iraq and control of energy is the key to global control in the twenty-first century. Indeed, they understood it well, putting their design in place with cold and infallible logic. In a just world, the United States would be subject to hundreds of billions of dollars in war reparations for international war crimes. They would be held accountable for the illegal attack upon a sovereign nation, the mass killings, the "shock and awe", and the destruction, for the "collateral damage", another word for killing and wounding innocent people. Yet the whole violent episode falls clearly within the context of American foreign policy since World War II. Why should the architects of the chaos wrought in Iraq feel any remorse? Indeed, they were only faithfully carrying out the "noble" agenda set out directly after the Second World War to ensure global control, to perpetuate US imperialism on a worldwide scale.

We know the instruments have long been in place, designed by the cold warriors, George F. Kennan, US Ambassador to Moscow in the 1950s, and architect of "containment"; Allen Dulles, an early Director of the Central Intelligence Agency; and his brother John Foster Dulles at the State Department. Every US President from Harry Truman straight through to George W. Bush lied to the American people about covert operations and foreign wars as their sons and daughters were sent off to kill others and sometimes die for the American empire. Almost every crime imaginable was carried out around the world under the deep cover of the American CIA. Covert actions were signed off by Presidents, almost weekly, in a long and bloody chain which continues. Today much of this activity has simply been privatized to US security firms like Blackwater USA, which the Iraqi Government attempted to expel from Iraq.

So while most certainly the war was illegal and criminal, this is not news.

Perhaps it is not even relevant in the context of the US record. US "National security" had always trumped international legality. The war was pre-planned way before the Twin Tower attacks of September 11, 2001, the hard intelligence in the hands of US officials being dismissed or ignored. Millions of dollars was paid by the CIA for fabricated and false stories from Iraqi exiles, such as Ahmet Chalabi and Ayad Allawi, while those most knowledgeable about the region were ignored along with the lessons of history. Members of the UN Security Council were bribed in early 2003 in an attempt to get an authorization for attack. The people of the US and the world were lied to and manipulated, while evidence of the weapons inspectors was ignored. The fix was in from the beginning with a US Government hell-bent upon war. The neoconservatives would break new ground as the time-tested imperative of racist "kicking ass" by colonial masters was taken to a new level. The bottom line is that the entire operation was naked imperialism under the ideological cover of a "war on terror". Secret prisons were set up around the world and people at home were stripped of hard-earned civil liberties.

This was not a new phenomenon, not essentially different from the earlier Cold War itself. The US had set up secret prisons as early as the 1950s. Korea, Vietnam, and CIA operations around the world, in hundreds of covert operations, from Iran, Guatemala, Chile, the Dominican Republic, Grenada, Panama, the Congo, to the Bay of Pigs operation in Cuba, and hundreds of others are now buried in dusty records. A bitter history which has burned deep scars in our brains. Carried out for "liberty", these operations were not, but rather for the American Empire, now bloated beyond all reason. All of this sworn by a long stream of US Presidents to be a noble enterprise, and believed to be, by the great majority of the American people, to the extent of their vast ignorance about global affairs.

So why should those in the White House today apologize? They simply follow in this long and honored American tradition, inherited from the last Cold War, and indeed from other colonizing imperialists, the French, the British, and other old European powers. They knew that they were not placed in power by the dollars of corporate America to listen to the voices of the American people from the grassroots. Walter Lippmann instructed the American ruling class well against the impending disaster the democratization of US foreign policy would bring in the 1930s. Rather, they were put into power, even if the Republicans illegally stole the election in 2000, to serve the needs of The Empire, which they did so well, even while carrying out grand larceny on an unprecedented scale against their fellow American citizen taxpayers. In the event, however, the potholes along the way have been a little more rough than expected. Not a little because global wars for empire are no longer acceptable in global public opinion. Not to be deterred, the brave leader at the helm of the American empire kept his eyes firmly on the prize. He was determined, as we are so often reminded. Nothing could stop him from bringing "freedom" to Iraq. "We will prevail."

In the week of September 10, 2007, the American people witnessed the charade in Washington, taking those who could recall, back to the Vietnam War. The General and his ambassador on Capital Hill, freshly back from the front. It was a Bush-Cheney-Rice-Rumsfeld-Gates production in collusion with Halliburton and dozens of other American corporate enterprises with contracts in Iraq and reaping vast profits. The Iraqi exiles had now enriched themselves beyond their wildest hopes, with tax dollars of working Americans and stolen oil funds. The seasoned war-weary Senators and representatives and the bright eyed steely and dangerous true believers, faithful neo-conservatives of the Congress, assembled in Washington. The Iraq "regime change" enterprise was on the rocks. In Congress, whether dissident or true believer, fellow travelers sought to steer the ship of state secure to Empire. If they talked of a change of course, the port they sought was nevertheless the same: that of power and the American Empire. There was the McNamara-like technician, General David Petraeus, Commander of US forces in Iraq, looking competent, doing his job, deploying a strategic campaign to show with his dozen or so charts that the escalation in Iraq, dubbed a surge, was working. We were back to Vietnam with the "best and the brightest," and once again the body counts and charts and all the props, that were not supposed to happen in this "cake walk". The hearing was held in the same room in the Cannon House Office Building where US military officials testified about the My Lai massacre in Vietnam in 1971. And there were the war protesters, the Code-Pink women, indeed the only voices from the grassroots, being dragged out by the police when they tried to speak. They were warned sternly by Congressman Ike Skelton, Chairman of the House Armed Services Committee, that "they would be prosecuted". The

American ambassador to Iraq, Ryan Crocker, looked trim and official struggling to put the best face on the fiasco. Chairman Skelton asked the American ambassador why the occupation was so slow in whipping the Iraqi Government into place, getting the "benchmarks" met. A new word for the dictates from the occupying American forces had been invented.

The ambassador eventually acknowledged that the Iraq Government was dysfunctional. The general recommended that the troops be cut back to the pre-surge level by mid-2008, just in time for the 2008 elections. The fraudulent claim that the war was leaping from success to success was pawned off upon the American people and the world, the foolishness of which no sensible person could miss. In the end, as with Vietnam, the truth was out, for those who wished to see the shambles that it was. It illustrated better than any textbook ever could, the true working of American "democracy"? Another war had failed. There was sharp questioning from the lawmakers for sure, but the war must go on in the name of Empire, enterprise and capital. "The business of America" is still business.

This charade, which one might see as comic theatre, was it not so deadly, came about because the truth is that the American Century is over. Unfortunately, the news has not yet reached Washington. There was way too much political consciousness around the world to suit the likes of George W. Bush and Dick Cheney. The occupation showed that people revolt when their country is occupied. One cannot just gas the local people out of existence, with poison chemicals, as Churchill once suggested when the British were stuck in the same boat as the Americans with their occupation of Iraq back in the 1920s.

That realization seemed to be seeping even into the political black holes of America after four years of lies from Washington had crumbled.

When the grassroots revolted in November 2006 and tossed a bunch of the pro-war bums out of Congress, the President took note. Bush clearly heard the democratic voices from America's hinterland, and being the democrat that he is, took immediate action. He understood what the people wanted and realized that they were serious and so must be crushed...the proper response for one so concerned as Bush for spreading democracy around the world...to others that is. The proposition of democracy in America was something else altogether. People had demanded the troops be pulled out of Iraq. He would send 30,000 more. People demanded an end to the war. He would make sure the war would go on till his last day in office and beyond. People demanded spending for social needs in America, and a cut-back for the war. Bush would ask the Congress for hundreds of billions of dollars more for Iraq and cuts in medical spending. When the newly elected representatives moved to end funding for the war, Bush depended upon his party to block the demands of the people. When the people demanded deadlines for withdrawal, and the Congress voted for them, the President vetoed the bill.

From his secret command post in Washington, Vice-President Dick Cheney pulled the strings and issued commands. Blind religious faith, ceaseless lies and the telling of half-truths prevailed in the face of impending disaster. All the fatal elements that destroyed the Presidency of Lyndon Johnson in Vietnam could now be seen again. But unlike Vietnam, Iraq had oil. Vietnam did not. Indeed, both struggles are at the heart of the American drive for empire. But, as the General and the ambassador reminded the people at the hearing, it was going to be a "long struggle".

Indeed, the US was not about to leave Iraq. The end would come some fifty years from now or on the day when the last drop of oil was pumped by the American companies controlling the Iraqi oilfields. Americans and Iraqis would go on dying. To what extent the Iraqis would succumb to the rule of the empire was yet to be decided by them and history. The US attack upon the sovereign nation of Iraq and its illegal occupation was driven by crazed men from their positions of power on behalf of the American Empire and corporate capital in the United States. America, as the exposed superpower in decline, had become the most dangerous country on earth, the nation that was most feared around the world, not because it was so powerful, but because its policies and policy-makers were power crazed and truly dangerous people. They saw themselves as infallibly rational. This was the historical cliff to which the American people, mostly good but naïve about the world, had been stampeded in ignorance and fear. But a nation cannot enjoy security, its people cannot be safe, by endangering the whole world. The reckless American policy in Iraq threatened the wider region and indeed the entire world. The US had become too dangerous for the world. But of course it always had been since it became a superpower after World War II.

The root of American imperialism is the belief, perpetrated in the Cold War ideological framework, that the United States has a God-given right to rule the whole world. This springs from the racist Wilsonian belief in American superiority and the right to force the "American way of life" upon the entire world. George W. Bush always talked about evil ideologies. But this American chauvinism was the real evil ideology, the blind prejudice that endangered us all more than ever and robbed a wide swath of the world's people of their freedom. It was not a pleasant truth for Americans that their penchant for "kicking ass" around the world was the root of terrorism. But the rest of the world already knew that the "war on terror" was just another excuse for empire, even if the Americans did not.

By mid 2007, both the President and Congress were lame ducks in the eyes of the American public and seen to be largely irrelevant in terms of what they wanted and needed. A CBS News poll showed that 77 percent of Americans thought the war was going badly, 47 percent said it was going very badly, 66 percent said the number of US troops should be decreased, 40 percent wanted all troops removed, 65 percent disapproved of Bush's performance, 75 percent said the country was headed in the wrong direction, and 70 percent said America was not respected around the world. A Reuters/Zogby Index of October 2007, showed Bush's approval rating at only 24 percent and only 11 percent had a positive opinion of the US Congress. While 56 percent said their own personal financial situation was good, only 26 percent gave a positive opinion of US economic policy and just 18 percent approved of US foreign policy.[89] Robert Fisk found that America was gripped by an irrational fear. America was said to be a country at war. But he found no sign of that. Perhaps many Americans had bought the ridiculous line of President Bush that if the troops could not win the war in Iraq, then the "enemy would follow them home."[90]

References

1. Hank Williams, "I've Been Down That Road Before." (1951)
2. On June 27, 2005, Defense Secretary Donald Rumsfeld remarked that the insurgency could go on another 12 years.
3. Chalmers Johnson, *Blowback: The Costs and Consequences of American Empire*. New York: Metropolitan, 2000.
4. Scott McConnell, "The Weekly Standard's War: Murdoch's mag stands athwart history yelling, 'Attack!'" *The American Conservative*, Nov. 21, 2005. Rupert Murdoch subsidized the *Weekly Standard*, edited by William Kristol, to the tune of $3 million dollars a year. Fellows at the conservative American Enterprise Institute published in the paper and thousands of copied distributed free around Washington. The paper was linked up to the new Fox News network, which would serve as the Bush Administration neo-conservative mouthpiece. After 9/11, 2001, the paper was

used to promote the overthrow of Saddam. "Their job was to divert America's wrath away from those who perpetrated the attack and turn it against those who did not." It was primarily the *Weekly Standard* which established the lie, after weeks and weeks of false stories, that Saddam was linked to Osama bin Laden. Writers such as Max Boot made the case for American Empire, an "imperialism based on racial harmony. George W, Bush was proclaimed "The Liberator" of Iraq in the weeks leading up to the invasion.

5. Kenneth Katzman, "Iraq: Elections, Government, and Constitution," CRS Report for Congress, Congressional Research Service, RS21968, June 15 2006. In both the January 2005 elections and the December 2005 elections for the 275 seat National Assembly, the United Iraqi Alliance won the elections (140 seats and 128 seats). This party is Shiite. In both elections, the Kurdish Alliance came in second (75 and 53 seats respectively). Coming in third in January 2005 was the Iraqis List, Iyad Allawi's party, winning 40 seats. The Sunnis mostly boycotted the January election. In the December 2005 election, the Sunni Iraq Concord Front came in third with 44 seats and the Iraqis List was fourth with 25 seats. The Constitution was approved in the October referendum by 78.6 percent. The Sunni Provinces of Anbar and Salahuddin voted against the Constitution by 97 percent and 82 percent respectively. Article 2 makes Islam "a major source of legislation." Article 39 allows families to choose between secular and Sharia Law to adjudicate family issues. The two apparatuses typically used to buy elections around the world by the US CIA were employed extensively. These are under the National Endowment for Democracy, namely, the National Democratic Institute (associated with the Democrat Party in the US) and the International Republican Institute (associated with the Republican Party). Money supplied through these institutions to influence the election included at least $122.5 million dollars. In addition, the CIA secretly sent an unknown number of operatives to rig the elections, but failed in significant measure.
6. The logic ran along the lines that the worse things got, the more hopeful the situation was, because it showed that the

insurgents were getting more desperate and frustrated. So if the US did not leave, thus "emboldening the enemy," the US would ultimately win...right around the corner. If the US left before the "job was done" then the enemy would follow them home. So the war crept on in six month intervals as the public waited for that magic turning point. All this could have brought a few laughs if it was not getting so many people killed.

7. The poor reporting was certainly not because footage of events was not available. Coverage on Turkish TV was excellent and far better on al-Jazeera. BBC and CNN bagan to cover up the reality of the war in daily reporting. In fact, CNN international has become insufferably boring, even unwatchable, given the repetitive running of corporate commercial ads. BBC, at once highly professional, headed straight south when Blair was Prime Minister and the best people fled to al-Jazeera in Doha.
8. The American troops in the country were not referred to as "foreign fighters," presumably being "Iraqi."
9. Alexandra Zavis, "46 Bodies Found in Wave of Iraqi Violence," AP, Feb. 23, 2007. Sam Knight, "Al-Askariye Shrine: Not just a major Cahtedral," World-Times Online, Feb. 22, 2006. Patrick Cockburn, "Destruction of holiest Shia Shrine brings Iraq to the brink of Civil War," The Independent, Feb. 22, 2007.
10. The Shrine at Samarra has existed since 944. It was built to the tombs of two ninth century imams, direct descendents of the Prophet Muhammed. These are Ali al-Hadi (the Tenth Imam) and his son, Hassan al-Askari (the Eleventh Imam). Samarra had been built as the new capital of the Abbasid Empire. Shias believe that the Twelfth or "Hidden Imam" went into hiding under the al-Askariya Shrine in 878 to prepare for his eventual return among men to punish the sinful, "separate truth from falsehood," and bring justice to humanity. He was known as "The Mahdi." The Gold dome was added in 1905 with 72,000 separate gold pieces.
11. Gilbert Burnham, Riyadh Lafta, Shannon Doocy, Les Roberts, "Mortality after the 2003 invasion of Iraq : a Cross-Sectional Cluster Sample Survey," *The Lancet*, Vol. 364, p.

1857, October 11, 2006. Some 1849 households were surveyed. This compared to about three million civilians who died in the Vietnam War. The interval level put the number at between about 400,000 and 900,000. Debora Mackenzie, "Enormous death toll of Iraq invasion revealed," *New Scientist*, October 11, 2006.

12. "U.S. Casualties Surge in Iraq," AP/MSNBC Oct. 12, 2006.
13. "Prospects for Iraq's Stability: A Challenging Road Ahead," National Intelligence Estimate, National Intelligence Council, Jan. 2007.
14. Michael Schwartz and Tom Engelhardt, "Surging Into Catastrophe in Iraq," TomDispatch, Feb. 12, 2007.
15. By October 2007, this would get to be such a problem that the US State Department began to assign diplomats to take up the 40 to 50 posts coming vacant in the US Embassy in Baghdad or risk being fired. It was called the largest call-up of US diplomats since the Vietnam War. Mathew Lee, "US to order diplomats to serve in Iraq," AP, Oct. 27, 2007.
16. Swartz and Engelhardt, "Surging into Catastrophe." And following information on the surge strategy in Baghdad.
17. *Ibid.*
18. Both Iraqi Prime Ministers, under the Americans, Ibrahim al-Jaafri and Nuri al-Maliki were members of the Da'wa Party, a shia party. This party was led by al-Jaafri, who was in alliance with Muqtada al-Sadr and his Mahdi Army. Moreover, it was widely acknowledged that the Interior Ministry in al-Maliki's Government was responsible for a large number of killings of Sunnis in death-squad activities as ethnic and sectarian cleansing was being carried out. In fact, the US occupation had unleashed widespread anarchy throughout the country.
19. *Ibid.*
20. *Ibid.*
21. *Ibid.*
22. *Ibid.*
23. Indeed, some police units became so corrupt and violent that they were disbanded.

24. Sabrina Tavernise, "Iraq Suspends Police Brigade in Baghdad," *New York Times,* Oct, 5, 2006.
25. *Ibid.*
26. Richard A. Oppel Jr. and Damien Cave, "U.S. Troops Lock Down Much of East Baghdad," *New York Times*, Feb. 11, 2007.
27. Patrick Cockburn, "A bloody message from Iraq: Nowhere is safe..." *The Independent*, 13 April 2007.
28. Muhammad Saeed al-Sahaf, Iraqi Information Minister under Saddam Hussein. It turns out that al-Sahaf's predictions about Iraq after the war were more correct than those of Tony Blain and George W. Bush.
29. Robert Fisk, "This was a guilty verdict on America as well," Robert Fisk, The Independent, Nov. 6, 2006.
30. Andrew Cockburn, "Bloodthirsty tyrant knew that defeat would cost 'every sliver of my flesh,'" The Times, Dec. 30, 2006. The death sentence was based on the liquidations of 148 men and boys of Dujail district in 1982. The article suggests that the hanging would spark more sectarian violence. Saddam had "ridden to power on a CIA train." Robert Fisk, "A dictator created then destroyed by America," The Independent, Dec. 30, 2006. "Arabs will ask what about the other guilty men? ...His execution will go down as an American affair..." Steven R. Hurst, "Thousands flock to see Saddam's Grave," AP, Dec. 31, 2006.
31. "Military revises Zarqawi account," *USA Today*, June 10, 2006; Brendan O'Neill, "Zarqawi; a Bogeyman Made by the US," Antiwar.com, June 10, 2006. Two 500 pound bombs were reportedly dropped on the house where Zarqawi was staying. Five other civilians were killed, including a girl between the ages of 5 and 7. His death would not really matter. He was not the towering figure that the US had made him out to be.
32. Late Edition, June 25, 2006.
33. Representative Representative Christopher Shays, a Republican, Late Edition, Sep. 3, 2006.
34. Aaron Glantz, "Antiwar Voters May Get Less Than They Bargained For," Antiwar.com, Nov. 11, 2006; Tom

Engelhardt, "Outlaw Empire Meets the Wave," Antiwar.com, Nov. 9, 2006.

35. Charlie Reese, 'Goodbye, Rummy," Antiwar.com, Nov. 11, 2006.
36. Late Edition, November 26, 2006.
37. James A. Baker, III, and Lee H. Hamilton, co-Chairs et al., "The Iraq Study Group Report."
38. Eli Lake, "Baker's Panel Rules Out Iraq Victory," *New York Sun*, Oct. 12, 2006.
39. Tom Engelhardt, "James Baker's Iraq," ZNet, October 13, 2006. There were plenty of hints before the report was released that the US would not be "cutting and running." The US some 55 military bases in Iraq and was rushing to complete construction on the largest US embassy in the world, equipped with its own missile system. Commanders on the ground talked about having enough ammunition for "the next four years." "Iraq a helluva mess: Baker," Agence France-Presse," October 18, 2006; Simon Jenkins, "America has finally taken on the grim reality of Iraq," The Guardian, October 18, 2006. The Baker Report was leaked in the third week of October, as the Administration delayed its official unveiling till after the elections.
40. Engelhardt, "James Bakers' Iraq."
41. Jim Lobe, "Jim Baker, Savior?" Antiwar.com, October 12, 2006. Simon Jenkins, "The US is radically rethinking its exit strategy, while Britain waits zombie-like for new instructions," *The Guardian*, Oct. 18, 2007. This was somewhat premature, given the flat rejection by Cheney of the Baker Report. The neoconservatives were prepared to slog on through the quagmire, disregarding the cost.
42. Ray McGovern, "Bush's Wooden-Headedness Kills," Antiwar.com, July 19, 2007. Bush thought he was on the right track in Iraq in the face of all the evidence to the contrary.
43. *Ibid.*
44. Deb Riechmann and Keven Freking, "Bush: I won't change strategy in Iraq," AP, Oct. 20, 2006.

45. Mussab al-Khairalla, "Saddam Hussein Sentenced to Hang," Reuters, Nov. 6, 2006.
46. "Hussein Trial adjourned amid courtroom rancor," CNN.com, Nov. 29, 2005.
47. The al-Anfal Campaign was carried out from 1986 to 1989 and is thought to have resulted in the deaths of between 100,000 and 200,000 Kurds through destruction of settlements, mass deportation, concentration camps, firing squads, and chemical warfare. The campaign has been characterized as "genocidal." The chemical warfare was directed by Ali Hasan al-Majid ("Chemical Ali").
48. "Iraq Government: Saddam execution might not need president's approval," USA Today, Dec. 27, 2006.
49. "Iraq is Split Over Saddam Verdict," CBS News, Nov. 6, 2006.
50. Andrew Rice, "Dead Man Squaking," Slate, Nov. 6, 2006.
51. Jennifer Loven, "Reports: Bush to replace top generals," AP, Jan. 4, 2007.
52. Robert Fisk, "Bush's New Strategy- the March of folly," *The Independent*, Jan. 12, 2007. "..History is littered with powerful men who thought they could batter their way to victory against the odds."
53. Stewart M. Powell: Bush could double force by Christmas," San Francisco Chronicle, May 22, 2007.
54. Pat Buchanan, "Cakewalk Crowd Abandones Bush," Antiwar.com, Jan. 5, 2007.
55. Marc Santora, "U.S. Commander Warns of Long Struggle in Iraq," *New York Times*, Jan. 15, 2007.
56. That is, it had a negative connotation with regard to Vietnam. Later in the year, Bush himself began to compare the Iraq war with the Vietnam war. Vietnam could be used to support Bush's bull-headedness only by turning history on its head and arguing that the US could have won if US troops had been kept longer in the country. There is no need to speculate whether this was based upon George W. Bush's ignorance of history.
57. Damien Cave, "250 Are Killed in Major Battle," *New York Times*, Jan. 29, 2007.

58. Ashura marks the 7th century death of Muhammad's Grandson, Hussien.
59. Linda Bilmes and Joseph E. Stiglitz, "The Economic Costs Of The Iraq War: An Appraisal Three Years After the Beginning of the Conflict," Paper presented at the ASSA meetings, Boston, January 2006. In October, 2004, the Congressional Budget Office estimated the Afghanistan and Iraq wars would cost $2.4 trillion assuming a large number of troops would remain in the region over the next decade. By October 2007, $604 billion had been spent. The White House was quick to dismiss the report as mere "speculation." Anne Flaherty, "Wars May Cost $2.4 trillion Over Decade," AP, October 24, 2007.
60. These wars were largely being put on the national credit card to enrich major US corporations and sink future generations in inordinate public debt for private capitalist accumulation. Joel Havermann, "War costs are hitting historic proportions," Los Angeles Times, Jan. 14, 2007. Thomas E. Woods, Jr., "What the Warfare State Really Costs," LewRockwell.com, Sept. 12, 2007. The article quotes the late Seymour Melman who pointed out that "the military industrial complex "elevates inefficiency into a national purpose, disables the market system, destroys the value of the currency, and diminishes the decision power of all institutions other than its own." Robert Scheer, "Bush Budget Delivers the Bacon," Truthdig, Feb. 8, 2007. "President Bush's budget has nothing to do with fighting terrorism but everything to do with pumping up the profits of the administration's generous political doners in the defense industry." Laurence M. Vance, "Counting the Cost," LewRockwell.com, July 28, 2007.This American Friends Service Committee suggested that the Iraq war cost $275 million every day ($3180 each second), but a more recent estimate suggests $720 million each day. This is $8333 a second. Kari Lydersen, "War Costing $720 Million Each Day, Group Says," *Washington Post*, Sept. 22, 2007. Of course, a large portion of it is simply legal theft by well connected US corporations, such as Halliburton and Blackwell USA. It is interesting that the American press was filled with articles on the massive overspending for wars with almost no

reaction from the public. This seems to be depoliticization with a vengeance.

61. Joel Havemann, "War costs are hitting historic proportions," *Los Angeles Times*, Jan. 14, 2007. Neil Abercrombie, "On war costs, Bush is master of disguise," *Boston Globe*, Mar. 5, 2007.
62. William Matthews, "Iraq War Costs Near Vietnam Levels," DefenseNews.com, Sept. 14, 2007. There were obviously much fraud in the system, with the small companies the most likely to get caught. For one example, a small parts supplier in South Carolina was paid $455,009 to ship three screws costing $1.31 to Iraq and $293,451 to ship an 89 cent washer to an air base in Florida. They collected $998,798 for shipping two 19 cent washers to an army base in Texas. While these examples seem most blatent, they are actually small compared to the billions directly transferred to Halliburton. A million dollar line item is often subcontracted for between $50,000 and $80,000. Tony Capaccio, "Pentagon Paid $998,798 to Ship Two 19-Cent Washers," Bloomberg, Aug. 16. See the film, Iraq for Sale, 2006.
63. House Resolution 2929 was passed in 2007 which bans funding for "new permanent bases" in Iraq, but means little, since it seems there are already enough in place. The "No Permanent Bases Provision" in an appropriations bill signed in 2006 seems to be another one of those pieces of legislation that the Bush Administration will simply ignore. Joe Volk, "Baseless In Baghdad," TomPaine.com, Oct. 13, 2006. Whatever the US is in Baghdad, baseless it is not. There is no sign that it ever will be as long as there is any oil in the country or the bases are needed.
64. David Phinney, "Asian workers trafficked to build U.S. embassy in Baghdad," Alternet.org, March 3, 2007. "Welcome to the new US embassy," *Times Online*, Sept. 1, 2007. The real cost was uncertain as the Kuwaiti firm building it had used substandard materials and some of the work would have to be done over.
65. The US, for public consumption, however, gave the opposite impression. Brigadier General Mark Kimmitt claimed that the US does not plan to leave military bases behind in Iraq,

Afghanistan and other Middle East countries. Rather, the "long war" would be turned over to local governments by training the locals for counterterrorism. The catch was that "the US would only consider keeping a permanent base in Iraq if asked to do so by the Government." That, of course could be easily arranged. The same officer had recently argued that Iraq was a fully sovereign country. Pat Reber, "US won't leave garrisons behind in Iraq: Senior US Officer," Presse-Agentur, Feb. 22, 2006. Senator John McCain, campaigning for the Presidency in 2007 said that the US would be in Iraq for the next 100 years.

66. Joshua Holland, "War on Iraq Coming to a Dead End in Iraq," Alternet, April 10, 2007.

67. Seymour M. Hersh, "The Redirection," *The New Yorker*, March 5, 2007. Hannah Allam, "Insurgents get a cut of U.S. aid to Iraq," Seattle Times, August 27, 2007; David E. Sanger, "Bush Is Said to Approve More Aid to Iraqi Sunnis Battling Extremest Groups," New York Times, Sept. 2, 2007; Paul Sperry, "A Surge in Bribes," Antiwar.com, Sept. 26, 2007.

68. "Iraq Sheik working with the U.S. Slain," MSNBC, Sept. 13, 2007. Earlier an ally of Abu Risha was blown up in the Monsour Hotel in Baghdad. Fassal al-Guood was a former governor of Anbar province and Sheikh of the al-Bu Nimir Tribe.

69. Marie Colvin and Sarah Baxter, "US bribe insurgents to fight al-Qaeda." *The Sunday Times*, Sept. 9, 2007. These groups were called "Awakening Councils," or "Concerned Local Citizens" (CLC's). This made these groups of tribal members, formerly working for al-Qaeda and killing American soldiers, seem like groups of citizens in some local town in the Midwest of the USA. Orwellian rhetoric had again reared its head. At the same time, it was realized that basing US security strategy upon putting the enemy on the payroll was risky. There was concern that they would become a separate military force in Iraq and again turn against the Americans. Indeed, this happened in Falluja before the assault there. The plan was to integrate a portion of these groups into the Iraqi Armed forces and to disband

the rest. The groups were said to have some success in infiltrating the insurgent group al-Qaeda in Mesopotamia and gaining intelligence for the Americans. How many Americans understand that the Americans brought al-Qaeda to Iraq and then put them on the US payroll all in the name of making the country democratic.

70. "Rising to the humanitarian challenge in Iraq," *http://www.oxfam.org/en/policy/briefingpapers/bp105_humanitarian_challenge_in_iraq_0707*, July 30, 2007. "NGOs: One-Third of Iraqis need immediate aid," *USA Today*, July 30, 2007. "Third of Iraqi Children Malnourished," *Herald Sun*, July 30, 2007.
71. "NY Times Calls Iraq a 'lost cause,'" AFP, July 8, 2007.
72. Eddie J. Girdner, "Another Bill of Goods and Democracy," *Turkish Daily News*, September 17, 2007.
73. Kenneth M. Pollack was director of research at the Saban Center for Middle East Policy at the Brookings Institute and Michael E. O'Hanlon was a Senior fellow in foreign Policy Studies at the Brookings Institute.
74. Michael E.O'Hanlon and Kenneth M. Pollack, "A War We Just Might Win," New York Times, July 30, 2007.
75. Glen Greenwald, "The really smart, serious, credible Iraq experts, O'Hanlon and Pollack," Salon.com, July 31, 2007.
76. Pollack's book, *The Threatening Story: The Case for Invading Iraq* (New York: Random House 2002) played off the title of Churchill's book, *The Gathering Storm,* which again suggested that Saddam was Adolf Hitler. Pollack had made a passionate plea for the invasion of Iraq and the overthrow of Saddam.
77. Jim Lobe, "Bush Campaigns to Sustain Surge," Antiwar.com, Aug. 23, 2007. A report to Congress from retired Marine General James Jones's commission of veteran and military chiefs on Sept. 7, said, of the "sprawling US military footprint in Iraq, "The unintended message conveyed is one of 'permanence,' an occupying force as it were." That message, nevertheless, seemed accurate enough. "US troop numbers in Iraq an all-time high" *Herald Sun*, Sept. 7, 2007. Patrick Buchanan, "Phase III of Bush's

War," Antiwar.com, Sept. 1, 2007. Buchanan pointed out the weakness of Congress allowed Bush to simply ignore it and go on with his war-making. Hillary Clinton, Barack Obama and John Edwards, campaigning for President all said in September 2007 that they could not guarantee that all troops would be gone from Iraq by 2013, the end of a four-year term. Clinton has reportedly admitted that she would still have troops there after two terms, 2017. Personally, I expect it would be a good bet. Beth Fouhy, "Dems can't make guarantee on Iraq troops," AP, Sept. 26, 2007. Some on the Republican side, campaigning for President, argued that now that Iraq was "broken" the US could not leave until it was fixed. This was former Arkansas Governor Mike Huckabee. Jacob Sullum, "The No-Exit Strategy," *Reason Magazine*, Sept. 12, 2007. "Buy Time and Pray for a Miracle," Cato-at-Liberty, Aug. 27, 2007. The intelligence community is betting that American troops will still be in Iraq ten years from now. Jennifer Loven, "Bush hopes to buy time for Iraq strategy," AP, Sept. 13, 2007. Springing off the inspiring Petraeus Report, Bush spoke from the Marine base in Quantico, Virginia, urging that the large number of troops must stay in Iraq. The weakness of Congress was seen in their failure to confront Bush on the war and work with Republicans who were also tired of Bush's policy. When anti-war organization MoveOn.org ran a full-page add in major newspapers taunting General Petraeus as "General Betray Us" the Democrats mostly expressed outrage along with the Republicans. Jonathan Weisman and Shailagh Murray, "Democrats Push Toward Middle On Iraq Policy," Washingtonpost.com, Sept. 13, 2007.

78. Robert Scheer, "The General Lies," *Truthdig*, Sept. 11, 2007. The British talking and waffling about pulling out the rest of their troops out seemed mostly tailored for domestic consumption and posturing for an election that Prime Minister Gordon Brown would have to face in the near future. The Foreign Secretary David Milliband, dodging questions left and right like a political weasel, even indicated that the ones which had been pulled out could be "redeployed." The British still had 5500 troops in Basra in October 2007. Late Edition, 28 October, 2007. Nick Juliano,

"Instead of going home, British troops headed to Iranian border," *The Raw Story*, Sept. 12, 2007.

79. Robert H. Reid, "Iraq: Blackwater guards fired unprovoked," AP, Sept. 20, 2007; Sabrina Tavernise, "Maliki Alleges 7 Cases When Blackwater Killed Iraqis," *New York Times*, Sept. 20, 2007. Daniel Howden and Leonard Doyle, "Making a killing: how private armies became a $129bn global industry," *The Independent*, Sept. 21, 2007. James Glanz and Sabrina Tavernise, "Security Company Faces Iraqi Criminal Charges," *New York Times*, Sept. 23, 2007.

80. Peter W. Galbraith and Tom Engelhardt, "The War is Lost," *TomDispatch*, July 18, 2007. Galbriath argues that Iraq has already broken up into three parts, for all practical purposes. Amending the present Constitution to satisfy all three constituencies remains highly problematical.

81. Juan Cole, "The Iraq War is Over, and the Winner Is...Iran," Salon.com, July 21, 2005. Ayatollah Khomeini's dream had come true. It was Khomeini who had pressured Iraqis in Iran to form the Supreme Council For Islamic Revolution in Iraq (SCIRI). This group took power in Iraq with the January 2005 elections. Both Jaafari and al-Maliki are members of Dawa, which was originally part of SCIRI. Now SCIRI controlled Baghdad and 7 out of 9 southern provinces. The US was disturbed when Jaafari visited Tehran in 2005 made numerous deals, but drew the line at Iran's offer to train Iraqi troops. Meanwhile, the US and Iraqis continued to fund the Iranian terrorist organization, Mojahedin-e Khalq against the Iranian Government. The neoconservatives ignorance of the Middle East, as well as their unwillingness to learn, seemed to know no bounds. The SCIRI was later changed to The Supreme Islamic Iraqi Council (SIIC) led by Abdul Aziz al-Hakim.

82. Anthony Shadid, "Across Arab World, a Widening Rift," *Washington Post,* Feb. 12, 2007. There was a tendency to see the strategy as one of "divide and rule" by the US, Britain and Israel.

83. William E. Odam, "Victory Is Not an Option," *Washington Post*, February 11, 2007. Odam is a retired Army Lieutenant

General, was head of Army intelligence, and director of the National Security Agency under President Ronald Reagan.

84. Michael Abramowitz, "Intelligence Puts Rationale For War on Shakier Ground," *Washington Post,* July 18, 2007. Stuart Nusbaumer, "The Surge isn't ending the insurgency but dispersing it." *The American Conservative,* May 21, 2007.While the Secretary of Defense, Robert Gates argued that Anbar province was a success story, after the US began to pay the tribal sheikhs not to work with al-Qaida, it appeared that the surge strategy had simply caused "squirts" moving the insurgents out of some areas and into others. Many other analysts were no more hopeful about the surge. Charles J. Hanley, "Historians offer dismal Iraq forecast," AP, Jan. 21, 2007. British historian Niall Ferguson calculated there was only a one in a hundred chance of a "happy ending."

85. "US seen retreating from democracy push," Reuters, Oct. 12, 2006. Ramzy Baroud, "The Logic Behind Rice's Grin," ZNet, Oct. 15, 2006.

86. Ramzy Baroud, "The Logic behind Rice's Grin," Znet, Oct. 15, 2006. Bush and Rice were forced to "abort democracy" to prevent "great loss" to US foreign policy.

87. Marc Santora, "US Commander Warns of Long Struggle in Iraq," *New York Times,* Jan. 15, 2007. "Big U.S. presence in Iraq until mid-2009: Commander," Reuters, July 30, 2007. Susan Cornwall, :Iraq Role to Last Years, Cost More: officials," *Washington Post,* July 31, 2007. H. Darr Beiser, "Bolten: Iraq won't end with Bush term," USA Today, Sept. 7, 2007. Ewan MacAskill, "Bush: there will be no pullout from Iraq while I'm president," *The Guardian,* Aug. 23, 2007. Robert Burns, "Army: Troops to stay in Iraq until 2010," AP, Oct. 12, 2006. Zoltan Grossman, "The Korea Rationale for Staying in Iraq: An Endless Occupation?" *Counterpunch,* Sept. 20, 2007. David S. Cloud, "U.S. Needs 'Long-Term Presence' in Iraq, Gates Says," *New York Times,* Sept. 27, 2007. Nancy A. Youssef, "Troop leels in Iraq likely to remain above 130,000," *McClatchy Newspapers,* Sept. 12, 2007.

88. "Pentagon ants smaller long-term presence," AFP, July 2, 2007. It was clear that the US military would be happy to see significant numbers of US troops pulled out if the insurgency could be quelled. However, there was no doubt that there would, at the same time, be a long-term presence of US troops in Iraq.
89. "Poll: Calls to Get Out of Iraq Escalate," CBS News, June 29, 2007. "Voters unhappy with Bush and Congress," Reuters, Oct. 17, 2007.
90. Robert Fisk, "The Crushing Fear that Stalks America," *The Independent,* March 24, 2007.

9

Iraq: The US Occupation of the Middle East and Global Hegemony

"Force, force to the utmost, force without stint or limit, the righteous and triumphant force which shall make right the law of the world, and cast every selfish dominion down in the dust." **Woodrow Wilson**[1]

"It is cruel and arrogant to attempt to block desperate social remedies to desperate social problems that local leaders elect to try when you have nothing better to offer." **Richard J. Barnet**[2]

"There are two things which a democratic people will always find very difficult, - to begin a war and to end it... All those who seek to destroy the liberties of a democratic nation ought to know that war is the surest and the shortest means to accomplish it."

Alexis de Toqueville[3]

"I know of no country in which there is so little independence of mind and real freedom of discussion as in America." **Alexis de Tocqueville**[4]

This chapter summarizes some general principles about the US colonial occupation of Iraq and US foreign policy. The US occupation of the Middle East is not a new phenomenon but merely a shifting of the regional US occupation from Europe to the Middle East as a basis for US Global hegemony. During the Cold War US hegemony was based upon the occupation of Europe and US satellites in East Asia, such as Japan and South Korea. Now the eye of the storm has shifted to the Middle East and South Asia.[5] After World War II, it was necessary to occupy Europe with a standing army and institutional tools such as the Marshall Plan, NATO, the CIA, and various other devices.[6] This was necessary in the Cold War era to ensure that Western Europe served the needs of US capitalism and remained outside the socialist orbit. It would ensure the availability of markets and production for the US economy and programs could be implemented through the CIA to control politics and prevent a democratic socialist Europe from emerging.

This approach, beginning with the European Coal and Steel Community, would eventually culminate in the Common Market and later the European Union. Now that the danger of a social Europe no longer exists, due to the establishment of the European Union, which has essentially locked the 27 nations of Europe into the IMF/World Bank system of capitalist neoliberalism, no European Union country can play its own game but must march lockstep to the dictate of the EU bureaucracy in Brussels.[7] Stripped of their sovereignty by the European Commission, the Central Committee of the European Union in Brussels, countries cannot serve their own national interests in terms of their political economy.

The Cold War was primarily about ensuring US hegemony over Western Europe and Japan and by extension as much of the world as possible and not about the "Soviet threat" except that the Soviet model tended to inspire third world countries to adopt socialism.[8] The so-called Soviet threat was largely a pretext for the occupation of Europe and operations against nationalism and national autonomy, that is, national liberation movements, around the world.[9] In the Cold War era, Middle East oil was secured by an arrangement with the Saudis to keep the oil flowing to American oil corporations, while it shored up anti-democratic and feudal forces in the region, prevented political development, and repressed democracy. At the present time a new deal is being forged with the Saudis for the next phase of US imperialism in the region.[10] British and French interests were minor irritants, such as in the Suez Crisis of 1956, and these countries were gradually pushed out of the region as the US increased its control.[11]

The real danger during the Cold War and after was regional assertion, national autonomy, which could threaten US and Israeli interests in the region. This arose with Saddam Hussein and Iran, first Muhammad Mossadegh and later the Islamic Revolution in Iran in 1979. It was this which threatened the US, not weapons of mass destruction. Nationalism had also threatened the US in South Asia, in India under Jawaharlal Nehru and with the Non-aligned Movement.[12] After the Cold War, it was logical that the "New World Order" would involve a shift of US occupation and hegemony from Europe to the Middle East. Due to the actions of Saddam Hussein in the late 1990s, the control of Iraqi oil was slipping out of US hands.[13] Oil was being marketed through Turkey and surrounding countries illegally. Iran was no longer in the US orbit; oil and the US grip on power there was no longer secure due to exploration and trading deals being made with China, France, and other countries.

This book argues that the US occupation of Iraq is a permanent occupation. The US is not going to leave Iraq.[14] At the current time, 2008, there is a lot of talk in the US about pulling the American troops out of Iraq and about the US "getting out of Iraq." This is not going to happen in any substantive way in the near future. The US will be essentially occupying Iraq as long as it is considered to be in its "national interest" and as long as it can possibly stay.[15] The oil is not going to run out soon, but even if it did, the US is installing permanent military bases for future use.[16] Presently, there are no forces which can dislodge the US from Iraq. It may be that the US sees the civil war as useful, to some exent, as a pretext for extended occupation until the

US base infrastructure is in place. The construction of long-life permanent buildings proceeds on the 12 large military bases in existence. Life can be made more difficult for American soldiers but the US can stay by paying the cost. It is mostly a matter of getting the US population to put up with the burdens, by instilling greater fear and possibly greater political control. Militant nationalism is not strong in the United States, but the state propaganda apparatus linked to the private corporate capitalist press is devastatingly effective. At the fulcrum is the Fox TV network, which has served as the mouthpiece of George W. Bush and the neoconservative storm-troopers and has established itself as the "most-watched" media. Given the high degree of depoliticization in the wider US population, these tools backed by Rupert Murdoch's media empire can sufficiently overcome most domestic opposition. No one knows, of course, how long this can be done, but so far the perpetuation of fear has served to intimidate most Americans and "keep the rabble in line." With the US "owning Iraq" the US presence there, it is hoped by the ruling class, will be taken for granted. This was the case with Western Europe, Korea, Japan and so on after World War II.

Currently the rhetoric which surrounds the debate about Iraq in the United States is highly deceptive and illusory and largely geared for public consumption. It is clear that most US presidential candidates are deplorably cynical in their dialogue with the American people about the future US occupation of Iraq. "We must bring the troops home now" and so on, usually is not said seriously and at most just expresses a desire to get the troops "out of harm's way," which might mean keeping them largely confined to the large military bases which have been constructed in Iraq.[17] There are at least four permanent and currently 12 large military bases, which have been established, although it is not clear at this point how many of these military bases the

US will want to claim as its own for the future. Perhaps all of them, if the situation permits, and if the more than 1000 existing bases which make up the "footprint" of the American Empire, is any indication. A fallback position would be to withdraw to Kuwait or to Northern Iraq in the Kurdish region which might become a fully independent state in future. As many troops as possible would be shifted back to the US and other areas, of course, especially when presidential election campaigning is underway. Colonial powers in general do not send more occupiers than is considered necessary.[18]

Further, there is currently considerable confusion in the anti-war movement in the US between the Vietnam War and the operation in Iraq. Iraq is not Vietnam and a major difference is that Vietnam was not a country which was the key to controlling global hegemony; although some tried to make it out to be such, it was not. The domino theory was just a pretext for the war.[19] But Iraq is different. Not only is it a "stupendous prize" in terms of oil, the control of that oil and the territory in the heart of the Middle East is seen as the key to the control of the entire region and to regions beyond. So the US will not give up its "stupendous prize." While part of the appeal is the huge profits being made by US corporations, there are far-reaching strategic considerations as well. Iraq, aside from being a huge base from which to operate in a wide region, gives the US great leverage over all the emerging potential future great powers, China, India, Russia, the European Union and so on. The first three, as potential alliance, pose a serious threat to US regional and global hegemony.

Consequently the US has established permanent, hardened, bases around the country and is building the world's largest US Embassy complex in Baghdad. A further element is that much of the occupation has been privatized to so-called "security firms." The most notorious of these is Blackwater USA, but at least 25 such firms are operating in Iraq with 180,000 "contractors." That is 180,000 mercenary soldiers from around the world are deployed and paid high wages, on the order of 2000 US dollars a day. The profits are great and the tab is sent to US taxpayers and future generations. It is a way of pumping value out of the US population to increase capitalist accumulation. The US monetary policy of sinking the value of the US dollar also forces every nation in the world to help pay for the US war in Iraq. China, which owns more dollars in its reserves than any other country gets hit with the highest bill. While some political candidates, both Democrats and Republicans, such as Hillary Clinton and Barack Obama, attempted to distance themselves from supporting the war, there is a basic consensus among the political class that US Middle East hegemony is to be supported. The US ruling class understands this. And a candidate can get in office and stay in office in the American system only with money from big corporations. That is the way the American system works.

The way the US "saves" a country is by destroying it. This means destroying the potential for the country to emerge and develop on its own. If the country does not have the potential to do this, then it is not a threat and so need not be destroyed. Once that potential is destroyed, then the US can reinsert the country into its global orbit and have access to the natural and human resources of the country for capitalist accumulation. In fact the notion of making Iraq "democratic" or "free" is synonymous with destroying the potential of the country to develop on its own or outside the US orbit. It also means destroying its potential to enjoy a degree of sovereignty outside the global capitalist order and play its own game.

War is the tool that is used to subdue a country, economically and politically, when the tools of the IMF, the World Bank and the World Trade Organization prove to be ineffective. Even when the US loses a war, technically, as in the Vietnam War, the US still wins the war if the country targeted is significantly destroyed. It must depend upon international capital, IMF and World Bank loans and so on.[20] The people are either significantly dead, to the tune of several million people, or further impoverished in a significantly isolated economy. Vast damage is done to the environment and ecology of the occupied country and the people are poisoned with Agent Orange or uranium weapons along with poverty, disease and death.[21] From the criteria of the neo-conservatives, and the corporate board rooms of the US and Europe, the war in Iraq has not been a failure, but an overwhelming victory. From a global strategic point of view this is correct, although in a dialectical way, great powers ultimately become overstretched and weaken themselves to be overtaken by rising powers.[22] Not only does the war reshape the political economy of Iraq, it forces the roll-back of social welfare in the US and pours massive tax dollars into corporate profits, rather than into social programs.

The war in Iraq, Operation Iraqi Freedom, has been a significant success in terms of increasing US global hegemony in the short term. This is true, as much as those who would like to roll back US global hegemony hate to admit. The fact that the war has been lost in technical terms and did not turn out as a crushing victory as on the drawing board, is significant but not serious enough to slow down the US neo-conservative drive for global hegemony. The neo-conservatives are significantly correct about their achievements. They have carried out a great historical coup and this was allowed by all the major powers of the globe, especially the hypocritical European states, such as France, Italy, Germany and so on, which did not significantly oppose the operation strongly enough to effectively challenge it. These European states are part of the global imperialist complex and go along with US hegemonic control. They would rather enjoy their wine, dining and café life than fight the barbarian hoards. That is being left to the crusading

Americans. Nicolas Sarkozy may have restored the respectability of "French" fried potatoes in America but the French like their café life too much to put many boots on the ground out on the frontiers of the empire. They have found an easier way of colonizing the peripheries of Europe through the European Union. This can be done through treaties and laws from Brussels while they enjoy their café life. The Europeans are ready to play second fiddle and observe the world from their cushy perch in the restaurants which fan out from the Berlaymont headquarters in Brussels.

The one exception to the above consensus is global public opinion, but this democratic force, in the event, has been forced aside by the Bush-Blair steamroller. Meanwhile the European elites are fine with this, as they are busy hoodwinking their own publics about the nature of the undemocratic European institutions.[23] That is, the Iraq War entailed crushing democracy on a global scale in the name of spreading democracy.

In terms of bolstering US hegemony in the Middle East, it is completely irrelevant, from the point of view of the neo-conservatives that at least two million Iraqis have died since the first Gulf War in 1991.[24] Some three million Vietnamese died in the war in Indochina, and around three million in the Korean War. The death of 3943 US soldiers, as of February 2008, and more than 30,000 casualties, along with thousands more lives disrupted and destroyed for mental health reasons and other health problems, is largely negligible. These are absolutely considered light loses by neo-conservative and even broader American standards. This might not be true of any other country in the world today, certainly not in many. Further, this neo-conservative perspective is essentially the same as that of Congress and a large portion of the American public, who seem too occupied to take what is happening in Iraq very seriously, except when it affects them personally. The death toll of

American military personnel in the Vietnam War reached some 59,000 officially, while the unofficial count was much higher, considering those who committed suicide. All of this is of minor consequence and not a real concern to the neoconservatives and the broader US ruling class, except as it affects their ability to get re-elected. The public will be massaged, manipulated, coddled, lied to, frightened and so on, and politicians will continue to fool votes out of them with false promises. One sees this very clearly in the current cynical and even callous remarks of Senator Hillary Clinton and Barack Obama and others as they now jockey for position and votes in the 2008 presidential election. They are grooming themselves as central and accomplished politicians to continue to play out their political careers. Politicians are mostly posture, little substance, less sincerity. This is not a politically partisan, political party game. At root, it is a ruling class game and the key players who have the potential to win in the political game are solidly part of the ruling class and compelled to deceive the public for their class interests.

From this ruling-class perspective, the war is won for them and the task is simply not to lose grasp of what is now in their grip with promises of future profits, disguised under the rubric of a "war on terrorism." What they are sorry about is that it did not turn out as historically neat as they would have wished. History proved to be quite untidy. If things had gone more smoothly, they would have eagerly claimed the glory. Nevertheless, the idea is to "get it while you can" and the ruling class have got it. Their Iraqi colonial empire is in place. Right now the neoconservatives are under heavy criticism, but broadly it is true that the ruling class believes that action in Iraq has served and will continue to serve US interests. That is why they hedged their bets and went along with the war on the hunch that in the end, America would gain significantly from enlarging the global empire. They bet on the Iraqi stock being higher but they will not get out of the war market because of a few rough waters. Their statements concerning Iran are quite militant and one has to believe that their protests of a strike would not be loud, even if forthcoming. From the ruling class perspective, much has been gained in Iraq and it is just a matter of "winning" in terms of containing the local "insurgency," the Orwellian term used for Iraqi national resistance. Most of the criticism is couched in the criticism that the war was mismanaged, not that the war was bad policy to begin with. Some politicians, like Senator Arlen Specter, say that "if we had known that Saddam Hussein did not have weapons of mass destruction, we would have not invaded." This is patently untrue. A determination was made to invade regardless of whether there were weapons of mass destruction or not. And he knows this well.

From the corporate capitalist perspective the operation in Iraq has contributed greatly to capitalist accumulation. Halliburton has made huge profits along with a whole range of American corporations extending their operations to a larger Middle East and South Asia region and linking up with local corporations. The US military, while often at odds with the White House, is in business and has tried out and developed some new tactics and US troops are gaining expertise in urban warfare which will be necessary in the continued global class struggle. Avenues are kept open to funnel more dollars from taxpayers away from social programs and into the military industrial complex which accelerates capitalist accumulation while keeping much of the cost of the war secret.[25] More of the inordinate theft from taxpayers is concealed. Neoliberalism has gained a foothold in the Middle East and in that respect is a triumph. It intends to integrate the Middle East more tightly into corporate globalization.[26] But more significantly, perhaps, the footprint of the Empire has been established. The beach head on the Tigris and Euphrates rivers in Baghdad is firmly in place with the almost one billion dollar US embassy complex being rushed into completion.

To be sure, there are many emerging problems down the pipeline, but these are contingencies are to be handled as time goes along in the war of attrition against nationalist resistance in Iraq. It is part of the long term imperialist effort. Indeed, the US at this point has little choice, given its posture in the world as the unchallenged global hegemon. Anything less would surely challenge and undermine its hegemony. There will be much collateral damage along the way and even possible massacres as in British times, but it is of little consequence from the ruling class perspective. The 2007 escalation, dubbed a "surge" by the spin-masters in Washington, is not working and the Bush Administration keeps playing with the dates, manipulating the American people and pretending that there will soon be "light at the end of the tunnel." This is the same old Vietnam Syndrome being played out again.[27]

The war in Iraq is part of a global class war. The war in Iraq, against the Iraqi people and nation to appropriate their resources, strategic location, oil, waterways, and so on, is a part of a global war, essentially a global class war which is being significantly waged against the whole world, including the people of the United States. The Cold War was the same kind of war, as was World Wars I and II. This all flows out of US messianic zealotry, saving the world from evil as embodied in the ideology of Wilsonianism.[28] This, of course, is just eyewash for the masses to blind them to the reality of becoming cannon fodder in wars that serve the interests of the ruling classes. The Cold War was based upon the false pretext of a Soviet threat, the threat of Communism, as noted above. The real threat was nationalism, and autonomous democratic development in the periphery, but it is true that a different kind of world, a different kind of economic system would threaten capitalist interests. This was a potential threat and largely a threat of democracy from the left. Convincing the people of this "threat" was finally successful with massive propaganda and misleading the public.[29]

The same is true of the new phase of this same global class war, the so-called war on terror.[30] This is disguised class warfare to prevent the rest of the world from slipping out of the neo-liberal capitalist world order and to appropriate and bring in peripheral regions which have not yet been completely integrated into the global neo-liberal system. The major difference with the Cold War period is that Keynesian economic policies with greater social welfare had to be utilized then as a result of the existence of state socialism. But the real danger was that the Cold War would end, so as the "Soviet threat" vanished with the Soviet Union, something had to be done to keep the global class war going. The "war on terror" saved the day and prevented the end of this war and presented the needed enemies which were missing. Former US Secretary of State, Colin Powell, talked about the problem of the US 'running out of enemies." The "weapons of mass destruction" were not found in Iraq. But the US found something more valuable. Or rather they created proxy enemies, like Abu Musab al-Zarqawi, and others associated with al-Qaeda, whom they could claim were a deadly threat to the United States.

But how does one create a war on terror? One must first create terror and ensure its future existence to keep the war going. This is the game that is being played out today. This then provides the ideological pretext for the continuation of the global class war.

Global terrorism has been created by the US in funding radical anti-Western groups and by US hegemonic policies. This continues at an even greater rate today. Global terrorism for the most part has been created by US actions and US and Western colonialist policies toward the emerging world which has resources needed by the West. There is actually nothing new about this policy which was used extensively by the British. The Muslim Brotherhood in Egypt, at the root of major groups across the Middle East and South Asia, was founded by the British to weaken

Egyptian nationalist movements. Israel founded Hamas in Palestine for the purpose of countering Palestinian nationalism. The United States, with the help of the Saudis, organized and funded the Mujahideen against the Soviet Union in Afghanistan, directly contributing to the emergence of the Taliban movement in Pakistan and Afghanistan and the emergence of al-Qaeda.[31] These policies proceed apace today as Western countries fund terrorist and resistance groups all across the Middle East and South Asia to pursue their "national interests." Examples are given by Seymour Hersh of the US funding of Sunni groups in Syria and Lebanon today against Hizbollah.[32] For example, to weaken Iran, the US is funding Kurdish, Tajik, and Baluchi resistance groups and the Mujahideen i-Qalk in Iran. There are many other examples. These policies often result in "blowback" in which these groups return to attack US and Western interests and US imperialist policies. But at the same time, blowback is exactly what the doctor ordered, what the US needs as a pretext to continue its global imperialist policies. It is also the Israeli policy to continue to provoke Palestinian terrorism. As long as it continues, Israel can continue to wage wars for more territory and give their colonial rule the sheen of legitimacy and so the game continues. In other words, global terrorism today is rooted in and clearly emerges from historical conquest, colonialism, neo-colonialism[33] and today's neo-liberal corporate globalization. It is the counter reaction to US policies of global hegemony.

In order to create the impression that the US is starting to overcome al-Qaeda in Iraq the US has started to fund Sunni tribal chiefs in Iraq. It is really a bribe which may succeed as long as the money continues. But in the end, funding and training both sides in a civil war, as in Iraq, is sure to be a disaster. As noted in Chapter Eight, one of the Sunni sheiks on the US payroll was killed in Iraq a few days after meeting George W. Bush at a military base in Anbar Province.

In order to contain and consolidate its occupation of Iraq and the entire Middle East, the US is creating the foundation and means for a far wider range of global terrorism. Noam Chomsky has pointed out that a recent highly credible study has concluded that the war in Iraq increased global terrorism by an order of seven-fold.[34] Now the US, according to Seymour Hersh, has embarked upon a dangerous plan to fund radical Sunni, including Salafist, groups all across the Middle East with the cooperation of the Saudis. This is but another chapter in the policies which led to the funding of the Mujahideen in Afghanistan and the blowback of September 11, 2001.[35] In this case, the objective is directed to the rise of the Shiite Crescent all across the Middle East, particularly Iran and Syria, but also against Shiite rule in Iraq. It is to weaken Shiite communities in Lebanon and Saudi Arabia. Terrorism and the "war on terror" are largely artificial creations of the West. This latest policy promises an even greater blowback in future, which possibly is what the US desires in order to unleash even more massive and deadly weapons against the Middle East. The British also entertained ideas about mass liquidation of the local population as seen in the statements of Winston Churchill about using poison gas against the local population when the British occupied Iraq.

Neoliberalism, capitalist globalization, and global capitalist accumulation are being furthered by shoring up obscurantist, religious, and feudal forces. This follows British policies in colonial times. The Islamic Brotherhood in Egypt, the root of al-Qaeda today, was founded by the British in Egypt to help blunt Egyptian nationalism. The British spurred religious movements in India among all three major religious communities, Sikhs, Muslims and Hindus in their divide are rule policies. This has led to radical religious based political parties today in India, The Sikh Akali Dal in Punjab, the Muslim League and the Hindu nationalist Bharatiya Janata Party (BJP). All are socially and politically backward, anti-women's rights and so on, but seen to be "democratic" within the context of an open civil society.

This thesis seems to be a contradiction in the post-modern era, but it is still compatible in the present historical era. The US used the Saudis to control the oil in the Middle East during the Cold War. This meant shoring up the most socially conservative, anti-democratic, politically regressive feudal forces, essentially a Wahabi regime. This served US capitalist interests, while any genuine political development under Arab nationalism was a threat that had to be curbed. This was true of the Arab nationalism of Gamal Abdel Nasser, Saddam Hussein, the Ba'ath nationalists and so on. In the same way, the US overthrew Muhammad Mossadegh in Iran and restored Shah Reza Pahlavi. The US depended upon feudal local rulers and also helped to nurture radical Salafist elements in the Saudi Kingdom. The US is launching a new campaign today to help ensure the future continued occupation of Baghdad and the entire Middle East. The project is designed to curb the rise of the Shiite crescent and keep a balance between Sunni and Shia elements, and this is being forged through an agreement with the Saudis as in the past.

This is essentially the same historical anti-democratic model, falling back on feudal forces and involving the US-Israel-Jordan-Saudi axis to weaken Iran, Syria, Hizbollah and Shia elements in eastern Saudi Arabia, as well as the now dominant Shia elements in Iraq. This is a sort of divide and rule strategy but a dangerous game. The US supported General Zia al-Haq in Pakistan in the 1980s, who allied with the feudal clerics to further Islamicize Pakistan. The Taliban movement was first born in the medressas of Pakistan. The Jamaat i-Islami was strengthened, to fight the Soviets in Afghanistan. Today Pakistan is a hotbed of Taliban sentiment. Progressive, liberal, and leftist elements have been squeezed out by the three major constituencies of the clerics, the military and the feudal landlords.

To the north, of the Middle East, the emergence of a more dynamic, quickly developing, westernized, more independent, modern Turkey is also somewhat of a threat. This is mainly because of the emergence of a strong anti-US nationalism that tends to challenge US hegemony, while being pro-modern and pro-western. In October, the popularity of the US in Turkey was the lowest of any country in the world with only nine percent of Turks favorable to US policies. The ruling regime in Turkey runs the risk of suffering a political backlash if it is seen to be tied too close to US interests.

The US has used and continues to use religious, fundamentalism, obscurantist and backward forces to further its goals and mainly to deter any threat to the prevailing political and economic order. Today religious, fundamentalist forces and political parties, such as the AK Party (*Adalet* ve *Kalkinma* Partesi or Justice and Development Party) in Turkey and the BJP (*Bharatiya Janata* Party or Indian People's Party) in India,[36] can be bought off and they generally follow the IMF/World Bank programs closely. They represent rising under-classes, including the petty bourgeoisie, socially conservative, who want to get rich. They are often anti-American but pro-domestic capital. They discredit and tend to weaken social, left, progressive tendencies that make a deep and fundamental critique of neo-liberal capitalism. So, objectively, they serve the purpose of furthering the neo-liberal capitalist world order.

In Turkey, the AK Party policies have served the cause of big business to the point of big business being widely criticized. Big businesses have been accused of caring only for their profits and not criticizing the Ak Party for undermining, to some extent, the old established nationalist secular order. Further, such parties inhibit a political and historical consciousness.[37] This is generally true of post-modernist trends and ethnic politics in general. It contributes to mental fragmentation and so serves the purpose of promoting corporate globalization. So the US generally does not have any problem with obscurantist and religious politics unless there emerges anti-imperialist and strong nationalistic elements. The Western spin is to see such politics as more democratic while the old established secularism is seen as anti-democratic. This is actually two different visions of "democracy," the Jacobin variety and the liberal variety. In any event, these reactionary nationalist and anti-imperialist forces can be used for US purposes, such as in the cases of Baluchi nationalism, Tajik nationalism, Kurdish nationalism and so on, to destabilize political regimes.

As far as religion goes, on the domestic side, fundamentalist obscurantism that prevents and inhibits political and social consciousness keeps people exploited, ignorant, parochial, politically and socially backward, docile and easy to rule. A racist and somewhat communal ideology makes people anti-Islam in the US. Religion has been used by Republicans in the US for political purposes in a whole bundle of non-issues, like abortion, gay marriage, prayer in public schools, placing the Ten Commandments on the court house lawn, research using fetal tissue, and so on, to obscure real economic and social issues like salaries, employment, medical assistance, education, and serving the state by shunting their youth to the military and praying over them when they die. Such religious obscurantism serves a very useful role in keeping the US population politically challenged and lacking a political and social consciousness. This is not as useful in European politics but it can be used to stabilize politics in a conservative direction. In the Middle East, it has been exploited by the West to prevent a push for more social welfare and so on. Where a more secular policy is followed, as in Turkey, in trying to suppress religious prejudice and obscurantism, the country is accused of repressing religious freedom.

It appears that political systems which have never had either a strong leftist movement, or a period of communist rule, produce a large class who lack political consciousness and who generally vote against their own long-term interests. This has been seen in recent years in both Turkey and the United States.

The US is now a major Middle Eastern power and will remain so for at least another fifty years. Nothing can now prevent this. Even though US global hegemony may weaken in general, US militarism will remain strong for the indefinite future. This is part of the new international order, in general. The US population, the Middle East region, and the world population in general, are behind the curve in understanding this. The Iraq War is often seen as a US invasion followed by the US troops going home, as in Vietnam. But this, as noted above, is mistaken. The neoconservatives have actually succeeded in moving the tectonic political plates of the world so that the US is a major Middle Eastern power in the same way that World War I and II made the US a major European and Pacific power. This is the real new global order. We know this was planned at the time of the first Gulf War. Afterward, the US Ambassador in Bahrain, in January 1992, said that "if the US plays its cards right, it will be the major power occupying the Middle East for the next 50 years or until the oil is essentially depleted, in the same way that the US occupied Europe and its Asian satellites for the 50 years following World War II."[38] This observation was supported by the United Arab Emirates and other countries in the Gulf lining up with the US to secure protection from the Iraqi regime of Saddam Hussein. The US saw the opportunity to exploit the favorable situation which had come about as a result of the first Gulf War in 1991. Now the neoconservatives have "played their cards right," certainly from the perspective of the ruling class, and we should acknowledge that they have succeeded, even if not brilliantly. They have moved the political tectonic plates of the earth. Regardless of how upsetting it might be for many, who saw the possibility of a more peaceful world after the cold war, the chess pieces have been moved and the game goes on. Rather than become a normal country in the global arena pursuing reasonable interests, the US elites opted to extend and increase their hegemony over the entire world. Most certainly, the fall-out is still going on. There will be many aftershocks to this global political earthquake, but the earth has moved to a new political geological era. A new order has been established.

The tectonic shift brought about by the occupation of Iraq is bringing new global forces into line which will strengthen the challenge to US global hegemony. Global public opinion has taken a radical shift against US global hegemony. The US image has suffered greatly so that the US is seen either as the great Hitler or the great Satan by large numbers of people. Certainly the US is no longer seen as the Great Savior and guarantor of peace, as after World War II. The earthquake has shattered that image of the US for good, but at the same time, there are emerging new alignments which will challenge the hegemony of the US. Those countries which are in the collective alliance of hegemony, the collective imperialism[39] of the US, the EU and Japan, will also be challenged in their global role. India, formerly a non-aligned country in the Cold War, may or not be pulled into the US orbit. It is not clear at this point how much autonomy it will retain. There is a threat to the US if India plays its own game, as China and Iran are doing, and is not closely integrated into the global capitalist imperial system. Iran, Venezuela, Bolivia[40], and Cuba have formed an anti-imperialist alliance and some other countries may participate. This is a further threat to US hegemony.[41]

There are other global factors that are not realized by the US population for the most part. First, and significantly, a number of countries, mostly big emerging markets, have caught up with the developed countries, essentially, in broad areas of development. That is, there is not very much difference between the life-styles of middle classes in a wide range of countries today. The average income is often less, but the essential development factors are there and the income for middle classes may not be very much less when the price parity index is taken into account. Some countries in this category include Brazil, India, Mexico, Turkey, China, Russia, and Indonesia.[42] The fact is that the middle classes are being squeezed all across the world. This means that these big emerging market countries do not have to depend so much upon the US or the West in the global economy.[43] They are able to assert more independence, especially if they can link up with resource rich countries such as Iran and Venezuela.

Secondly, the US is itself a declining empire. As the US declines as a result of imperial overstretch, emerging countries are strengthened.[44] For the most part, today China is playing a very clever game in the sense of a global strategy. The US decline is seen in a number of factors including the massive and increasing debt and its deficits: the budget deficit, the trade deficit, and the current account deficit. There is declining social welfare and a major environmental crisis.[45]

Third, US culture and the life-style in the United States is in a state of crisis. The knowledge and lack of a global outlook of most of its people is a negative factor.[46] One finds essentially a parochial mindset, often religiously fundamentalist, and sometimes racist,[47] among the people. This means that the people can easily be caught off guard and fall back while looking out for terrorists from the Middle East. In fact, the greater threat is the incredible introverted world view of most people in America and the ease by which they can be dominated by the ruling class. In fact, the society and people are being decimated by the socially destructive policies being made by their rulers in Washington.

Most Americans are naïve about the world and the vast ignorance of the typical American, following the political and class repression of the working class from the McCarthy purge in the 1950s, persists today. If Americans are incapable of understanding the world, then they are incapable of joining it. If Americans had a more internationalist mindset, perhaps they could see themselves as part of the international order or community with common interests, rather than "American."

The consciousness of many around the world transcends their nationality to a more global level. It seems to be the case to a greater extent in Europe than in America. This is partly geographical. America is so vast and so far away from the rest of the world that the rest of the world seems distant and outside of their consciousness. For many Americans, there is a very big distinction between being "in the US" and being "outside the US." On the other hand, such a distinction of being abroad is not very great in Europe and other parts of the world where countries are generally small, close together, and similar in culture. It appears that US culture is increasingly weak in some aspects, such as social stability and family stability. Individualism and lack of inclusion of the urban underclass in social welfare produces a relatively large class of alienated people and the world's largest prison population, both absolutely and in per capita terms. There is nothing for many to fall back upon as the family structure is very weak. Shunting needy people into churches for social assistance, as the neo-conservatives attempted to do, is not only regressive, but cynical and a denial of people's social and political rights. A generation in America was greatly debilitated by the ravages of the Vietnam War and now another generation is being ravished by the brutal occupation of Iraq.

Fourth, the after-shocks of the US occupation in the Middle East will have to play themselves out in both domestic and international politics over the next 25 to 50 years. This is not likely to happen in a way similar to the way US hegemony in Europe and East Asia played out during the Cold War. This is more like a colonial situation which will take its great toll in money and lives. Now, the Turks say, "We have a new neighbor, the USA." The US is correctly seen as the de facto ruler in Iraq. While there will be much dissent in the US, propaganda and the instillation of irrational fear will probably largely overcome this resistance, and the Iraq invasion may be seen by a significant majority as noble, or at least with noble intentions in future. The historical memory of Americans is exceedingly short. The effort to overcome US hegemony by countries around the world is likely to have increasing success. The US and its capitalist allies, however, will do all in their power to sabotage and overcome such anti-imperialist movements. The big emerging powers will continue to strengthen as the US declines, in turn, creating their own contradictions.[48] Whether one can be optimistic about a global working class movement is a larger question.[49] At some point, it may become clear to large populations both in rich and poor countries that the established global political and economic system is not working for them and must change.[50]

References

1. Speech at Baltimore, Maryland, April 6, 1918. Quoted in J. William Fulbright, *The Arrogance of Power*. New York: Vintage Books, 1966, p. 253.
2. Richard J. Barnet, *Intervention and Revolution*. New York: Meridian, 1968, p. 276.
3. Alexis de Toqueville, *Democracy in America*. New York: Mentor, 1956, p. 278.
4. Alexis de Toqueville, *Democracy in America* (Two Vols.) New York: Alfred A. Knopf, 1945, p. 263.
5. James M. Cypher, "From Military Keynesianism to Global-Neoliberal Militarism," *Monthly Review*, 59 (2), June 2007, pp. 37-55. While the neo-conservatives in the Bush

Administration have promoted US militarism with a vast propaganda effort, the main thrust of US hegemony is structural dating from World War II.

6. Recent studies include Tim Weiner, *Legacy of Ashes: The History of the CIA* (New York: Doubleday, 2007), and Francis Stoner Saunders, *The Cultural Cold War: The CIA and the World of Arts and Letters* (New York: The New Press, 1999).
7. The consolidation of this system is to be finalized in some form of a European constitution, but this has run up against some stiff opposition from sections of the population who understand what is afoot. Eddie J. Girdner, "A Spectre Haunting Europe: The European Constitution, The Budget Crisis and the Limits of Neo-liberal Integration," *UluslararasiIliskiler (International Relations)* , Vol. 2, No. 7, Fall 2005, pp. 63-85. Eddie J. Girdner, "The Magic Circle of Madness: How Europe Lost its Soul," *UluslararasiIliskiler (International Relations),* Vol. 3, No. 12, Winter 2006-2007, pp. 101-126.
8. Walter LaFeber, *America, Russia and the Cold War 1945-1980* (4th ed.). New York: John Wiley and Sons, 1980; William Blum, *Killing Hope; U.S. Military and C.I.A. Interventions Since World War II.* Monroe, Maine: Common Courage, 2004; William Blum, *Rogue State: A Guide to the World's Only Superpower*. London: Zed Books, 2002.
9. Noam Chomsky, *World Orders, Old and New*. New York: Columbia Univ. Press, 1996. Noam Chomsky, "Imminent Crisis: Threats and Opportunities," *Monthly Review*, 59 (2), June 2007, pp. 1-19.
10. Seymour Hersh, "The Redirection," *The New Yorker*, March 5, 2007.
11. John M. Blair, *The Control of Oil*. New York: Vintage Books, 1978; Larry Everest, *Oil, Power and Empire: Iraq and the US Global Agenda*. Monroe, Maine: Common Courage, 2004.
12. On Indian politics: Srinivas C. Mudumbai, *United States Foreign Policy Towards India, 1947-54*. New Delhi: Manohar, 1980; W. H. Morris-Jones, *Politics Mainly Indian.* Bombay; Orient Longman, 1978; Dilip Hiro, *Inside India Today*. New York: Monthly Review Press, 1976; Sankar Ghose, *Changing*

India. Bombay; Allied Publishers, 1978; John Kenneth Galbraith, *Ambassador's Journal: A Personal Account of the Kennedy Years*. Boston; Houghton Miflin, 1969; Lloyd I. Rudolph and Susanne Hoeber Rudolph, *In Pursuit of Lakshmi: The Political Economy of the Indian State*. Chicago: University of Chicago Press, 1987; Paul R. Brass, *The Politics of India Since Independence*. New York: Cambridge Univ. Press, 1990.

13. Background to the US invasion and occupation of Iraq: Andrew Cockburn and Patrick Cockburn, *Saddam Hussein: An American Obsession*. London: Verso, 2000; Kenneth M. Pollack, *The Threatening Storm: The Case for Invading Iraq*. New York: Random House, 2002; Geoff Simmons, *Targeting Iraq: Sanctions and Bombing in US Policy*. London: Saqi Books, 2002; Milan Rai, *War Plan Iraq*. London; Verso, 2002; Robert Fisk, *The Great War For Civilisation: The Conquest of the Middle East*. New York: Alfred A. Knopf, 2006.

14. This is pretty explicit in what officials of the Bush government are saying explicitly. It was seen also in the David Petraeus hearings in Washington recently. There is much in the US national and world press that documents this. Bush says the model is Korea, which the US is still occupying with no official end to the war. A more realistic model is the occupation of Palestine by Israel, where Israel must have the water resources of the West Bank and control the population. War protesters in the US seem to be thinking of Vietnam, where the US pulled out the troops and left after 12 years or so. But Vietnam did not have oil and was not seen as the key to global control.

15. I have tried to address some of these issues elsewhere: Eddie J. Girdner, 'Blood for Oil: Sacrificing America's Youth to Empire and Capitalist Accumulation," *Mainstream*, 43 (25) June 11, 2005, pp. 11-19; Eddie J. Girdner, "Empire of Terrorism: War, Hubris, and American Tragedy," *Mainstream* 42 (44) Oct. 23, 2004, pp. 20-26; Eddie J. Girdner, "The Short End of the Stick: The Middle East and Global Security," *Turkish Review of Middle East Studies*, No. 17, 2006, pp. 99-120.

16. A list of these US base facilities in Iraq is given in Johnson, Chapter Four. Chalmers Johnson, *Nemesis: The Last Days*

of the American Republic, New York: Metropolitan Books, 2006.

17. Marc Santora, "U.S. Commander Warns of Long Struggle in Iraq," *New York Times,* January 15, 2007; Major Garrett and Trish Turner, "Bush Surprises Senate Aides with Unexpected Interruption of White House Meeting," *Fox News*, July 17, 2007; Joshua Holland, "Coming to a Dead End in Iraq," *Alternet*, April 10, 2007; Peter W. Galbraith and Tom Engelhardt, "The War is Lost," *The New York Review of Books*, August 16, 2007.

18. Of course, in some respects, it is a new ballgame now in the sense that the more war and occupation is carried out, the greater can be the grand theft from the taxpayers in no-bid contracts to the corporate establishment hogs in the dollar-creek. The looting of the public treasury becomes truly institutionalized in perpetuity, or at least until the empire collapses. It is possible to kill the goose that lays the golden egg, as history has shown.

19. On Vietnam: See Le Duan, *The Vietnamese Revolution*. New York, International Publishers, 1971; Stanley Karnow, *Vietnam, A History*. New York: Viking, 1983; Harrison E. Salisbury, *Behind The Lines-Hanoi*. New York: Harper and Row, 1967; Gerard Chaliand *The Peasants of North Vietnam*. Middlesex, England: Penguin, 1969; Wilfred G. Burchett, *The Second Indochina War: Cambodia and Laos*. New York: International Publishers, 1970; Robert Templer, *Shadows and Wind: A View of Modern Vietnam*. London: Penguin, 1955.

20. John Perkins, *Confessions of an Economic Hit Man*. San Francisco: Berrett-Koehler, 2004.

21. Eddie J. Girdner, "Waste, War and Toxic Imperialism: The Political Economy of Depleted Uranium," *International Journal of Environment and Development*, 1 (2) Dec. 2004, pp. 281-300.

22. Paul Kennedy, *The Rise and Fall of the Great Powers*. New York: Vintage, 1989.

23. In technical terms, a "democratic deficit." In reality, a near dictatorship.

24. Many books have been published on the conduct of the US occupation: Michael R. Gordon and General Bernard E. Trainor, *Cobra II: The Inside Story of the Invasion and Occupation of Iraq*. New York: Pantheon, 2006; Evan Wright, *Generation Kill: Devil Dogs, Iceman, Captain America and the New Face of American War*. New York: G. P. Putnam's Sons, 2004; Aaron Glantz, *How America Lost Iraq*. New York: Jeremy P. Tarcher/Penguin, 2005.
25. Neil Abercrombie, "On war costs, Bush is master of disguise," *The Boston Globe,* March 5, 2007; Joel Havemann, "War coss are hitting historic proportions," *Los Angeles Times*, Jan. 14, 2007.
26. On imperialism and corporate globalization: Harry Magdoff, *The Age of Imperialism: The Economics of U.S. Foreign Policy*. New York: Monthly Review Press, 1969; William K. Tabb; Richard J. Barnet and Ronald E. Muller, *Global Reach: The Power of the Multinational Corporations*. New York: Simon and Schuster, 1974; William k. Tabb, *The Amoral Elephant: Globalization and the Struggle for Social Justice in the Twenty-First Century*. New York: Monthly Review Press, 2001; Michael Abramowitz, "Intelligence Puts Rationale for War on Shakier Ground," *Washington Post*, July 18, 2007.
27. Robert Dreyfus, "Surge Mentality: White House in Denial," *The Nation*, July 30, 2007; Adam Hochschild and Tom Engelhardt, "Over the Top in Iraq," *Tom Dispatch*, Jan. 22, 2007; Stewart Nusbaumer, "Beyond Baghdad," *The American Conservative*, May 21, 2007; Patrick Cockburn, "A bloody message from Iraq: nowhere is safe..." *The Independent*, April 13, 2007.
28. Arthur Silber, "Dominion Over the World (VIII): Unwelcome History—Religion, the Progressives, Empire and he Drug War," May 16, 2007.
29. That a strong system of propaganda to shape public opinion to the needs of the ruling class was clearly seen by Lippmann and others who proceeded to develop the public relations industry to that end. Walter Lippmann, *The Public Philosophy*. New York: Mentor, 1955.

30. Massive propaganda has been used to build fear among the American public, first in the false "intelligence" before the war and in instilling fear ever since the invasion. Robert Fisk, "The crushing fear that stalks America," *The Independent,* March 26, 2007; "Coming War With Iran," (Interview with Lt. Col. Karen Kwiatkowski (ret.) *Truthdig*, March 2, 2007. This article shows how military officers were ordered to go along with false "intelligence" which served a political agenda.
31. Background can be found in: Jason Burke, *Al-Qaeda: Casting a Shadow of Terror*. London: I.B. Tauris, 2003; Ahmed Rashid, *Taliban: The Story of Afghan Warlords*. London: Pan Books, 2001; Peter Marsden, *The Taliban: War and Religion in Afghanistan*. London: Zed Books, 2002; Mahmood Mamdani, *Good Muslim, Bad Muslim: America, The Cold War, and the Roots of Terror.* New York: Pantheon, 2004; Robert Baer, *See No Evil: The True Story of a Ground Soldier in the CIA's War on Terrorism*. New York; Crown Publishers, 2002; Richard A, Clarke, *Against All Enemies: Inside America's War on Terror*. New York: Free Press, 2004.
32. Seymour Hersh, "The Redirection," *The New Yorker*, March 5, 2007.
33. Richard J. Barnet, *Intervention and Revolution: America's Confrontation with Insurgent Movements Around the World.* New York: Meridian Books, 1968.
34. Noam Chomsky and Tom Engelhardt, "What if Iran Had Invaded Mexico?" *TomDispatch*, April 6, 2007. The increase in terrorism is referred to "the Iraq effect." The study was carried out by Peter Bergen and Paul Cruickshank using government and Rand Corporation data. Michael Swartz and Tom Englehardt, "Nine Paradoxes of a Lost War," *Tom Dispatch*, October 16, 2006.
35. Seymour Hersh, "The Redirection."
36. The AK Party (Adalet ve Kalkinma Partesi, Justice and Development Party) in Turkey presents itself as largely secular although it also embraces religious tendencies which raises suspicions of all those in the party, including Prime Minister Recep Tayip Erdogan. The Bharatiya Janata Party

(BJP) in India is more deeply religiously oriented. Both parties can be said to have strong bases in the petty bourgeoisies. Eddie J. Girdner, "The Twilight of Refah: Turkey and the Islamist Welfare Party," *Scandinavian Journal of Development Alternatives and Area Studies* 18 (4). December 1999, pp. 31-49. Eddie J. Girdner and Nitish Dutt. "Challenging the Rise of Nationalist-Religious Parties in India and Turkey," *Contemporary South Asia*, 9 (1) 2000, pp. 7-24.

37. The AK Party, while pursuing policies which may militate against the long term interests of the working classes in the long run, have provided significant social benefits to the underclasses, such as expansion of housing, subsidized food and fuel, free school books, new roads and parks and expanded medical care. Social welfare policies still translate into votes in Turkey, unlike the US, as seen in the July 22, 2007 Parliamentary elections. They have broadened their appeal to both the big bourgeoisie on the one hand (with neo-liberal policies) and the marginally poor on the other (with considerable welfare benefits). AK Party won a landslide 47 percent of the votes. The secular elites primarily oppose their policies which seek to relax curbs upon further Islamization, such as the proposal to allow students to wear headscarves in universities.

38. Informal briefing at the US Embassy in Manama attended by the author.

39. See Samir Amin, "US Imperialism, Europe and the Middle East," *Monthly Review* 56 (6), Nov. 2004, pp. 13-33.

40. See *Monthly Review* 59 (3), July-August 2007, Special Issue: Revolt in Latin America.

41. On US global hegemony and US decline: John Pilger, The New Rulers of the World. London: Verso, 2002; Samir Amin, *The Neo-liberal Virus: Permanent War and the Americanization of the World.* New York, Monthly Review, 2004; Noam Chomsky, *Failed States: The Abuse of Power and the Assault on Democracy*. New York" Metropolitan Books, 2006; Chalmers Johnson, *The Sorrows of Empire: Militarism, Secrecy, and the End of the Republic*. New York: Metropolitan Books, 2004 and *Nemesis*.

42. Eddie J. Girdner, "Globalization and the Turkish Economic Crises," *Zeitschrift fur Turkiestudien (Journal for Studies in Turkey)*, 17 Jahtgng 2004, Heft 1-2. Eddie J. Girdner, "China as a Capitalist State: From Primitive Socialist Accumulation to Neoliberal Capitalism," *The Turkish Yearbook of International Relations*, No. 35, 2004, pp. 121-144.
43. When the sub-prime mortgage crisis was taking hold in the United States and some US and European banks were facing bankruptcy in August-October 2007, there was an economic boom in new housing in Turkey with banks flush with money to loan on new mortgages. The dollar plunged against the Turkish Lira. On the other hand, the overvalued domestic currency, linked closely to the global economy, made the Turkish economy extremely sensitive to global financial instability. The vast amount of dollars flowing into Turkey from Iraq has also helped the economy to boom. The Americans in Iraq are living off Turkish exports.
44. See the trilogy of books by Chalmers Johnson: *Blowback*, *Sorrows of Empire* and *Nemesis.*
45. Some recent useful books on the US political economy include: Molly Ivins and Lou Dubose, *Bushwhacked: Life In George W. Bush's America*. New York: Random House, 2003; Greg Palast, *The Best Democracy Money Can Buy*. London: Plume, 2003; Si Kahn and Elizabeth Minnich, *The Fox in the Henhouse: How Privatization Threatens Democracy*. San Francisco: Berrett-Koehler Publishers, 2005; Eddie J. Girdner and Jack Smith, *Killing Me Softly: Toxic Waste, Corporate Profit and the Struggle for Environmental Justice*. New York: Monthly Review, 2002.
46. The quality of American life and values in the 1950s and 60s are penetrated in Edward Abbey, *Confessions of a Barbarian: Selections from the Journals of Edward Abbey, 1951-1989*. Boston; Little, Brown and Company, 1994.
47. Eddie J. Girdner, "Religious Fundamentalist and Racist Tendencies in the Electoral Arena in the United States: Political Fringes or Mainstream America?" *Gazi Universitesi Iktisadi ve Idari Bilimler Fakultesi Dergesi (Gazi University, Economics and Administrative Sciences Faculty Journal)* 4 (1) Spring 2002, pp. 11-30.

48. It is not clear, indeed, whether the world will survive the struggle for global hegemony as the US struggles for supremacy with the arming of space and development of a new generation of weapons of mass destruction. See Noam Chomsky, *Hegemony or Survival: America's Quest for Global Dominance*. New York: Metropolitan Books, 2003.
49. Eddie J. Girdner, "Neo-liberalism and Class Formation on a Global Scale," *Nature, Society and Thought* 19 (2), 2006, pp. 225-231.
50. "The middle classes could become a revolutionary class, taking the role envisaged for the proletariat by Marx." This is according to a report of the UK Ministry of Defense. *Global Strategic Trends, 2007-2036*. UK Ministry of Defense.

10

Conclusion: US Global Hegemony and the "War on Terrorism"

"The security of the civilized world depends on victory in the war on terror and that depends on victory in Iraq." **George W. Bush (August 31, 2006)**

"..You know one of hardest parts of my job is to connect Iraq to the war on terror."

George W. Bush (September 6, 2006)

"The Iraq conflict has become the 'cause celebre' for jihadists, breeding a deep resentment of US involvement in the Muslim World and cultivating supporters for the global jihadist movement."

National Intelligence Estimate (April 2006)

There was actually a good reason why the effort to connect Iraq to the "war on terror" was so difficult for George W. Bush. There has never been any real connection between Iraq and the war on terror. The US invasion and occupation of Iraq, as in Afghanistan, has actually created terror, as the intelligence agencies of the US and Great Britain accurately predicted. A report completed by the intelligence agencies of the United States in April 2006 and leaked to the press in late September of the same year, reported that rather than curbing acts of terror, the US invasion of Iraq had caused "Islamic terrorism" to mushroom around the world.[1] President George W. Bush and former British Prime Minister Tony Blair had long argued that Islamic terrorists were attacking the United States because they hate the

"American way of life" and "American freedom." However, the National Intelligence Estimate (NIE), based on the findings of sixteen intelligence agencies in the United States, including the Central Intelligence Agency, and at a cost of over 40 billion dollars, made no mention of such a reason. According to the NIE there are primarily four factors which have contributed to terrorism: the invasion and occupation of Iraq, the entrenched grievances of the people in the region, the slow pace of reform in the Middle East, and pervasive anti-American sentiment.[2] In other words, the best intelligence that the United States can produce confirms that today terrorism is primarily a reaction to the foreign policies of the United States and Great Britain in the Middle East. These are precisely the facts which both US President George W. Bush and former British Prime Minister Tony Blair argued against. The Director of the Central Intelligence Agency (CIA) in the United States, General Michael Hayden, has stressed that new jihadist cells were likely to emerge. "If this trend continues, threats to the U.S. at home and abroad will become more diverse and that could lead to increasing attacks world wide."[3] The report confirmed that not only is Bush wrong in telling the American people that the war in Iraq has "made them safer" but that "the Iraq conflict is the primary recruiting vehicle for violent Islamic extremists."[4] The Bush Administration, in the run-up to Congressional elections a month later, in November 2006, tried to put the best spin on the leaked report, and suggested that the voters would not be influenced by the report. Officials of the Bush Administration seemed to be saying that the American people should ignore the most comprehensive report on terrorism ever produced by US intelligence agencies and believe the President instead. It was clear that in the Bush Administration politics would once again triumph over intelligence, as happened before the beginning of the Iraq War. The President's popularity ratings continued to fall.

At about the same time, a report from the Government Accountability Office noted that the political process in Iraq had sharpened the country's sectarian divisions, polarized relations between its ethnic and religious groups, and weakened its sense of national identity.[5] This result was precisely the opposite of that which had been predicted by the Bush Administration in moving toward elections in Iraq. It must be remembered that the best face was put on the elections as the United States desired to delay elections in Iraq as long as possible, as we have seen, to avoid the wrong parties from coming to power. However, the US was forced to hold elections after the insistent demands of Grand Ayotollah Ali al-Sistani. The report from the Government Accountability Office pointed to the great increase in violence between Sunnis and Shiites and attacks on US forces, which were reported to be running at some 800 per week at the end of September 2006. The Iraqi Health Ministry reported 2660 civilians killed in Baghdad alone in September 2006. In May 2003, there were some 100 "insurgent" attacks. This increased to 4500 attacks in July 2006. One half of these were against US forces while a quarter of them were on Iraqi security forces and a quarter on civilians. The security situation in Iraq was seen to be deteriorating, further threatening economic progress.

In October 2006, the medical journal, *The Lancet*, reported that some 655,000 Iraqis had been killed since the US invasion in March 2003. This was about 2.5 percent of the Iraqi population. This study was a follow up to the report by the same researchers in 2004 that reported that 100,000 Iraqis had died. About 31 percent of the deaths were caused by the US led forces. The report noted that "Iraq is descending into bloodthirsty chaos."[6]

Moreover, electricity remained extremely inadequate, with Baghdad having less that six hours of power a day, on average, and other areas having less than eleven hours per day. Two years later, by February 2008, there was still a

3,000 megawatt deficit of electricity in Baghdad, little clean drinking water and the sewage plants were mostly broken down, unable to handle the demand, and leading to a large pool of open sewage in the city.[7] It was not clear if power could be restored to 24 hours a day even within the next ten years. The US, on the other hand, reported that reported that 76 new health clinics had been constructed country-wide, 1885 new schools had been built and 1604 schools repaired. It was also clear that many Iraqi troops remained loyal to sectarian and political interests rather than to the national interest.[8] Ethnic and sectarian cleansing of Baghdad neighborhoods continued.

The Bush Administration refused to acknowledge that the wars in Afghanistan, Iraq, and Lebanon were colonial wars directed against local peoples to strengthen US global hegemony. It was pointed out by many that even the concept of a "war on terrorism" was a flawed concept that made no sense. No nation can fight a war against a "tactic."[9] Terrorism is a tactic that is being used against a system which the global superpower has imposed upon them. What the US was really fighting was the legitimate reaction to US foreign policy which militates against the interests of the people of the Middle East. It is the same fight that the US waged against the people of Vietnam in the 1960s who dared to defend their national interests. These wars were not labeled a "war against terrorism" but as wars to "stop communism." They were "counterinsurgency wars" against people who rose up in revolt against colonial domination from the French in Indochina and now against US forces in Iraq. When those in the south of Vietnam fought against the US invasion, they were said to be "insurgents," the same name given to Iraqis who oppose the US occupation. They were said to be "guilty of internal aggression."[10] Indeed, if the nations of the Middle East possessed nuclear weapons, they would be in a much better position to defend their interests without using terrorism. The "war on terrorism" would be won, but the war against US imperialism, the real war they are fighting, would indeed go on using different tactics.

The "revolution" launched by the neoconservatives from the banks of the Potomac in Washington increasingly showed up the rulers to be impostures in "new clothes" as the eighth year of George W. Bush's Presidency began. The entire world was increasingly appalled at the reckless hubris of the "civilized world" which endangered everybody. In fact it was difficult to find a single initiative of the Bush Government which had not achieved the opposite of what was intended.[11] Political instability had increased from Lebanon to Pakistan. Iran, labeled a member of the "axis of evil" by George W. Bush, had been strengthened greatly by the war in Iraq, as had Hezbollah in Lebanon. Opposition to US policies in Jordan, Saudi Arabia, Egypt and Pakistan had increased. By early 2008, the US was spending at least $15 billion a month on the wars in Afghanistan and Iraq, with no one knowing the end-strategy for either war. While things were said to be getting significantly better in Iraq with the "surge" strategy, the situation in Afghanistan had clearly deteriorated for US and British forces.[12] Where a degree of democracy had come into play, such as in Iran, Egypt, Palestine (bringing Hamas to victory in the December 2005 elections), and Turkey, the results had generally militated against US policy in the region.

In the United States, there continued to be an erosion of support for President Bush among the population as people lost faith in all the claims of the neoconservatives about making them safer. For those who took a sober look at US foreign policy, it seemed that disaster was not far over the horizon if there was not significant change. However, the spin put on the "surge" strategy led most people to believe that the US was winning the war in Iraq by the end of 2007. As the US Presidential campaign got underway, the US economy seemed to be the overriding issue. People were concerned with losing their home, their job, and being able to afford health care as the economy weakened. Iraq, however, remained a critical issue and most people wanted the troops to be withdrawn. Changing the president would be refreshing but the real problem was systemic. the US system of global imperialism would still be in place.

By February, 2008, at least 3945 members of the US military had died in Iraq since the start of the war. More than 30,000 had been wounded. There had been 171 British soldiers killed in Iraq with a total of 126 killed from other members of the "coalition of the willing."[13] Almost all of the British forces had gone home. Reports from the ground continued to be bleak, in spite of efforts of the Bush Government to put the best face on the situation, until the additional 30,000 surge troops were sent.[14] In mid-August, 2006, Colonel Pete Devlin, Chief of Intelligence for the US Marine Corps in Iraq, had reported that it was unlikely that the US would be able to secure Anbar Province, stating: "There is almost nothing the US Military can do to improve the political and social situation there." Another US Army officer stated that: "We haven't been defeated militarily but we have been defeated politically and that's where wars are won and lost."[15] The situation in Afghanistan was equally dismal with the Taliban making a rapid recovery. Taliban fighters were learning faster than the occupying forces, making "brilliant tactical moves" while the west was making "appalling strategic mistakes."[16]

It seemed that the realization of the disaster might be gradually filtering through the obfuscating media even in the United States. By the end of August, 2006, about two-thirds of Americans opposed the war and 60 percent believed that the war had increased the chances of a terrorist attack. Some 43 percent said they were embarrassed by the US image overseas. And 58 percent of the people said that President Bush did "not inspire confidence."[17] A study by two prominent economists in the United States estimated that the economic costs of the war would lie between one trillion and two trillion dollars.[18] This made the estimate of US Defense Secretary Donald Rumsfeld at the beginning of the war of $50 to $60 billion laughable, were it not for the fact that the nation was in the process of being bankrupted for future generations. The Iraq war had turned out to be a huge program for impoverishing the American people to the tune of over two trillion dollars, while the real beneficiaries were the defense and construction contractors such as Haliburton and a long list of others.

The United States had followed in the footsteps of the British in attempting to impose imperialism on the Middle East by occupying Iraq, with similar results. Actually, it appeared that the US would suffer an even bigger disaster than the British had in terms of the occupation itself. All of the agonizing about "what went wrong" was a futile exercise in rationalization. The war itself was wrong and no tactics could have made US imperialism acceptable to the Iraqi people who were determined to defend their national interests.[19] As Chalmers Johnson pointed out, it is absurd for a country to attempt to impose its system of government and economy upon another country. Such imperialism is grounded in "hubris, racism and arrogance" and is likely to ultimately fail.[20]

The United States continued to lose the "war on terror" on the ground even while the ideological sands of the neoconservative shibboleth were rapidly running out. Hardly a day passed which did not discredit the Bush Administration in its warnings of what lay ahead. Nor was there any evidence that the Israeli-Palestinian conflict would be seriously addressed. While the Israeli Army mostly completed its withdrawal from southern Lebanon at the end of September 2006 and more United Nation's Interim Forces in Lebanon (Unifil) troops arrived in Lebanon, under UN Security Council Resolution 1701, nothing substantial had been changed by the war. The Ehud Olmert Government proceeded to expand new housing units in a major expansion on the West Bank. The expansion was clearly illegal as explicitly stated by officials of the Bush Administration. More discrediting information had surfaced about the illegal use of cluster bombs in southern Lebanon by Israeli forces during the war, where some 160,000 shells were fired, many into villages, and cluster bombs were dropped in 450 settled areas. At least 200,000 people were unable to return to their villages, which was part of the purpose of using the bombs which became mines, in the first place. Under international law the use of such bombs, as indiscriminate weapons, is prohibited. It would take some two years to clear most of the bombs and the Israelis would not provide the maps of where the bombs had been dropped.[21]

At the other end of the region, it was clear that anti-American tensions were running higher in both Afghanistan and Pakistan. It was learned that the US CIA had paid Pakistan millions of dollars for some 350 suspects in the "war on terror," even though such payments are illegal under US law. In Pakistan, the military ruler, General Pervez Musharraf, revealed that Deputy Secretary of State, Richard Armitage, had threatened to bomb Pakistan back to the stone-age if the country did not reverse its policy of supporting the Taliban and support the United States after September 11, 2001. The US Ambassador to Pakistan had made a list of demands on the Pakistan Government including over-flight rights and the right to use naval ports and air bases. There was a major separatist movement in the province of Baluchistan, being brutally suppressed by the Pakistan authorities, while the Pakistan military had been largely defeated in battles against the tribes in Waziristan.[22] By late 2007, large battles were being fought between Taliban militants in Swat and Pakistani forces, with hundreds of Pakistani soldiers being killed. Pakistan threatened to disintegrate with the assassination of former Prime Minister Benazir Bhutto.

The crises looming on the horizon was that between the United States and Iran. While the United States has acknowledged that Iran has the right to enrich uranium for peaceful production of power, Washington irrationally defended what was also acknowledged to be a double standard, that is, allowing Israel, Pakistan and India to have nuclear weapons while stating that force would be used to prevent Iran from enjoying the same right. There was no way such a policy could be made plausible or rational within the larger global arena. It was not clear whether the US would actually move to begin a strategic bombing campaign against Iran and further raise tensions in the region.[23] However, there were continued signs that preparations might be under way in late 2007.

At the same time, it was clear that the United States was again using deception as had been done in the case of regime change in Iraq. According to the CIA and other intelligence agencies, Iran was not likely to develop a nuclear bomb before 2010. The National Intelligence Estimate which argued that Iran was a "strategic threat" was clearly unrealistic. This approach was seen in a report in *Time Magazine* which argued that Israel would "have the capacity to carry out Ahmedinejad's threats to eliminate Israel" once it had a bomb. Such a statement is indeed ludicrous. Even if Iran had as many nuclear bombs as Israel, it would still be suicidal to attack Israel as the country would end up destroying itself. The argument was made as if the author had never heard of the principle of deterrence. Moreover, while the neoconservatives tried to convince the American people that air strikes would be relatively safe and easy, more realistic analysts, such as former Centcom Commander, Anthony Zinni, pointed out that at some point US ground forces would be necessary in a war against Iran, making the whole concept of attacking Iran a "dumb idea." Still, the larger public could not be sure just how irrational the Bush Administration neo-conservatives might be and whether they would go ahead with strikes. From the neoconservative goal of imposing maximum chaos on the Middle East, bombing nuclear facilities in Iraq was perfectly rational. In October 2007, President George W. Bush warned US allies to toe the US line of facing down Iran or possibly face "World War III." A danger was that both US President George W. Bush and Iranian President Mahmoud Ahmedinejad seemed to hold to a messianic vision believing that they were backed by God in the defense of their respective positions.[24]

The driving force behind George W. Bush's "apocalyptic" policies in the Middle East was an ideology which, itself, embraced massive state terrorism to forward US global hegemony. It wove together three ideological strands: the views of conservative republican pragmatists who substituted the September 11, 2001, attack for Ronald Reagan's "evil empire," the views of the neoconservatives in the Bush Administration who saw themselves as revolutionaries, and fundamentalist Christians in the United States who supported Zionism in Israel and saw the Bush Administration as carrying out prophecy written in the Bible. This resulted in the dangerous apocalyptic view that whatever the Administration did was right, a view in which President George W. Bush appeared to believe.

Nevertheless, by late 2007, doubts had begun to creep into the minds of even some mainstream neoconservative believers. The Project for a New American Century (PNAC), whose close circle of 27 founding neo-conservatives provided much of the drive for the wars in Iraq and Afghanistan, appeared to be greatly weakened, if not heading toward closure. According to reports, the organization began breaking down after the invasion of Iraq. Its adherents had pushed its agenda through editorials in the conservative US press, including the Wall Street Journal, Fox News, the Weekly Standard, and the Washington Times. The future existence of the group was in question due to the dispute between those who criticized the US for not sending enough troops to Iraq and pursuing a harsher agenda toward regime change in Syria and Iran, as well as demolishing Hezbollah and the current Bush Administration strategy.

Meanwhile the Bush Administration, having lost its last shred of credibility in its claim of being interested in bringing democracy to the Middle East, fell back upon making the ludicrous argument that the "war on terrorism" was equivalent to the war against the Nazis in World War II and that those who wished to conduct diplomacy with those opposed to US policies, such as Iran, Syria, Hamas and Hzbollah, were "appeasers." The forces in the Middle East who opposed US policies were labelled "Islamofascists" and said to be spreading Islamic fascism. In the words of George W. Bush: "They are successors to fascists, to Nazis, to communists and other totalitarians of the 20th century."[25]

Ultimately the Bush Administration's policies toward the Middle East have achieved precisely the opposite of what they set out to achieve. It has been the most catastrophic US foreign policy in history. Seeking to increase US global hegemony, the US has in fact been weakened. Seeking to contain Iran and weaken or collapse the Islamic regime, Iran has been greatly strengthened. Seeking to bring regime change and establish a stable democracy in Iraq, the overthrow of Saddam has brought chaos and sectarian strife, even throwing in doubt the territorial integrity of the country. Seeking to rid Afghanistan of the Taliban, the overthrow of the regime has only strengthened radical Islamists as an insurgent force and thrown Pakistan into greater political instability. At the same time, the US harnessed itself to a military dictator, General Pervez Musharraf. Seeking to contain the Muslim Brotherhood in Egypt, the group has only strengthened and threatened the Mubarak Government. Seeking to contain Hamas, the party was elected democratically. Unable to take power due to the repudiation of the results by the US and Israel, Hamas took over the Gaza strip. The wrong party was elected and so "democracy" was seen to have failed. Seeking to crush Hezbollah in Lebanon, the organization only grew stronger. Syria, which has largely avoided the conflict, along with Jordan, has become a haven for refugees fleeing the chaos in Iraq. The emerging Kurdish Regional Government in northern Iraq with the operation of the Kurdish Workers Party (PKK) threatened peace in southeastern Turkey, forcing the Turkish military to bomb Kurdish villages across the border in Northern Iraq and fomenting Turkish nationalism and sharper anti-American sentiments in Turkey.

In a larger sense, the entire world has become more anti-American in reaction to the dangerous policies of the George W. Bush Administration. Future generations of Americans have been saddled with an enormous debt, which has not brought freedom to Iraq and Afghanistan but has greatly enriched a few large American corporations. American citizens have lost significant rights and freedoms under fears about terrorism. And the American people themselves are losing economically and falling into greater poverty and inequality. More jobs are being exported under free trade pacts such as the North American Free Trade Agreement (NAFTA). The United States Government has failed to aid their own citizens properly in disasters, such as Hurricane Katrina in 2005.

The Surge and After

Realizing after the 2006 mid-term elections that the situation was critical and that the US was losing the battle to secure Iraq, the Bush Administration changed strategy. An additional 30,000 troops were deployed primarily to secure Baghdad. This "surge" strategy was only partially successful. The more risky strategy was that of banking on the "Awakening Councils" or "Concerned Local Citizens" groups (CLC's). These actually were deals made between the

US forces and Sunni militias whose members had previously been working as insurgents in Iraq in league with al-Qaeda. What was sometimes not mentioned was that the US was putting the tribal sheikhs and their members on the US payroll and essentially bribing them to work for the Americans and not for al-Qaeda. By February of 2008, there were said to be 80,000 Iraqis signed up to Awakening Council groups with members being paid some $300 a month and up. About 9,000 of these council members were being processed to join the Iraqi security forces, the Army and police. Some of the Awakening Councils were being infiltrated by al-Qaeda and at least 100 members were killed in a two month period.[26] What was going on behind the scenes was largely concealed in the US press, the stress being put on the argument that the "surge was working."

Nevertheless, a closer examination of events on the ground showed that the situation remained very uncertain. No one know how long the tribal sheikhs would continue to work for the Americans and it remained uncertain as to what would happen when the Americans were no longer there to pay the "Awakening groups." It was said that about 25 percent of these groups would be integrated into the Iraqi Army and the rest would be disbanded so that they could not form an independent force to fight against the US and the Iraqi Government. What would prevent this, however, is unclear. Many of the insurgents had simply been pushed out of Baghdad and Anbar Province to move further north or south where new battles were required to diminish their strength.

In February 2008, for example, Operating Phantom Phoenix, launched on January 8, 2008 was continuing. This was billed as a "countrywide assault by US military and Iraqi military forces on al-Qaeda. As a part of this operation, a 'decisive battle" against al-Qaeda was about to be launched in the northern city of Mosul. Mosul had previously been considered a quite peaceful area. Local residents were afraid of what would happen as they stocked up on food and fuel. On January 23, munitions stored by the insurgents had blown up in the city killing 60 people in Sanjili, a suburb. Iraqi national security advisor Muwaffaq al-Rubaie made the statement: "The battle that our armed forces will launch will destroy terrorism and the criminal gangs and outlaws in Ninevah." Of course, the battle was actually being launched by the US military, which still hesitated to trust the Iraqis with such an operation.[27]

Operation Phantom Phoenix involved the dropping of 40,000 pounds of explosives on the southern outskirts of Baghdad on January 10 in just ten minutes by US bombers and jet fighters. This assault on houses and citrus groves was followed by a ground attack by US soldiers. Arab Jabour, where the bombs were dropped, was believed to be controlled by al-Qaeda and some 12 people were arrested that day. It was reported that nine US soldiers were killed the first two days of the Operation north of Baghdad in Diyala Province. Some of the US soldiers were killed trying to clear out a booby-trapped house where they believed arms had been stored. At least 273 people had been killed in Diyala in December, although the numbers killed were way down in Baghdad from previous months.[28] Nevertheless, the fact that this type of operation, one of the biggest air-strikes of the war, was taking place close to Baghdad almost five years since the beginning of the war did not inspire confidence that US forces could continue to control a country the size of Iraq. There are millions of houses in the country where arms could be stored and hundreds of villages. The US forces appeared to be just moving the problem around from one place to another. Clearly the Iraqis wanted the US out and al-Qaeda was still there in sufficient numbers to keep the Americans busy and in the country.

US soldiers continued to operate in Diyala Province, clearing abandoned houses of arms with the support of the Iraqi Army and "Concerned Local Citizens."[29] Still the

Americans did not quite trust the Iraqi Army to do the same job and getting the local Sunni tribes on their side was tough going.[30] While billed as a huge success in the US press,[31] one had to be somewhat skeptical about the ultimate outcome of the surge and the alliances with Sunni militias. A similar attempt to ally with insurgents failed in Fallujah just before the big battle in 2004. Many of the tribal leaders, it was noted by journalists, "will shake the hand of anybody who he thinks can get him money and power." However, some members of the CLCs had not fared so well. Not only had some been assassinated by al-Qaeda, some continued to be killed in US operations against al-Qaeda. Another report from the village of Tal al-Samar about 30 miles south of Baghdad revealed that when American war planes bombed some houses, they killed at least nine civilians, members of the Sunni al-Ghrir Tribe, all innocent of al-Qaeda affiliation. This was not an isolated incident but continued to happen time and again around the country.

In another case, some 25 members of an "Awakening Council," allied with American forces, were killed north of Baghdad. The leader of the group, Mansour Abid Salim of the Taji Awakening Council, said the Americans had mistaken his men for al-Qaeda militants.[32] Presumably it is not easy to distinguish al-Qaeda militants from pro-American militants, at least for the American soldiers. At the same time, attacks "using Iranian-made roadside bombs," were reported to have risen to the highest level in a year in a "key part of Baghdad." These included the more powerful armour-piercing roadside bombs called explosively formed penetrators (EFPs). US troops and neighborhood security units were being targeted.[33]

One could not have a great deal of faith in the security arrangements even in Baghdad, even at this late date. Even as the numbers in the Iraqi Army and security forces increased to over 500,000, it was common knowledge that they were infiltrated by insurgents. In the same way, the US was using awakening groups to infiltrate al-Qaeda to gain intelligence.

On the first weekend in February, around 100 people died in bombs in two markets in Baghdad as two female suicide bombers blew themselves up in these markets. One of the bombers struck the Ghazil pet market killing 62 people. The other struck a market in Baghdad Jadida killing 37 people.[34] These incidents reminded everyone that the situation remained delicate and security had by no means returned for the people.

The beginning of February also saw one of the 18 "benchmarks" met when the "de-Baathification law," which was passed by Parliament on January 12, was issued. The law was meant to allow lower-ranking Baath Party members to reclaim their government jobs. However, under the law, 7,000 former Baathists still employed by Iraq's security services were scheduled to be dismissed. It was not clear how many former Baathists would try to reclaim their jobs. In many cases, it was clearly dangerous as former Baathists were still being target and killed merely for having past membership in the party.[35] For many it was already history and they would not risk returning to work.

It seemed that the post-surge strategy would focus upon at least four goals. First to "stand up the Iraqi security forces." It is somewhat ironic that the US still thought it would be years before the Iraqi Army could be depended upon to provide security. Secondly, the CLCs, whose members were former members of insurgent militias, were to provide security in their neighborhoods. Third, the US would try to broker local deals between Sunni and Shiite leaders to preserve the peace and make deals with former militants like Moqtada al-Sadr. Finally, renewed efforts would be made to pour resources into construction projects to preserve the gains made so far and to develop civil society and the economy. To a degree, the strategy appeared to be working marginally better, but the Americans were passing out a lot of money around the country and after alienating almost every faction in the country it was not sure how long the CLCs would remain friendly to the occupying forces. The situation might turn worse again any time and no one really knew what would happen as the American troops remained in the country.

The Iraq war was taking its toll on more than just Iraq and the economy in the United States. In 2006, there were 336,000 homeless veterans in the United States. A new wave of homeless vets had been brought by the mental illness caused by multiple deployments to Iraq and financial troubles, as many veterans were unable to hold a steady job or keep their families together when they returned. Often their marriages split up. The incidence of post-traumatic stress has been more severe on Iraq war veterans than Vietnam War veterans due to the multiple deployments and the constant stress caused by improvised explosive devices. There is no safe zone for American soldiers in Iraq. Similar to the Vietnam War, now Americans want to put the Iraq war behind them and move on, but this means that the veterans are left behind with their shattered lives in the excessively individualistic American culture which seems to forget quickly. The facilities provided by the Veterans Administration falls far short of meeting these former soldiers' needs. They often become addicts to alcohol and drugs and end up living on the streets.[36]

In January 2009, the United States would have a new president. There was emerging a new wave of idealistic youth in the United States. These youth were often full of enthusiasm with the rise of Illinois Senator Barack Obama in the presidential primaries and believed that if he could win the Presidency, America could change its ways and head in a different direction. They believed the troops would be quickly withdrawn from Iraq. Senator Hillary Clinton told people that if she won, it would be the end of cowboy diplomacy around the world and she would send prominent people to tell the world that the Americans were changing their policies. Meanwhile, on the Republican Party side, Senator John McCain, the most pro-war of the presidential candidates, seemed certain to win the Republican nomination as the primaries continued in February of 2008. He claimed that it was the "success" of the "surge" which had made him the leading Republican candidate, in spite of the unpopularity of the war. For John McCain, the new hope of the neoconservatives, the US would remain its presence in Iraq for the next 100 years.[37]

One has to admire the idealism of American youth who desire to see an altered America, which would join the rest of the world rather than forge ahead to remain the overbearing superpower which rules the globe. However, much of the rhetoric of the presidential campaign was naïve and quite unrealistic. The institutions of American capitalism and imperialism are global and to change this would require profound, even revolutionary, change in the system. The US would remain an imperialist power far into the future, even as its power waned and the dollar shrank in value. No one should have doubted that whoever was to be elected President of the United States in November 2008 would be forced to carry on the imperialist agenda to further shore up US capitalist accumulation. This agenda would continue under the rubric of "US national security interests," meaning primarily the interests of corporate capital. This would certainly be true of Hillary Clinton who seemed to be the most likely of the candidates to become President. The big corporate class is the primary constituency, the de-facto ruling class in the United States of America. The demise of the US global empire was likely to be a long historical process and changing the president's face was little more than window-dressing. Black or white, male of female, or European or African descent was not going to go far in addressing the root of the problem. The Democrats would certainly win in November 2008, but they would be saddled with new institutions put in place by the neoconservatives, such as the Patriot Act, and how to deal with the occupation of Iraq would still be on the agenda.

George W. Bush's proposed budget for 2008 left little doubt which direction the US would continue to go for some time. The President proposed a seven percent increase in defense spending in the $515 billion for the US military. But only $70 billion of this was for the wars. Another $200 billion or so would be needed for the wars but had not been included in the budget. The President proposed to eliminate 47 educational programs and to eliminate 151 programs altogether. He proposed to cut $200 billion from health programs, when the US already falls far behind most rich countries in health care and 47 million Americans have no health insurance at all.[38] The three trillion dollar budget would add some $400 billion more to the national deficit, already standing at $9.25 trillion dollars and increasing by $1.5 billion a day. Every citizen in the United States owed more than $30,000 of this huge debt which would be almost ten trillion by the time Bush left office. The budget would include an economic stimulus package or $145 billion dollars, but much of this would be for protecting tax cuts for the wealthy rather than putting money into the pockets of the poor for consumption or education. A trillion dollars had been spent in Iraq already and no one could see the end. If America was still a democracy in any real sense of the word, then the people were most certainly not taking advantage of their democratic rights.

It would be up to the American people to ensure their economic well being, their legal rights and their freedom in future. It would be up to them to restore the image of the United States grounded in foreign policies which truly respected and defended the equal rights of people everywhere. It would be up to them to demand real change, not just window dressing. And it would be up to them to restore the American Republic. It was not clear if it would take a revolution, but it would certainly take more than a presidential campaign. In carrying out regime change in Iraq, the "revolutionary" neoconservatives had made considerable inroads in regime change at home in their attempt to demolish the central tenets of the US constitution which guaranteed freedom, democracy, liberty from the state, and civil rights. The American people allowed George W. Bush to expand the Empire but destroy the American Republic.

References

1. Philip Shenon and Mark Mazzetti, "Study of Iraq War and Terror Stirs Strong political Response," *New York Times*, Sept. 25, 2006. David Millikin, "Leaked intelligence report rocks Bush election stance," Agence France Presse, Sept. 24, 2006. Mark Mazzetti, "Combative Bush Releases Parts of Terror Study," *New York Times*, Sept. 27, 2006.
2. Mark Mazzetti, "Combative Bush Releases Parts of Terror Study."
3. Mark Mazzetti, "Combative Bush Releases Parts of Terror Study."
4. David Millikin, "Leaked intelligence report rocks Bush election stance."
5. Drew Brown, "Iraqi elections believed to have worsened divisions, report says," *McClatchy Newspapers,* Sept. 12, 2006.
6. Sarah Boseley, "655,000 Iraqis killed since invasion," www.znet.org, October 12, 2006. Borzou Daragahi, "Iraq Disputes Claim of 600,000 War Dead," *Los Angeles Times,* October 12, 2006.
7. "Baghdad drowning in sewage: Iraqi Official," Agence France Presse, Feb. 3, 2008.
8. Drew Brown, ""Iraqi elections believed to have worsened divisions."
9. Charley Reese, "Slipped His Moorings," Antiwar.com, Sept. 12, 2006.

10. John Pilger, *Hidden Agendas* (London: Vintage, 1998), p. 560.
11. Helena Cobban, "The incredible shrinking U.S.", Salon.com, June 9, 2006. By the time of the US presidential election in 2008, the George W. Bush Presidency was so unpopular that not a single candidate of any party wanted to be in any way associated with the government. Bush had alienated practically the entire political community.
12. Deborah Haynes, "Iraqis fear surge is a temporary lull instead of permanent peace," *The Times*, Jan. 1, 2008. Clearly there was some improvement in security in parts of Baghdad, but this seemed to be due in large part to the completion of ethnic and sectarian cleansing of some key neighborhoods, and dividing up neighborhoods behind security walls. It was also partly due to the US making deals with and paying local militias to keep out al-Qaeda elements. There was also a ceasefire by the al-Mahdi Army in effect. On the other hand, many people in Baghdad were not hopeful about the future. The American people were being told that the "surge" of 30,000 extra troops had succeeded, but this was largely a myth. Some 20,000 US soldiers were due to be withdrawn by July 2008, but troop numbers would still be higher than before the beginning of the "surge" in January 2007.
13. "2701 members of US military dead since start of Iraq War," Associated Press, Sept. 24, 2001.
14. Tom Regan, "US intel report: Iraq's Anbar province 'politically lost," *Christian Science Monitor,* Sept. 11, 2006.
15. Tom Regan, "US intel report: Iraq's Anbar province 'politically lost."
16. Tom Regan, "US intel report: Iraq's Anbar province 'politically lost."
17. Tom Regan, "Polls show opposition to Iraq War at all-time high," *Christian Science Monitor*, Sept. 1, 2006. "Growing doubts about war on terror," MSNBC, Sept. 1, 2006.
18. Linda Bilmes and Joseph E. Stiglitz, "The Economic Costs Of The Iraq War: An Appraisal Three Years After The Beginning Of The Conflict," Presented at the ASSA Meetings, Boston, January 2006. (posted at various sites on the

Internet). Craig Lambert, "The $2 Trillion War: Iraq Black Hole." *Harvard Magazine.*

19. Thomas Gale Moore, "Understanding Why Iraq Is a Disaster," Antiwar,com, Sept. 12, 2006.
20. Chalmers Johnson, "Exporting the American Model," *TomDispatch*, May 3, 2006.
21. Scott Wilson, "War Turns he Tide for Israeli Settlers," *Washington Post*, Sept. 25, 2006. Michael Slackman, "U.N. Force Is Treading Lightly on Lebanese Soil," *New York Times*, Sept. 25, 2006. Meron Rapaport, "What Lies beneath," *Haaretz*, Sept. 8, 2006.
22. Musharraf," Agence France Presse, Sept. 25, 2006.
23. Chris Moore, "Will the US Again Attack Iran-This Time Without Saddam?" Antiwar.com, Aug. 28, 2006.
24. Paul Craig Roberts, "Crisis Is Upon Us," Antiwar.com, Sept. 25, 2001. Chris Moore, "Will the US Again Attack Iran-This Time Without Saddam," Antiwar.com, Aug. 28, 2006. Michael Duffy, "What Would War Look Like?" *Time*, Sept. 17, 2006.
25. Jim Lobe, "Fascism Frame Set Up by Neocon Press," Antiwar.com, Sept. 2, 2006.
26. Mike Lanchin and Mona Mahmoud, "Iraq Signs up to Awakening Movement," BBC, Feb. 4, 2008.
27. Mujahed Mohammed, "Mosul residents stock up ahead of decisive battle," Agence France Presse, Feb. 3, 2008.
28. Stephanie Gosk, "U.S. warplanes flatten safe havens," AP, Jan. 10, 2008.
29. One wonders what the "Concerned Local Citizens" were, in fact, concerned about and if it was the same as what the American occupation forces were concerned about. It must be said that the Americans had ingenuously coined a nifty label for those they had managed to co-opt, to make it look just like a group in some suburban neighborhood in Ohio, where people might be on the lookout for a robber.
30. Jonny Dymond, "On Patrol with the US Army in Iraq," BBC, Feb 3, 2008.
31. Mark Kukis, "Turning Iraq's Tribes Against al-Qaeda," *Time*, Dec. 26, 2006.

32. Lauren Frayer, "9 Iraqi civilians accidently killed," AP, Feb. 4, 2008.
33. "Rise in Iran-made bombs in Baghdad district-US," Reuters, Feb. 3, 2008.
34. Sam Dagher, "Market bombings: Baghdad locals want security, not Iraqi police," *Christian Science Monitor*, Feb. 4, 2008.
35. Qassim Abdul-zahra, "New law Allows Baathists to reclaim jobs," AP, Feb. 3, 2008. Ned Parker, "Former Hussein supporters live in fear in Iraq," *Los Angeles Times,* Feb. 3, 2008.
36. Erin McClam, "New Generation of homeless vets emerges," AP, Jan. 20, 2008.
37. Jim Lobe, "McCain is Now the Neo-Con Candidate," Lobelog.com, Feb. 2, 2008.
38. Even those who do have health insurance are also vulnerable as revealed in Michael Moore's winning documentary "Sicko" on the US health care debacle.

Index

D

F

G